More Praise for *Italian Neighbors*

"Elegant . . . It details with affection and dry wit [Parks']
initiation into the byzantine complexities of Italian social life, a
fascinating mix of conservatism and lawlessness. . . . Parks'
beautifully modulated account shows him and his wife
gradually being incorporated into the town's rituals and
rhythms as the seasons change."

Chicago Sun-Times

"When it seemed that everything that could be said about Italy
and the Italians had already been said . . . here comes a delightful
and insightful new book that even the most occasional reader
will find truly amusing, genuinely informative, and indeed,
absolutely fascinating. . . . [Parks'] sparkling style and his keen
sense of observation and understanding of the ever-varied
cultural facets of his adopted country readily become apparent.
From the first few lines, they are woven in a lively tapestry
that will continue to haunt you long after you have finished
this witty and stimulating book."

Book World

"Proper pastry shop etiquette, attitudes toward gardening and
pets, the ritual of sharing home-bottled wine, and the careful
progress of conversation and confidence are all lovingly
detailed. . . . His portrait of the village becomes a vibrant
symbol of all the places we call home."

Booklist

"Zestful."

Kirkus Reviews

ITALIAN NEIGHBORS

Also by Tim Parks

Loving Roger
Tongues of Flame
Home Thoughts
Family Planning
Goodness
Juggling the Stars

ITALIAN NEIGHBORS

OR,
A LAPSED
ANGLO-SAXON
IN VERONA

Tim Parks

Fawcett Columbine • New York

To protect the privacy of individuals, some names have been altered.

A Fawcett Columbine Book
Published by Ballantine Books

This edition published by arrangement with Grove Press, Inc.

Library of Congress Catalog Card Number: 92-97332

ISBN: 0-449-90818-6

Cover design by Georgia Morrissey
Illustration by Mark Strathy

Manufactured in the United States of America

First Ballantine Books Edition: July 1993

10 9 8

AUTHOR'S NOTE

I OFTEN FIND IT USEFUL, or at least amusing, to think of a book in terms of a gesture, a mood, a posture. In which case the gesture of this book might be that of a busy but inexpert fellow dashing about the narrow confines of his territory waving a net on the end of a long stick. It's not a butterfly net, by the looks of it. It's altogether too big for that, huge in fact. But it might be a will-o'-the-wisp net. Which would explain the extremely fine silk mesh, the random way it is being waved. And if we were to ask this frantic fellow what particular species of will-o'-the-wisp he is after? He stops, out of breath, surprised at our interest. Well, some of the most common, he pants: national character, a sense of place, the feeling people, place, and weather generate. And how is he getting on? He shrugs, pouts, as if to say, this is a mug's game if ever there was one. Will-o'-the wisps—you know—the thing is, even when you do catch one for a moment you have a terrible job recognizing them, and then when you pin them on the pages of your book they immediately lose all color and shape. Anyway, he is spending most of his time picking truisms, clichés, and caricatures out of his net. Not to mention the mere grit and chaff the air is full of. You leave him to get on with it. He rushes off, apparently at random. And it seems that in his desperation he's beginning to wield his net quite wildly, and perhaps in not altogether legitimate fashion, sweeping backward in time when he ought to go forward, allowing the fine fabric to fill with all kinds of things from moments years apart and places, even dimensions, far from contiguous. You shake your head. Whatever it is that finally gets catalogued in his book, obviously this is not a man you'll be able to trust on such imponderables as documentary authenticity.

ITALIAN NEIGHBORS

AFA

Hᴏᴡ ᴛᴏ ꜰᴏʀɢᴇᴛ ᴛʜᴇ ᴅᴀʏ we arrived in Montecchio? How to even begin to describe the weather to someone who has not been in the Veneto in July? For the weather must surely have played its part in how things went.

We're not talking about heat, really. Or that's only part of the problem. The temperature is maybe only 88 or 90, which is not impossibly hot. One has managed with 95 and more on beaches down south or in the mountains. But there is no sunshine with this heat today, no blue sky, no color, no air. Above you—and it doesn't seem very far above you either—is a uniform, oppressive, at once damp and gritty grayness, the sun only a suspicion somewhere, a blond thumbprint, a smudge. Nor is there the slightest inkling that this strange, simmering, spongy atmosphere is going to roll itself up into some kind of raincloud or liberating storm. There's not a breath, not a whisper of wind.

You don't notice it perhaps in the town, but as you leave

3

Verona, heading east, you suddenly become aware how miserable visibility is. The hills immediately to the north whose cherry blossoms you enjoyed so much in spring, the toothy peaks of the Alps which were so dramatic in sharp and slanting winter light, have all disappeared. Perhaps you're not seeing more than a couple of miles. And if—and God forbid—you were to turn south into the Bassa Padana itself, Po-bound across the open plain, you might well find, beyond Nogarole Rocca, toward Mantua, a sort of brilliant gray heat fog, so dense the world will seem a haze and the other cars ghosts, and the vines and fruit trees and towering maize and tobacco plants one vast steaming minestrone of a landscape. . . .

But we are going to Montecchio, which, like Verona itself, lies at the foot of those first now invisible hills that mark the beginning of the long climb up to the Alps. And curiously it is the Alps, one is always told, which are one of the guilty parties as far as this weather is concerned. But only in the sense that they shut out the merciful winds that might otherwise blow away everything that makes the atmosphere in the plain so unpleasant: the slow accumulation of exhaust fumes, the exhalations of a thousand pig and chicken factories, and the abundant insecticides that hover and mingle in the stale air over what otherwise, or in other weather, would be scenes of exquisite beauty.

The local name for the whole phenomenon is *afa*—or *lo smog* (pronounced "zzzmog"). One picks one's shirt away from armpits and feels uncomfortable about the crotch. The only thing close to it in British terms perhaps is a packed Friday-afternoon rush hour on bus or train when the *Standard* has taken up half its front page to tell you WHAT A SIZZLER!

But just at the moment we are traveling behind the rusty white Fiat 127 of our future *padrona di casa*. We are going to see and, we hope, move into a 1200-square-foot flat in the outlying village of Montecchio. Hence our own car, an aging tangerine Volkswagen Passat, is loaded to the stops with all our worldly belongings; the trunk is held down by shotcord over piles of boxes, the handlebar of one of our bicycles is creeping down the windshield.

Across the toneless, almost invisible countryside, the narrow road is flanked by low cement walls, deep flood emergency dikes, dusty poplars, cypresses, vines. We pass an occasional peasant figure, broad-butted on his puttering *motorino*, helmetless, cigarette in the corner of his mouth. Or it might be a woman, shopping bag between fat knees, kerchief tight on gray hair, monumental somehow despite precarious movement, the face so grimly set. Other vehicles our cautious guide chooses to overtake are a tractor with an aging dog balancing on the mudguard and a three-wheeled *furgoncino*, a sort of motorized wheelbarrow with tiny cabin, handlebar drive, and a pile of scrap metal rattling perilously behind. Meanwhile we ourselves are overtaken by bikes so white and fast my side mirror doesn't appear to register them, space-suited riders flashing into the distance, and then of course the usual chase of black or metallic Mercedeses, Alfas, Lancias, BMWs. It was a traffic mix, a social mix, with which one was to become familiar.

Perhaps ten minutes out of town, without any noticeable change of speed, we find we are in a built-up area again; first a loose alignment of stuccoed houses, then the broad open space of Montecchio's main, Montecchio's only real piazza: small shops, tall cedars in two patches of scrubby green, a gas pump with a weighbridge for trucks, a war memorial. All at once, the buildings close in, the road narrows drastically, the pavement on each side rises to three feet above ground level. Stout legs and slim are barely a foot from the passenger window. And still the traffic doesn't change speed. We emerge, cross a bridge, wind left past the glaring heterogeneity of a huge new red-brick church, then more bridges, ditches and streams, until, just before the road climbs out of the village and into the hills, our would-be *padrona* indicates left and we are in Via Colombare.

Narrow, perhaps two hundred yards long, and straight as straight, Via Colombare achieves an exquisite confusion of invading suburbia and peasant tradition. It is where *furgoncino* and Mercedes both come home to lunch. Closely packed along either side, the houses are all different: two, three, or four stories, one facing this way, one that, some centuries old, others new, handsome or poverty-stricken, crude or lavish; one pink-stuccoed, one blue, one green, many with just bare, pitted concrete the same grim color as today's unpromising sky. There may be a new Alfa 75 drawn up outside one door, and a decrepit straw-hatted grandfather on rickety chair parked outside the next. To add to the sense of emblematic collision, from the far end of the street a painted Madonna gazes from her shrine in the wall of a cherry orchard, right along the flat ribbon of patchy asphalt to where a derelict bottling factory is due for redevelopment opposite.

There is no sidewalk in Via Colombare. The front doors of most of the older, poorer houses thus open directly onto the hot asphalt. Their owners have to remember to keep their window shutters tied back lest a truck (presumably lost) carry them away (one day an old stone balcony went). And where the newer houses of urban arrivals or *contadini* made good are set back from the road, or perhaps there is a garden, the welcome breathing space that might result is lost because of the obsession with tall and elaborate iron railings as an indicator of wealth. Likewise gates must be tall and iron and complicated and where possible rendered all the more impressive by the addition of little brick and stucco shelters with terra-cotta roofs.

It was by these gates, as we parked the car, and by the humbler doorways with their fly curtains, as we climbed out, that the street's inhabitants had begun, if not quite to gather, then at least to appear: a heavy woman with the alibi of a broom, a man not quite intent on forcing his dog into the trunk of his car, others with no more excuse than the walls or railings they were leaning on. And it was impossible not to get the feeling that they were there to watch us. Not in any way suspiciously, not with hostility. But with curiosity, yes. With definite and considerable interest.

Well, we felt uncomfortable enough with the heat, the humidity. It was possible we looked out of sorts. And of course we were aware by now that Italians don't drive bright orange cars (or bright yellow or green cars for that matter) and that the owners of such cars are looked upon with a certain amount of condescension and immediately understood to be Germans, an epithet more or less synonymous with bad taste. Then despite our new Verona plates we still had that old GB sticker on the back, and so could be, what, from *Gibilterra*, it has often been suggested. Yes, we were used to all this; in a mild lighthearted kind of way perhaps we even cultivated it, for it is fun to be foreign, at least for a year or two. But however far out in the country we were, an orange car and an air of disorientation and discomfort were not usually enough to get ten or fifteen people hanging around their doors in the glaring heat to watch us. And so soon after lunch too. Did they know something we didn't? Were they expecting a show?

Our future *padrona* was nervous, clumsily pushing the wrong key into the gate of what was certainly the most modern building on the street: newish lime-green stucco with a *graffiato* finish, huge, broad, quite superfluous Californian eaves, double-glazed glass front door, a large terrace balcony for each of the four flats. She made no comment on the watching faces around us; they did not surprise her. Was it safe to assume that what they knew, she knew too? And why had she insisted, so uncharacteristically for an Italian, on arranging our meeting at a time when most people were resting, shutters half drawn, dazed by the combination of heavy lunch and humid heat?

Quite unprompted now, and in a nervous attempt to be offhand, this dry, thin-faced, intelligent woman with her small bright brown eyes was telling us about some gynecological problem she had. She'd been to the clinic again this morning. All the tests doctors made one do nowadays. The time, the expense. Especially when one more or less had to go privately if one was to get any decent service. But who could afford to risk the unnamable diseases? You know how it is. Her hand was shaking. She was having terrible trouble with her bunch of keys, forcing quite improbable versions into the lock on the gate.

My wife and I exchanged glances, looked about us. The sun did not so much lie along the street like a white hot poker, as it would do later in August and September; it was more that the whole scene, the scarred asphalt, the flaking stone or cement of the walls, the gardens, the vines, the dusty ivies, were fizzing with light. Everything glared.

"Eccoci!" The gate snapped open. And at that precise moment Lucilla appeared on a balcony above us and began to shout, or rather to yell, to shriek, to scream.

Lucilla was, is, a short, squat woman, big-breasted, fat, more than round-faced, tinted hair thinning almost to baldness, teeth with the quality of bones, set apart from each other and slightly protruding. Certainly the general impression she gave us that first day in Montecchio was not improved by the fact that every feature was contorted with rage.

This, then, was what the inhabitants of Via Colombare had been waiting for. The tubby woman danced and screamed on her balcony. Her voice filled the air in the narrow street. She pointed down at us, waving her arm as if to hurl anathema and excommunication.

I had been in Italy just over a year at the time. I lay no claims to being a linguist, but I think I had reached the point where I understood perhaps 80 percent of what was spoken directly to me, and say 50 percent (far more than enough) of what was merely said in my presence. But that afternoon I could identify not one syllable of what Signora Lucilla was so urgently bawling.

I turned to Rita for help. She understood very little more than I did. This was not apparently the local dialect. Which was reassuring. On the balcony above us the little woman continued to be galvanized by rage. A quite extraordinary energy. As if determined to spit out her teeth at us by dint of shrieking.

"Pazza," Signora Marta said firmly. "Crazy." She was refusing to look up and acknowledge the tirade. *"Completamente pazza.* It's the *afa."* By great good luck she got the key to the glass front door first time and we were inside; there were creamy marble stairs, a feeling akin to coolness, tropical plants, a reduction in the noise level, but absolutely no time to lose. Up we panted past the two ground-floor flats on the first landing with their funereal polished-wood doors and round brass knobs; on we rushed to the second landing, where an identical pair of doors again faced each other like diametrically opposed choices in some Masonic trial. Our *padrona* knew to go left. Out came the keys again amid growing nervous-

ness. Ah, *finalmente!* But no, there was still the security lock. And Lucilla simply exploded from the door opposite.

Later I came to think of Lucilla's story as something that in England would be exclusively the stuff of nineteenth-century novels—child labor and deprivation, uncertain inheritance, death-bed fawning, wills burned or buried and others with forged signatures or clauses added under duress with the complicity of generously bribed physicians—a world where money was not sensibly regulated by the likes of pension funds and insurance policies. I remember planning a novel around Lucilla, but then thought nobody would believe it, they'd think I'd been reading too much Dickens, was stealing passages from *Middlemarch*. Hence in describing now the scene that followed, it seems natural to use expressions like "her bosom heaved," for heave it did, and greatly; or "eyes and cheeks were blown out with apoplexy," for blown out they most certainly were. Smaller even than I had imagined, and bigger-breasted, Lucilla stamped a high-heeled foot as if to strike sparks from the marble. Her heavy jowls quivered. The blue print dress stretched and strained about her. Tears of rage rolled down her cheeks. And now we began to understand something. Her shouting had resolved itself into a simple chant of *"È mio, è mio, l'appartamento è mio!"*—It's mine, it's mine, the flat is mine! She grabbed the other woman and shook her. She spat. As for ourselves, it was as if we hadn't existed. Which was just as well.

Still fumbling with her keys—I wished she would give them to me—Signora Marta at last lost her nerve. So far she had been playing cool city woman to this ill-bred peasant savagery. Now she too began to shout. "You need a doctor, signora, a *psicologo!*" And in her eagerness to get away from the unpleasant scene, she yanked quite viciously at the key in the security lock and it snapped in her hands.

Silence. Surprise. Then Lucilla was saying, *"Grazie Gesù, grazie!"* Behind her back, after swiftly making the sign of the cross, her hands seemed to be trying to loosen some girdle or brassiere. Her face was purple: *"Maria santissima, grazie!"* The key had broken. We couldn't get in. It was a sign from God. It was proof of her claim to ownership. She was weeping for joy. Signora Marta led us in a hasty retreat down the stairs. As we drove away, the onlookers were already converging on the house for news of how the battle had gone.

IELLA

OVER ESPRESSO IN A BAR back in Verona, Signora Marta endeavored to reassure us. That ignorant old *strega*, witch, had run the cleaning company for which Marta's uncle—Patuzzi—had done the accounts. When the company was sold off, Lucilla and her brother Giosuè and sister-in-law Vittorina had built the *palazzina* in Via Colombare together with Patuzzi so that they could all retire happily together. Lucilla's daughter had been supposed to move into the fourth flat but hadn't wanted to be near her mother. Signora Marta pouted thin lips and tapped a city nose, as if to say, "And we know why, don't we?" In any event, Lucilla had somehow got it into her head that the whole *palazzina* had been built with her money—that is, the company's money—and that all flats would revert to her or her heirs on the death of the occupant. "Can you imagine anything so crazy?" Uncle Patuzzi had died a year ago. His wife, Maria Rosa, Marta's aunt, had hung on in the flat a year longer, but was ill, infirm, and constantly harangued by an ever more threatening Lucilla, with whom she had never *andata d'accordo*, being herself from an altogether different social class. Now the old lady, *poveretta*, had gone into a home, mainly to escape Lucilla, and she, Signora Marta, as future heir and present administrator, needed to make some money out of the place, if only, as we would surely appreciate, to pay the various bills and taxes. No sooner were we actually in the flat than Lucilla would accept the situation, this afternoon's outburst being anyway mainly due to this abysmal weather, which could play havoc with anyone's nerves.

Well, Rita and I had spent most of our life together looking for rented accommodation. We searched twice in Boston, three times in London, and this was our second time here. We knew that finding a place is tough and that the more generous and idealistic the tenancy laws are, the tougher it becomes. Italy's laws were/are idealistic in the extreme, with a sort of permanent freeze on evictions, since no political party seems ready to face the flak of unfreezing the situation; the same might be said of almost every area of Italian politics. What's more, we had no place to stay. So it was agreed that no sooner had the locksmith done his job—and Signora Marta had a friend who had another friend, who knew something about locks—than we would try again under cover of darkness.

Thus it was. Poor Lucilla must have been in bed, or deafened by her television. Signora Marta had her keys carefully labeled. Barely a minute after the cars had been parked, their doors clicked quietly shut, we were tiptoeing into the flat. Under a forty-watt bulb, Marta made us sign something on the kitchen table to the effect that we promised to leave in exactly one year's time or at any moment thereafter when she should so desire. Of course, such a contract could have no legal validity, since wise Signora Marta had no intention of declaring us as tenants and getting caught for tax on her rent. But as one discovers after a while, Italians lay great store by the signing of pieces of paper—*documenti*, they insist on calling them. There is a certain ritual attached to the practice, a warding off of evil spirits, and an appeal to the notion of honor which, people feel, should take precedence over legal quibbling, if only because it is generally more convenient to keep the government out of things.

Satisfied, but still nervous, Signora Marta gathered up her piece of paper. Here was the bank account number to pay the rent to: at the Banca Popolare di Verona in Piazza Nogara: 300,000 lire. Apparently she didn't have time to show us the place. If we had any problems finding anything we could call her on the phone. The furnishings, she could guarantee—and she made the gesture of someone in a hurry—were excellent. Her uncle and aunt had been people of considerable culture, well-educated, much-traveled. We would find books and art works that were *estremamente interessanti*. If there was anything left in the drawers or cupboards we could store it in the *solaio*, the attic, upstairs. The key was on the bunch. *"Va bene?"* This thin nervous woman took more than a cursory look through the Judas hole in the door, drew a deep breath, whispered *arrivederci*, and scuttled off down the stairs.

So far we had barely looked about us. Now we explored. And discovered that none of the light bulbs in the flat were any more than forty watts, so that even the parlor's grotesque five-armed chandelier dripping with globules of smoky glass cast only a dim glow of sad pomp. For such a cultured man Uncle Patuzzi had been doing remarkably little reading of an evening.

Still, minor shortcomings of this variety could easily be remedied, we thought. Likewise the array of department store Madonnas, Sacred Hearts, Sant'Antonios, and clumsy bric-a-brac crucifixions that stared down from every wall could be removed and stored away with minimum effort. And the orange and green floor tiles did have a smooth, clean, cool feel to them; the window fittings were, by London standards, quite luxurious, while the bathroom, with walls tiled almost to the ceiling, hardwood toilet seat, and handsome creamy beige bidet and bath, was palatial. Certainly when one remembered the bed-sitting rooms and miniflats of Acton and Willesden, this was a very well appointed place indeed.

But the furniture . . . Well, we had seen it elsewhere, so it was not entirely unexpected. But depressing all the same. So many

Italians, even young Italians, will move into the most modern buildings, light and airy with attractive ceramics and fittings, only to clutter the space with heavy coffin-quality furniture which affects the antique and noble but achieves only the cumbersome and uncleanable. Casting sad shadows into the bargain. Thus, a dark-stained console with twisting candlestick legs was shedding neat piles of sawdust to let us know the woodworms were at work. Veneer was blistering on a mammoth bookcase with surely anachronous frosted-glass doors, while above the sofa a teak-framed mirror with cracked silvering found forty-watt reflections of a darkly noble dinner table opposite. Venturing as far as the bedroom, and rather disconcerted now, it was to find great, square, black-varnished head- and footboards supporting a sagging boat shape between, reminiscent of the bed in a school-of-Veronese *Death of the Virgin* I had recently seen in a local church. On opening dusty chests, dark wardrobes, deep drawers, we discovered that all without exception were full to overflowing with the worn-out possessions of thirty years ago.

In need of air, we rolled up plastic slat shutters and walked out onto the main terrace balcony into the luminous, breathless heat of the evening. Across the street, in front of an older peasant house with fine pink stucco, a group of people our own age were laughing, drinking, smoking, and playing Ping-Pong under a fluorescent tube strung up between two tall cypresses and whirring with moths. In the street, despite the hour, their numerous children kicked a football among the cars, including our own, bicycles still on top, strips of chrome hanging off the sides. We sat on the arms of an old armchair that Uncle or Auntie Patuzzi had abandoned out here to make a home for spiders and provide the stuff of birds' nests. The sharp tock-tocking of the Ping-Pong ball, the laughter of adults and children, the background whirring of crickets, was not unpleasant. And would have been pleasanter still with a glass of chilled wine in one's hand. That was something to look forward to. Walking to the far end of the balcony, we saw a young man maneuvering his sober blue Lancia into a makeshift garage of corrugated iron and cinder block. Then came the strains of the news program from perhaps three or four open windows. What time was it, eleven o'clock? At midnight we could expect the first fresh stirring of the air. And we intended to be naked on the bed for that.

This has always been one of the pleasures of high summer here. You have been uncomfortably sticky all day. Maybe you've showered twice, tried shorts, long cotton trousers, T-shirts, tank tops, exchanged shoes for tennis shoes, tennis shoes for sandals, sandals for bare feet, had the fan on top speed blowing your papers about while you're typing, sucked ice cubes, put your legs in a bucket of cold water, etc., and nothing has worked. The heat seems to come from inside you. Comfort is unimaginable.

Naturally, you feel irritable. Toward evening, you look at the sky, listen to distant thunder, watch the heat lightning playing over low hills, and you know that it won't rain; so often the elements put on this show just to tease. Going to bed you must decide: the open windows and the *zanzare*, the mosquitoes, or the closed windows and the heat. Inevitably you opt for the mosquitoes, because in the end, at least around Verona, there aren't that many.

You lie there naked. The idea of any superfluous contact with your body in the form of a sheet, pajamas, is unthinkable. Through a kind of breathy intimacy the summer darkness has, you listen to chatter, facetious variety shows, card games and music from other open windows; because nobody in the entire neighborhood is asleep, nobody would dream of installing air conditioning so as to be able to turn in at the normal time (and even mosquito nets are rare). Everybody is waiting for it to happen. Until at last, around midnight or shortly afterward, like some good spirit suddenly moving across the face of the earth, or the touch of a lover's finger dipped in cool water, the air stirs, it shifts, it breathes, and the notion of freshness becomes imaginable again. Almost immediately the sounds fade, the TVs snap off, the children cease to shriek and chatter, Via Colombare is falling asleep.

It would have been an hour or so later on this particular night that Vega began to bark. I am not exaggerating when I say of Vega that I have never heard another dog sound so deeply disturbed, so much an *anima in pena*. She bayed, wailed, was at once furious and desperate. In fact I remember asking Rita which circle of the *Inferno* we might be in.

The third or fourth time the beast woke us up, I went out onto the tiny balcony of our bedroom at the back of the house away from the street. On a raised terrace not five yards away, the other side of a narrow canyon of garden between, a big golden Labrador strained a long chain to paw at flaking shutters barring the back door of an old peasant house. It howled rather than barked, perhaps moaned rather than howled. And as I watched, enjoying the now cool night air on my skin, somebody threw something at the creature from an upper window, food perhaps, for the dog was immediately scrabbling excitedly among the terrace sweepings between a Cinquecento and an Alfetta.

Back in bed, the apparent relief of silence was short-lived. The insidious whine of a *zanzara* hovered just above our pillows. Up in a flash, light on, a dusty accountancy magazine of Patuzzi's grabbed from the bedside table, within a minute I'd reduced the thing to a bright red spot of blood on the graying tempera wall.

"I wonder, you know," I asked, coming back to bed, "I wonder if the yuppies and artsy guys and retired professors checking through real estate agents' lists of farmhouses in Tuscany have been adequately filled in on these details." My wife, who always seems ready for questions of this kind, remarked that first the weather was never this unpleasantly sultry in Tuscany, second that local dialects there were all more or less comprehensible, since they formed the basis of modern Italian, and third, and most convincing, that anybody who could afford to buy a farmhouse in Tuscany need not have somebody else's hunting dog breathing down his neck, and would doubtless have screen windows installed before moving in. As far as we were concerned, however, she continued, there was just the small problem that we were not so fortunately placed vis-à-vis our bank accounts, and furthermore that there were so many Brits in Tuscany that our linguistic skills would not be in the kind of demand that might allow us to pay a hefty rent.

"Plus the fact," she added, *"che tu porti iella."* You bring bad luck.

Only months later, when I took the liberty of saying the same thing to a business acquaintance, did I appreciate that such an accusation is one of the worst things an Italian can say to somebody. Had I known, we would doubtless have argued long into the night.

PASTICCERIA
MAGGIA

Aₘ I ɢɪᴠɪɴɢ ᴛʜᴇ ɪᴍᴘʀᴇssɪᴏɴ I don't like the Veneto? It's not true. I love it. I'm going to tell you some wonderful things about it. When I've finished I hope you'll be wishing you'd been here as well, at least for a little while. But like any place that's become home, I hate it too. And of course you can't separate the things you love and hate: you can't say, let's move to so-and-so where they have the cappuccino, the wines, the lasagna, the marvelous peaches, the handsome people in handsome clothes, the fine buildings, the close-knit, friendly secretiveness of village life, but not, please, the howling maltreated hunting dogs, the spoiled adolescents on their *motorini*, the hopeless postal service, the *afa*. You can't do it. It's a package deal.

In any event, the morning after our unnerving arrival we doubtless set off to find the village bar/pasticceria and console ourselves with the pleasanter side of the arrangement, make ourselves known, see the lay of the land. And for anyone moving to

Italy, this is a habit I really can't recommend too warmly: frequent your local bar, and if possible bar/pasticceria; frequent it assiduously, decorously, even religiously.

Timing is important. In general, if you want to order a cappuccino with brioche you should try to arrive before ten-thirty. Of course, you could still order the same things later, but this would be a declaration of your foreignness. And while Italians usually seem to like foreigners, the foreigners they like most are the ones who know the score, the ones who have caved in and agreed that the Italian way of doing things is the best. For this is a proud and profoundly conservative people, as careful observation of ordering at the bar will confirm. And a tightly knit one too. How is it that they all instinctively sense, without even glancing at stylish watches, that such and such a time is the moment to switch to their *aperitivi*? How they chuckle and grin when a German orders a cappuccino rather than an espresso after lunch, pouring that milk onto an already full stomach. And here's a curious detail: espresso is always okay, twenty-four hours a day, even *corretto* (i.e., with grappa), but cappuccino has a very definite time slot: eight to ten-thirty. Trivia? No, good training. When the full complexity of these nuances becomes apparent—because the *digestivo*, the *gingerino*, the *prosecco*, all have their right times and contexts too—you will be less surprised by the labyrinthine process of, say, switching your driving license to an Italian one or sorting out your position vis-à-vis the health system. There is an order to all things; follow it, even when it borders on the superstitious and ritualistic.

Warning. If the first sip of your cappuccino tells you that long-life or *UHT* milk is being used, change bars before you have invested too much time here. Use of UHT milk (all too frequent, alas) indicates that either you are far far out in the sticks where the urbane delights of the cappuccino have never really been understood, or that this is a bar where most people (men) are ordering grappa or wine, or if they are ordering coffee are putting grappa and wine in it, not milk. A typical confirmation that you are in this variety of bar might be that the *barista* replies to your Italian, whether competent or hesitant, in defiantly incomprehensible dialect, quite probably revealing that dental work and oral hygiene are not high on the list of personal priorities. No matter how characteristic you might find this UHT bar, how picturesque its old wooden chairs, dusty pergola, sports trophies, sentimental paintings hung askew, and weather-beaten old characters arguing volubly over games of *briscola*, the fact is that ultimately you have no business here, you will never be accepted however many times you come. You are only making these doubtless very wholesome people feel slightly uncomfortable.

Another scene which is definitely to be avoided is the bar where you are invited first to pay at the till, then present your receipt to the in this case smartly dressed, even uniformed, *barista* behind his polished pink granite bar under a row of fashionable halogen lights. Reasons? First because this is probably a bar where if you want to sit down you will have to pay for waiter service, and hence having picked up your coffee and taken it to your seat, you will be scolded, perhaps quite severely, and invited to pay a surcharge. Payment for seating is of course perfectly understandable in the busy city center, but not really desirable if you plan to be in that bar as frequently as I'm suggesting. But the second and more important reason is that this is not the sort of bar where the same people come and relax every day and can thus, as weeks and months pass by, be placed and identified and become a part of your life. No, this is a busy bar. A business bar. A tourist bar. And we are not interested in any of those.

I cannot claim to be widely traveled, but I have lived in London, Cambridge, Boston, spent fairly long periods in Switzerland, in New York, holidayed in most of Western Europe. You can draw your own conclusions. In any event, I'm now going to stick my neck out and say that I honestly know of nowhere, nowhere, where the whole experience of ordering and consuming coffee and a pastry is, *or could be*, more pleasant than in Pasticceria Maggia, Piazza Buccari, Montecchio. And we selected it from five or six other candidates that very first Sunday. Obviously we had a nose for these things by now.

You enter through a glass door polished only seconds before you arrived, display windows to either side frothing with colorful goodies, since Italians will always favor the most extravagant packages, however miserly the contents, and are always ready to renew their long love affair with crinkly cellophane and foil, ribbons, bows, and tinsel flourishes of every kind. Opposite you, as you adjust to a pleasant but not excessive dimming of light, is a long bar with attractive curved corner, polished wood to the front and yellow travertine on top. Behind and above is the typical array of bottles, mainly *amari*, *digestivi*, distillations of this and that (artichokes, rhubarb), things you have never heard of and most probably will never learn to like; to the left is the seating area, just a handful of tables, to the right a great glass counter with four tiers of small and dainty biscuits, cakes, and pastries.

Needless to say, the whole arrangement has a cleanliness, smoothness of line, sureness of touch, unthinkable in England, but without the antiseptic feel of the same thing in Switzerland, the self-consciousness of anything that is not a fast-food chain in the States. Tense as you may well be after negotiating that main street where the crosswalk marking faded years ago, depressed perhaps by a broken fountain full of litter, you can hardly help wondering, as you push in through the door, at the way this same people so infallibly reproduces these two starkly contrasting environments: anarchy without, ceremony within.

But now we're here, by all means let the ceremony begin. You close the door on the busy, dangerous world outside, glance around. The girl serving is small, dark, pixieishly attractive, and loves to be looked at. So look. And take a seat. The first times we went to Pasticceria Maggia I remember experiencing a sniff of anxiety over the question of seating: was there space for us? Later one realizes that part of the civilization, the magic, of the place is that there always seems to be just enough space for everyone who wants to sit. Good. You settle into a comfortably cushioned chair. The simple red tablecloths are pleasant without creating the impression that you must be paying for them in some way or other. The cappuccino (and this is so important) is absolutely right: dark strong coffee at the bottom, thick creamy foam above, with, on request, the *cappuccio*, or hat of bitter cocoa sprinkled on top. Add just a dusting of sugar, use your spoon to draw up a little coffee and mix it with the foam. Now spoon up the frothy sweetened milk between bites of brioche and relax.

To spin things out, it's a good idea to try to get hold of one of the newspapers the bar is legally obliged to buy for its customers. Don't worry if the thick pink *Gazzetta dello Sport*, by far the most widely sold daily, seems a little daunting at first. Sportswriting is almost the only journalism with any verve to it here (and in lots of other places for that matter), and the Sunday edition will have the first division soccer results from England even if it never quite stretches to cricket. After a while you learn not to be ashamed of a residual interest in the home country.

On another table—wait until somebody kindly passes it to you—is *L'Arena*, Verona's local newspaper. Since they are talking about the agricultural fair, a headline proudly announces that the city is *L'ombelico verde d'Europa*—the Green Belly Button of the European Community. Well, there are the two scrubby patches of green outside the window in Piazza Buccari. . . . The fact that a member of the local government is under investigation for corruption barely gets four column inches. For this is his party's newspaper. Turning a page, yesterday's dead stare at you from identity-card photographs—you can look for the features of some hated employer—while advertisements opposite offer tickets for tonight's *Aïda* at the Arena, Shakespeare at the Teatro Romano, ten or twelve channels of TV viewing.

Why am I advising you to do all this? Because, quite apart from its simply seeming the height of relaxation and civilization, it is impossible to be a regular customer here at Pasticceria Maggia, to soak up the chitchat around you, to be sweetly served and smiled at by that pretty *barista*, to browse through the local scandals in the paper, watch bicycle races passing by amid honking and cheers across the street, without gradually beginning to feel that you are getting into the spirit of things.

People begin to nod to you. Beginning disconcertingly with the child-size village idiot in his deerstalker cap. But you will gain respect by putting up with his badgering. Smile, show no embarrassment. Say: *Salve, Moreno, tutto bene?* He's a nice boy in the end. And here's an invitation to teach your doctor's struggling daughter English, a request that can be politely turned down after having discussed at length the inadequacies of the education system (the *Arena* will keep you informed). On a weekday morning around ten you can score points by greeting the post office workers coming in for their long coffee break. These are not your favorite people when they refuse to look up at you from behind their murky little windows and then start weighing your postcards and forgetting whether Britain is part of the European Community. Now you can enjoy perhaps glancing at your watch and smiling too brightly as they lean on the bar and discuss what shopping they have to do. Frustratingly, they are unperturbed. They even seem friendly, as if the bar were a place of truce. Perhaps they will serve you faster if they see you here a lot. Or when those British football oo-lee-gans commit one of their regular atrocities, you can agree with local youngsters poring over the strident *Gazzetta* that your fellow countrymen are a degenerate lot, though pointing out in their defense that the performance of the national team, at least till Gazza came, has often been almost an incitement to insurrection (nothing more welcome to Italians than gently running down *la perfida Albione*; they feel extraordinarily competitive in our regard).

As the months pass and you continue to sit and sup, you will doubtless be approached by the ex-priest Lorenzo, now converted to ecology and admirably determined to save Montecchio's famous ditches. He will ask you to sign something and you will sign it. In the corner old men are muttering over Verona's relegation prospects; soon you will be able to talk about that too. After mass on Sunday mornings (did I mention the tiny crucifix on the wall above the liquor?) it will be the eight widows who put two tables together and confabulate in low voices, forming, in winter, a wall of fur coats. Even they will begin to smile at you after a year or so, perhaps wondering how long your own wife will outlast you.

Maybe you spot your butcher, your greengrocer, your dentist. Somebody asks you if you can do a translation for him. He runs a picture-frame company. No invoice required. For heaven's sake.

Somebody walks over to mention a friend who has failed his exam at the university a couple of times and needs a helping hand. "Perhaps you'll remember the name if it's you doing his oral." "Well, I'm afraid I shouldn't really . . ." "Virgilio, he's called. Virgilio Gandini." Somebody else is having trouble with the American instruction manual to the sprinkler system for his lawn. And that somebody knows another somebody who could fix the wobbly bearings on your car. . . .

It would be a foolish resident of Montecchio who did not at least occasionally pop into Pasticceria Maggia, a shortsighted newcomer who did not invest in at least a couple of years' worth of cappuccinos. . . .

Coming out on that first occasion, the morning after the evening before, I remember we almost ran into two grinning young carabinieri sauntering in in their beautiful uniforms with the scarlet-striped trousers and white breast straps. Something that might have been an elongated black beer can swung from a handsome belt, complete with trigger. A tall dark girl appeared from the kitchen holding two trays of cannoli and various other pastries; there were smiles, some relaxed flirtation. The *barista* minced. They ordered their cappuccinos. Cigarettes were lit. One crouched down to chat to a little child, asking predictably: What is your name, where do you live? Nobody seemed at all concerned by the submachine gun the other was fingering as he spooned sugar over his foam.

Outside, we found their small, dark blue 850cc Fiat van parked in the middle of the small road, blocking anyone who wanted to get by. A radio could be heard calling them with some urgency. Should we go back in to tell them? But no. They are having their cappuccino. They only have a few minutes before it's *aperitivo* time. They wouldn't want to be disturbed.

LAGHETTO SQUARÀ

With all that unpleasant unpacking and sorting out awaiting us back at the flat, we might well have chosen to make a detour before returning to Via Colombare that morning. Anything to stave off the evil day. We would thus have discovered how, following the line of the hills coming down from the north, the village of Montecchio, gray-green with dust and heat, is crossed, crisscrossed, by perhaps a score of small, lively streams bubbling swiftly through stone and grass and following a complex system of sluices which divert the water to feed neglected sheep dips, duckponds, irrigation ditches, and great flat scouring slabs at the bottom of broken steps where the occasional older woman can still be seen scrubbing her husband's underwear with a soap stick. The through road from Verona thus corners sharply left, right, and left again, as it gropes for the two key bridges that will allow it to continue on its way to the outlying village of Olivè. With all the dips and curves it takes in the process, the sudden widenings and narrowings, the canyon-high curbs followed by treacherous gutters and unexpected cambers, this chameleon strip of paved road confers upon the village a splendid sense of the haphazard ad hoc, as if the asphalt had been put down in thick fog to reach the scene of some emergency, or, more likely, festival.

Geography, we discovered, is immediately mystified in Montecchio. Paths cut this way and that. One watercourse flows over, beside, under another. House, factory, farm, supermarket, all stand next to each other, though higgledy-piggledy, or are even built one inside the shell of another. The most obvious routes are blocked by dikes or long stone walls. Apparently parallel streets mysteriously lose all contact with each other. So that for the first few weeks one feels a sense of admiration, even bewilderment, at seeing how confidently, and above all how fast, cars shoot through streets where, because of the lack of sidewalks, so many corners are blind. Such things as traffic posts are unknown, of course, and certainly undesired. Only a memory of a white line haunts the thoroughfares like some sermon heard and ignored long before, with the result that the sharp bends and corners of the main street are viciously cut by motorists and cyclists alike, especially during siesta time, when it is not generally supposed that anybody could be coming the other way.

Tires screech between the narrow walls of a bridge and into the tight bend immediately afterward. A Vespa swerves: the little boy sitting in front of his father has grabbed the handlebars. Wrists precariously interlocked, a fourteen-year-old on his *motorino* pulls a younger girl on her bicycle up the slope of a dike, finding time to rev and buzz his buzzer as he does so. Somehow, beneath it all, the sleepy underlying village serenity persists, is always there, but there to be constantly violated by this indomitable dionysiac principle on wheels. Here comes a moped reared up for fifty yards on its back wheel, overtaken by a Porsche in second at forty, roaring past the new church straight into the vicious turn by the drugstore. So that if Via Olivè was not in fact laid in a fog or a drunken stupor, one can only presume that it was conceived as a practice track for apprentice race drivers, stunt artists, and other would-be suicides. All of which inevitably takes its toll of those heedless elderly cyclists in trilby and shirtsleeves, headscarf and blouse, who wind and wobble about one-handed as they clutch walking stick, fishing rod, or shopping bag. As so often in Italy, the picturesque is combined with a sharp edge of danger.

The first bridge, around which cars will be loosely parked for butcher, barber, and cobbler, takes you over a dry flood-overflow ditch. Perhaps five yards deep, seven wide, and straight as a die for miles, this unfortunately necessary piece of engineering slices the village in half with a ribbon of brambly scrub, Coke cans, bottles, and other discarded trophies of summer nights. As we were to discover later, the fact that such a considerable obstacle has still been bridged only to one end of the village is a matter of smoldering political recrimination in Montecchio. For us that first morning it merely meant that the bar was perhaps five minutes farther away than it need have been.

Having crossed the ditch, one follows the road past the new church, past a single AGIP gasoline pump, perfectly at home beside a handsome stone arch, and arrives at the second bridge. More attractive than the first, this spans a tiny river, the Fibbio, which flows beneath windows and balconies, linking ponds where men stand fishing under NO FISHING signs, taking the mountain rains southward toward the Adige, the Po, the Adriatic.

Returning from the bar that morning, we doubtless turned left here to follow the stream a little way to its source, since this was also the direction for Via Colombare. And so would have made our second delightful discovery of the morning: at the bottom of a little dead end, not two hundred yards from our new flat, a great battered waterwheel was thrashing away in magnificent dereliction. The discovery was all the more welcome when we found that if we stood on a little bridge a few yards downstream of the wheel, the air was mercifully cooler, sparkling with bright droplets, damp and breezy.

Did we go on to the Laghetto Squarà that morning? I imagine we did. The little path behind the wheel would have been too inviting to ignore with anything more than an hour before lunch. It's stony underfoot. There are tall sagging fences to protect an extravaganza of peppers, eggplants, young tomato plants. Water is everywhere: tiny streams gurgling through the vegetable patches, the small river rushing at the millwheel, and to the right, through a Roman arch framing rusty silos, a stagnant pond with stone surrounds which presumably once had some industrial purpose. There are big blue dragonflies and livid green surface weeds. A scooter buzzes urgently at a blind corner, forcing one to step smartly aside, and then the path emerges into the open space of Laghetto Squarà.

What happens here is that spring water rising beneath an abandoned seventeeth-century church flows out under its rotting door and bubbles across the path into a small square lake, the *laghetto*. There are tall plane and poplar trees around it, a stone embankment this side, and grassy banks the other, with three or four sluice gates. At the edge, the glass clearness of the water allows you to look down two or three yards onto abandoned Roman building stones, pollution-fed weeds, and that characteristic assortment of junk that people all over the world feel obliged to throw into attractive expanses of water: old tires, a shoe, electrical appliances.

It's sad. Despite the obvious attraction of Laghetto Squarà, nothing has been composed or finished, nothing appears to be tended or even cleaned. For this is the public sector, not the private commercial world of the bar. Indeed, it's difficult to imagine the *comune*, the local government, having spent anything on the place in the last ten years, aside from paying someone to prune the surrounding trees with extraordinary ruthlessness (because paid, we later discovered, in the form of firewood procured).

Yet precisely because of this neglect, the *laghetto* hangs on to a quality it might lose with transformation into some modern notion of the recreational picturesque; it retains its weathered, rather haphazard air of simply, naturally, being there. You sit by the waterside on a big square stone fished out from the bottom some years ago; there are faded Roman inscriptions on its bumpy surface, a date, a few letters suggesting the name of an emperor. Spring water chuckles over the shale path to your left; the hills are behind you, the lake, the busy village, and the plain in front. "So," you think, "this is the water table—I am at the foot of the Alps." Kids throw themselves into the lake in their underwear. Girls scream, protesting they don't want to be pushed. And maybe they don't. It's a little more comfortable here than back in the dusty streets. A lizard basks just a few inches from your foot, reminding you how long you've been sitting still. Montecchio, you feel, may turn out to be okay.

FANTASMI

I⊤ ⊤ook us two long hot days. We made friends at Brandoli, the local supermarket, where three trips were required to accumulate the necessary boxes, and we moved a whole culture from flat three up into the suffocating *solaio* below the roof.

Should we have paid more attention to what we were moving? Would I know more about Italy if I had read all the various diaries and letters with attention? Perhaps so. But old bric-a-brac, old clothes, old medicines, old shoes, old files, accounts, newspapers, rags, toiletries, shopping lists, votive items, paperbacks, military hats, jewelry boxes, camp cooking equipment, and tins upon tins of assorted nuts, bolts, and nails have a very bad effect on my morale. Where another might find each item numinous with meaning, I feel overwhelmed by a sense of insignificance. I think of mountains and mountains of such relics multiplied for every household in every corner of the world—varying of course from country to country, each with its own cultural matrix, its own peculiar makeup, implying this value and that, but in the end just debris, life's parings waiting to be thrown out—and all I want to do is to see the back of it all as fast as possible. I'd never make it in archaeology or anthropology. Thus what I did save from our supermarket boxes for a moment's examination, and what my memory and my wife's now offer me in the way of details of that marathon cleanup, can only be scraps, clues, hints to the character, life, and times of Umberto Patuzzi—or "Il Professore," as we were later to come to think of him—and of his still-vegetating wife, Maria Rosa. Had we known how intriguing these people were to become to us, we might have paid more attention.

Signora Marta had said her aunt and uncle were well traveled, and indeed the gigantic frosted-glass-and-peeling-veneer cupboard in the *salotto*, or parlor, was stacked with sufficient tourist brochures to keep an agency going for a couple of months in high season—except that these brochures dated back ten, twenty, even forty years. The oldest, in alphabetically ordered piles, for the most part extolled cheap hotels in the local mountains or on the nearby Adriatic coast, with fragile brown-and-white photographs giving ample evidence of the fifties' building spree. Tuscany, Elba, Abruzzo, Rome, and Sicily followed close behind, like pieces in a rapidly expanding and now colorful jigsaw—Technicolor seas and gaudy local delicacies—until with the sixties' boom, mass prosperity, and the Italians' love affair with the automobile, here came the first price lists for hotels in Austria, Switzerland, Yugoslavia. Pile after pile of them. The most recent and lavishly seductive exhibits featured the Azores, the Bahamas, pensioners' package trips to Florida.

Clearly there was material for a couple of Ph.D.s in this cupboard, but nevertheless straight into our Brandoli boxes it all went. We were in a hurry. An essay on holiday destinations as an expression of Italian economic development over the last three decades was not what we had in mind. Except that here, beneath the brochures, was a photograph album. Well, who can resist at least glancing at photographs?

Such was Patuzzi's love of the road and his car that he must have had the habit of getting someone, presumably Maria Rosa, to snap him by exotic road signs, as others might want to record their presence at the top of mountains. So here he is, in black and white, full head of virile hair brushed back, thin aquiline intelligent nose, arriving in Trento with stout climbing boots around his neck and a knapsack on his shoulders; he has the confident satisfied look on his face of someone who has just been admired for making an intelligent remark, or at the very least has eaten a good lunch. 1937, says the spidery hand. And here he is again, in color now, balding, but still sporty, in wool trousers and green anorak, by a sign that tells us *Wien*. We flick through page after page of these things: mountain villages, hotel billboards, *autostrada* exits; until finally, most recent and most extraordinary, here is a much older, weathered, bent Patuzzi, leaning on a stick, by black lettering on a white road sign announcing *Praha*, with, beside him, and even more extraordinary, a very recognizable Lucilla. That does put a new slant on things. More a ménage than a condominium perhaps? Could she even be right about ownership of the flat? Or am I jumping the gun?

Farther back in the cupboard are some collector's items from the war days: an army hat, a school textbook ("Describe your feelings—of admiration and gratitude—on contemplating a photograph of Il Duce"), and a stack of the macabre *Signal* magazines: tabloid-size, in German, with Italian translations; these offer comic-strip propaganda, mainly directed against—well, against us. *"Bombe sull' Inghilterra!"* one enthusiastic piece is entitled. Is this, I sometimes wonder, why the young men in the bar still feel such rivalry? And what had friend Patuzzi done in the war apart from reading such heady stuff? (Later we learned that Lucilla had been begging for bread on the streets of Vicenza.)

Farther back still (I said the cupboard was huge, and it was) was a rather more harmless (and more numerous) collection of magazines going under the enigmatic title *NAT*. A moment's close attention to the inside cover revealed that these letters stood for *Nuova Alta Tensione*, and it took only a few seconds' leafing through them to appreciate that such tension was presumably meant to be created in the lower abdominal area by late-fifties and early-sixties pin-ups of Brigitte Bardot, Jane Fonda, Sophia Loren, and a host of lesser names, photos of such breathtaking touched-up tameness you wondered how people managed after all the bomb-toggling excitement of wartime. Was Patuzzi slipping them in between his accountancy journals as he walked out of the *tabaccheria*? Did he read harmless gossip about bathing beauties between toiling over accounts on the great ugly desk in the second bedroom which clearly had a longer history than this house? At what point had Lucilla come in, if she had? Beneath a photo of a tiny delicate-featured girl from the south, a caption was still telling us twenty-five years later that Mariangela Rainaldi, a devout Catholic, presently worked as a party hostess but was eager to become a film star.

In the drawer to Patuzzi's bedside table we found a long shoehorn, a catechism, an Alpini hat (the famous Italian mountain regiment), a long-expired tube of hemorrhoid cream, an oval silver-framed photo of a solemn Maria Rosa, and a long piece of thick leather with a handgrip at one end and a heavy ball of lead tied to the other. What on earth for?

But there was a problem with rubbish now. Not that we felt we could throw away anything precious, like the diaries full of additions and subtractions in figures of eight and nine digits, the replies to letters Maria Rosa's brother must have sent to a number of marriage bureaus in Paris—no, everything that should be preserved for prying eyes more patient than our own would be preserved. All the same, there was much in the way of old toothbrushes and toiletries from the early seventies that would be missed by no one. Who needed to know that Il Professore had cleaned his teeth with Pasta del Capitano?

Unable to locate anything inside or outside the flat that remotely resembled a garbage can, we eventually tiptoed downstairs to make ourselves known to the Visentinis in the flat below Lucilla's (the one that had been meant for her daughter). Presumably they would be able to tell us what the score was.

We knocked lightly on the door. A voice asked who we might be, for nobody will ever open in Italy until identity is declared. Security, even in the remotest villages, is at New York standards. We explained. Came the sound of a heavy lock turning over once, twice, three times, and the door opened. A wispy, attractive little woman in pink tracksuit stood before us and immediately insisted we come in.

Well, we were in the same country, the same village, the same building even, in a flat that in structural terms was a straight mirror image of our own, and yet on stepping into *casa Visentini* we were immediately in a different world. Everything here was modern, pleasantly styled, clean as a pin, with a light touch to the ornaments, the lithographs on the walls, the low, modern, comfortable sofa. If there was perhaps just one thing in common with our own accommodation, and with so many other homes I have been into in the Veneto, it was the desire for a certain formality, a certain achieved composition in every room, ritualistic and ceremonial. "Cozy" is not a word one would normally apply to an Italian interior, nor would the owners be proud to hear their furnishings thus described. The briefest glance at the Visentinis' showed that the whole domestic environment had been most painstakingly arranged, nothing left to chance, nothing haphazard. Everywhere lines met and diverged in clean, carefully calculated, stylish angles. The exact opposite of the world outside.

And at first Orietta and Giampaolo were as guarded and rigidly polite as their furniture was attractive and composed. Yes, we were invited in, and with kindness. Indeed, they insisted we come in. For this was the right thing. But it was not clear what we were to talk about. They did not want to be drawn immediately on the for us burning issues of a hostile Lucilla and a howling dog. Giampaolo in particular was poker-faced. The rubbish, he explained, was usually placed in a large shared plastic garbage can which was then put outside the gate for collection every morning. However, Lucilla had removed this bin on our arrival, making it abundantly clear she did not want us to enjoy the use of it.

The Visentinis offered no comment on this state of affairs. Presumably we must procure a can of our own.

I then asked about the garage Signora Marta had mentioned. Tall and serious, but handsome too, and with something boyish about him somewhere, Giampaolo led me downstairs to a semibasement where, to the right at the bottom of the stairs, a very big area the size of a whole flat served as the shared condominium garage. I was immediately impressed by the positively licked cleanness of the smoothly finished red-brick tiles that had been chosen for the flooring: no oil stains, barely visible tire marks. Attractive as it was, this simply didn't seem necessary for a garage.

Four parking spaces had been marked out between cement pillars. To the far side was Giampaolo's gleaming white twin-carburetor Alfa Romeo Giulietta, just in front of us a minuscule Fiat 126, again white. The other two places were empty.

I asked which was my space. Giampaolo said this one on our right was flat one's and so belonged to Vittorina (Lucilla's sister-in-law), and the space to the left of the Giulietta at the far end was flat three's, our own. But, he warned, neither space had been used since the death of the male members of those households: Umberto Patuzzi and Giosuè Zambon. This was a question of respect. He showed me the small crucifixes on the pillars beside the spaces. Lucilla, he said, was a superstitious person, but not ultimately an unpleasant one. It was merely a question of time.

I remarked that if using the garage meant war with Lucilla, forget it, it didn't matter, my car had little bodywork worth saving. This did not bring a smile, and in retrospect it occurs to me how foolish such jokiness is amid a nation of car worshipers. A man who has spent six months of his *stipendio* buying a twin-carburetor Giulietta that he hardly ever uses does not want to hear that others are quite happy to get by with a ten-year-old rusting VW Dasher. And bright orange at that.

Before returning to the women upstairs, Giampaolo made a point of showing me the communal *taverna*.

A *taverna* is a large basement or semibasement room situated beneath a modern *villetta*, *palazzina*, or small condominium of central or northern Italy, and it is dedicated to partying. It must have a large, preferably enormous fireplace, suitable for barbecuing; a selection of strictly labelless wines, Alpine-style pine furniture, one long banqueting table, an area with sink for washing dishes, and perhaps a stereo. On the walls, as was the case in Via Colombare, decorations should include old posters showing views of the mountains or the country, some hunting trophies (here, remarkably, a surely fake cheetah), and such things as old swords or shotguns. In Via Colombare there were Patuzzi's wooden skis from perhaps forty years ago.

It should be said that old houses do not have *taverne*. Only new ones. For the *taverna* is the contemporary Italian's dream of the past, an exercise in urban adaptation and nostalgia. That is to say, this big below-ground party room attempts to recreate, for the modern flat dweller in his cramped condominium, the feeling of those huge old country kitchens with their abundance of game, polenta, and local wine which still take up such a large space in the national consciousness. Thus in many a *taverna*, often beneath the most uninspiring prefabricated structures, you will find that the occupants have bought an authentic old *pietra serena* fireplace to install in the wall, or, if they cannot afford the real thing, then at least a decent imitation, with an impressive array of black iron fire-tending implements. Tables likewise tend to be old or to look old, and you must have at least one ornate high-backed hard wooden chair which no one ever sits on.

When a couple of condominium families get together to invite their friends to eat here, on the evening of *ferragosto* perhaps (August 15), or on April 25, *la festa della Liberazione*, they expect these furnishings, particularly the splintery pine benches and fake oil-lamp light fittings, to induce a mood at once of merriment and traditional wholesomeness, the rightness of family and friends enjoying the fruits of their labors around the common hearth. As if for the space of an evening, the officeworker or shopkeeper or pharmaceutical salesman could enjoy the healthy repose of the *contadino* after the grape harvest; as if, like some Jungian subconscious, the *taverna* could be used to store away a primitive past and all its richness.

My own experience is that like so many dreams, the *taverna* is better in the dreamer's imagination than in the realization. Happier the Veronese choosing his fireplace and barbecuing instruments than the same irritated fellow trying to enjoy them. You go to a *taverna* party in a damp basement, unheated and unaired since the last binge, and quite possibly you will catch your death despite the most stifling weather aboveground. The chimney doesn't draw properly, because it is rarely used. You eat off a miscellany of plates, survivors of other dinner services once used upstairs; you drink from dusty glasses that no amount of rinsing will clean, perhaps because there is no hot water in the basement sink. Items of cutlery are found to be missing. Your knife doesn't cut very well. Conversation booms about the bare cement walls. After about an hour or so, just when the wine and barbecuing are beginning to take the chill off the place, the condominium dog-in-the-manger comes downstairs to complain that the noise is making it impossible for him to follow the latest episode of some favorite *telenovela*, a recycling of *Dallas*, *Dynasty*, or whatever. He is reassured, amid much contrition and invitation to join in (for this is by definition a wholesome party), then promptly forgotten, though remaining perhaps as a nagging subconscious irritation.

The food begins to arrive. You eat the flesh and sometimes it seems the bones and feathers too of blackbirds and small pigeons, crushing, as instructed, Maltese-sized heads between your molars so as to suck out the brains inside. Which are indeed toothsome. But pitifully small. While all around the table people are trying too hard to be jolly.

Out come the carabinieri jokes (right angles boiling at 90 degrees and so on), the shaggy dog stories of bureaucratic odysseys ("so when I went back for the third time he says that since my birth certificate was from another province and dated prior to 1959, the whole procedure should have been done by mail with the office in Rimini . . ."). There is much loud guffawing, head-shaking, glass-filling. "No, you must have another *uccellino*. You must. They're *squisiti* and I've already cooked it now." The thing falls on your plate with a definite resemblance to those hapless little corpses one finds on wet pavements in spring. Accordion music strikes out from the stereo. Six couples launch themselves into traditional dances in six square yards. Loud giggles. Somebody burns himself on a hot poker left sticking out of the hearth. Etc., etc.

The *taverna* seems to induce this behavior, this determination to be festive at all costs. Indeed, almost any *taverna* party has the flavor of those New Year's Eves when you simply can't feel there is anything to celebrate and wish you had stayed at home. But then my wife constantly tells me I'm a *gufo*, an owl, a spoilsport. She thoroughly enjoys these occasions. In my defense, I would merely say that whatever the surroundings I always love the wine, I can even tell with my eyes closed more or less which of the local varieties I'm drinking, and if only we could be having it in well-ventilated accommodations upstairs with some tortellini *al dente*, followed perhaps by a plate of finely sliced rare horsemeat and a little *tiramisù* straight from the refrigerator, I would be in *paradiso*.

Throwing open the iron door, drawing me to the threshold to gaze inside, Giampaolo Visentini was obviously a *taverna* fan. Perhaps for him the *taverna* represented some unthinkable loosening up, or an occasion when the more difficult social skills could be replaced by simple prowess with the barbecuing fork. In any event, showing me the gloomy place (I remember antlers and crossed ski poles on thin whitewash) he began to betray the first signs of life and enthusiasm. Did I like barbecuing? Did I like grilled eggplant? And *bruschetta* (toasted bread with olive oil and garlic)? I said yes, yes I did. And was I interested in bottling my own wine? The people in his company always clubbed together to bring a truckload of casks from a particularly good vineyard in Friuli. If I would like to split a cask of Cabernet or *prosecco* with him I should let him know in good time. We could buy in October and bottle next spring. The price was low and the quality excellent. I said to count me in at once, I was always ready to give something a try. By the time we were climbing the stairs again there was a feeling we might just make it as neighbors.

Then, running the gauntlet of Lucilla's door to get back through our own, we heard our phone ringing for the first time. Signora Marta, perhaps, having forgotten to tell us where the serious books and spare light bulbs were kept. Or one of the numerous schools and agencies we had immediately passed the number on to.

"C'è il dottor Patuzzi?" a confident older man's voice asked.

I froze.

"*Parla Giordano. Una questione di documenti.*"

"But Patuzzi's dead. He's been dead two years and more."

"But his name's in the phone book," this voice objected.

"He's dead," I said.

"*Ah. In quel caso non insisto.*" And the phone went, well, dead.

Rita said: "It's if they say, 'Patuzzi speaking' you should start worrying."

But somehow it seemed that when you had just cleaned all of a man's junk out and read a few of his letters and seen his well-thumbed girlie magazines and his boyhood skis and a crucifix by his parking place, then *fantasmi* were not an unreasonable proposition.

RESIDENZA

IT WOULD HAVE BEEN some weeks later we tried to change that entry in the phone book. We phoned SIP, the telephone company, and were told that in order to have our names in the phone book with that number we would need a recent certificate of *residenza in bollo* (that is, with a few thousand lire worth of special stamps on it) and signed renunciation of the number by Patuzzi, or his heir. The *contratto* for the phone would then be shifted, for a small charge, into our name and the bills would be addressed to us.

By the standards one has grown used to, this seemed something of a breeze. A check at our local *comune*, a pleasant enough little office with the inevitable crucifix, an impressive collection of rubber stamps, and a large computer on line to the city registry, provided the information that for certificates of residency we would need either proof of ownership of the said flat as first home or a written statement from the owner that we were tenants there. This should be on *carta bollata*—legal paper with, again, a few thousand lire worth of stamps on it.

So we rang Signora Marta. She was very polite but unable to understand why we wanted to change the name, "referring to the number in the phone book." Couldn't we simply tell everybody who wanted to phone us what our number was? We explained that there might be people who wanted to track us down for work. We were *liberi professionisti*. But if, she objected, they knew of our names, then they could ask the people they'd heard of us from, *non è vero?*—people who would surely have our telephone number or know someone who had it. Telephone directories were thus demonstrated to be entirely useless.

No, she added, the point was, it would be extravagant if we were only staying for a year. Because when we were gone we would of course renounce the number, so as not to be listed under it anymore and have bills for it in our names, at which point she could if she chose have the line disconnected, but then God knew how long it might take to get it reconnected and how much that would cost. The result being that she would most probably have to take the number on in her own name (rather than Patuzzi's). And since she already had a phone number, this number (Via Colombare's) would be registered as a second home phone, meaning much higher basic bills even if she made no calls.

So many conversations in Italy follow these serpentine paths, with new laws and regulations constantly raising their ugly heads to turn the most obvious ways forward into dead ends. With the creeping sense of paranoia that results, you occasionally find that people have been imagining rules that don't actually exist, simply because they seem to be the kind of thing the government would invent to make life more difficult and hence probably has. Was it really true, for example, that Marta would be obliged to register the number in her name? Couldn't she register it in a child's or grandmother's? Or was it that if she did that they would then have to switch their *residenza* to Via Colombare with all the problems that entailed?

I proceeded cautiously: when we left the flat, I said, if she asked us to leave it, that is, and we rather hoped she wouldn't because we liked it here, then this would presumably be because she had decided to sell it, or had found someone else to live in it, and in either case the new occupants would want to take over the phone, wouldn't they?

"Not if they already have one in their own name elsewhere," she came back. "Or if they want to retain residency in another province."

Who could have thought of this before starting the phone call? Then when I had already given up and offered a cool *arrivederci*, she suggested by way of an olive branch: "I don't mind writing to say that you live there, though, if you need to have *residenza* for other purposes."

How to explain the elusive yet all important significance of "residency" to a Brit who merely lives where he lives and acts accordingly? Can we hazard a definition? Residency means that the state now recognizes that you live where you live, or say you live (e.g., in the province of X at such and such an address), and henceforth will distinguish you from all the people who live in another province, or country, or who do, yes, live in X but whom the state does not recognize as living where they live (in X), either because those people want to be recognized as living elsewhere (where they don't live) and have managed by some scheme to achieve this, or because they can't get hold of some precious *documento* that would allow them to demonstrate that they do in fact live where they live (in X), and must thus continue to be recognized as living where they no longer live (in Y or Z, for example).

But does it actually matter? Well, yes. Once the state recognizes that one lives where one lives, there are all kinds of benefits: the right to register your car in the area (otherwise you will have to travel to Y or Z to register it), the right to register with a local doctor, the right to apply for local state jobs, the right to have access to certain services and benefits, the right to pay lower phone and utility bills, the right to vote, and most important for us, a 2-percent reduction on the amount of income tax withheld at source on free-lance services.

"Va bene," I told Signora Marta; if she could write such a letter we would be very happy. *"La ringrazio."*

But I was puzzled. She hadn't wanted a formal rent contract. I had half suspected that this was why she hadn't wanted the phone number in our name: she didn't want it to be in any way official that we lived here. And now on the contrary here she was offering to help us get residence. A calculated risk? Generosity?

"The flat," Rita suggested, "is officially owned by Maria Rosa, who is gaga in a nursing home. How is anybody to know that we are paying into Marta's account?"

Still . . . life is complicated. In any event, the drift seems to be that the government makes well-meaning but complicated laws and people very sensibly get smart and get around them. For example, there was this business Marta had mentioned that second homes carry much higher utility bills—a popular tax-the-rich measure. However, it is quite common in Italy for the middle and even lower-middle classes to rent their real home in the city where they work and possess a small holiday flat (second home) by the sea, by one of the lakes, or in the mountains. Result: many people register themselves or their wives or children as residents in the holiday home, so as to avoid higher bills. This in turn will create all kinds of other problems. On election day, the registered residents will have to travel a couple of hundred miles to vote in some place whose local politics they know nothing about. So they don't vote, you object. But in Italy if one doesn't vote three times in succession, one loses certain rights . . . etc., etc. Bureaucracy is a huge tangle of sticky string in which every attempt to loosen one knot tightens another.

And checks, or *accertamenti*, to make sure that each citizen is contributing his length of string to this tangle, are quite common. A few weeks after moving into Via Colombare, I went out on the balcony to see who had buzzed our bell and found a seriously fat man in uniform sitting on a moped with big dispatch boxes. Montecchio's local *vigile*. Taking some papers out of one of these boxes, he asked me something. I asked him if he could please speak Italian. He politely switched from dialect to something more comprehensible, upon which it emerged that he had been asking me whether I lived where quite obviously I was living (wearing pajamas, a piece of toast in my hand). I said I did. He then asked if he could come and see. And in my kitchen he explained at length about the *tassa sui rifiuti*, the garbage-collection tax. This apparently was paid not by the owner or even the renter of a property but by the head of the household actually living there *whether or not resident*—that is, they wanted the money, and red tape was not a problem (similarly, it is perfectly normal for a foreigner to file an income tax return without having a work permit). The person in question was me, I said. I would pay. He scratched his head, cocked it to one side, eyed me carefully from his tubby face. *"Bon,"* he said.

The *vigile* then wrote something amazingly painstakingly on his sheet of paper. While he worked, I noticed how clean his uniform was, how well ironed his shirt, how white the little pouch on his belt. It was another day of sultry heat. Despite the weight of flesh beneath all these clothes and accessories, he was not sweating.

He asked me my name. Then asked me to spell it. Fair enough. We got through Parks quite rapidly, and were speeding through Timothy (Torino Imola Monza Otranto—I say it in my sleep sometimes) when we ran up against the age-old problem of Y. "Hotel, Epsilon," I finished. He hesitated, raised his head, blew out his cheeks, narrowed his eyes. What was epsilon? "Epsilon," I said, "is a letter." *"A sì?"* he said. It was clear that he was used to being *preso in giro*, made a fool of, and so had developed these mannerisms—the suspicion, the slow questioning, the stare—to make himself seem less gullible.

Having studied me for a sufficient length of time, he decided I was not the type, said: *"Sì, sì, sì, d'accordo,"* and scribbled something down, I didn't dare ask him what. But then I had the idea of pulling out my English driving license and offering it, *per una verifica*. Offended, he waved it away.

"Residenza?" he now inquired, for even if it had no bearing on

my paying this tax or not, it was important to write it down. Three or four times.

I was applying for it, I said.

"*Stato di famiglia?*" (A document describing relationships within the family—who is the mother, the father, the head of the household, who the breadwinner, who dependent.)

I was waiting for my marriage certificate to arrive from England.

"*Professione?*" For everybody must be classified according to his profession.

I told him teacher. Rather flatteringly he wrote down *Professore.*

Then just as he was leaving I made the foolish mistake of remarking that we didn't have this residency business in England.

Again he was clearly concerned that he was being made fun of. There was the same cocking of the head, the puzzlement. He was one of those fat people who are terribly graceful, nimble almost, very aware of their bulk. He turned on his heel away from the door in almost a dance step, pushed back his cap, and lowered himself onto a seat at my kitchen table. This was a serious matter.

How was it possible, he asked, for us not to have residency? We didn't.

So what do you do? When you move.

You move, I said.

And the registration plates on the car?

You leave them as they are.

And your identity card?

There are no identity cards.

And the doctor?

You go and register at the nearest doctor's office.

He clearly didn't believe me. It couldn't be that easy. Not that I was lying. But I must be ingenuous. There was so much I hadn't understood. He was wondering how he could prove this to me. He had prickly Latin black hair cut short under his cap, and he scratched at it slowly, tugged at the tubby lobe of an ear. Then he had me.

How, he asked, would the postal system work?

In what sense?

How would they know where to bring the mail to, when you moved?

I tried to be equable, offhand. Somebody wrote your address on an envelope, affixed a stamp of the appropriate denomination, and the postal service would take it to that address and ask no questions.

The man got up and left in polite disgust. Obviously it was not a country for *vigili*.

I was not surprised a few weeks later when the first garbage bill arrived addressed to Parks Thimothj. As for the phone, if you open Verona's very handsome telephone directory, you will still to this day find the name of Umberto Patuzzi covering up for whoever is enjoying the pleasure of SIP's services at Via Colombare 10, flat three. Doubtless the gas bills are still in his name too. And the electricity bills, despite the curious fact that these actually include the modest charge of seven thousand lire a year for the votive light over his grave . . . a second home?

L'ANIMALE
DOMESTICO

JULY. DOG DAYS. The heat, that is, and Vega.

We had settled down in the flat, and bought a few hundred-watt bulbs, only to realize what an attraction they were to the moths and mosquitoes. We had got used to the tock-tock of midnight Ping-Pong from across the street, discovered that something of a breeze could be created by opening all the windows of the flat simultaneously and waggling one of the communicating doors, eaten our way through mountains of watermelons (to every season its antidote), and dedicated a shelf of the refrigerator to bowls of sliced peaches swimming in Valpolicella.

We had even made our first tentative peace with Lucilla, offered our help around the house should she ever need it, assured her we would take no part in the court case pending in which Marta and Maria Rosa were to be accused of having dashed to Il Professore's bank security box only moments after his heart attack and burned the will naming Lucilla his sole heir.

"But who was Il Professore?"

"Why, Umberto! Patuzzi! A wiser man never lived. A real *professore*."

As I had been for the *vigile*.

"*Un uomo squisito*. His death was such a terrible blow." Tears had a way of forming rapidly in Lucilla's veiny eyes. We shook our heads. And our assiduousness and sympathy (genuine, actually) had its reward in the reappearance, on about day ten, of the communal garbage can and the prospect of talks about one of those sacred spaces in the garage. Downstairs in the flat beneath our own (and hence opposite the Visentinis), the more timid, perhaps dour Vittorina seemed ready to follow whatever lead her volcanic sister-in-law would suggest. All, or much, was coming right.

There was just the problem that night after night our sleep was ruined by the howls of Vega scrabbling at her master's shuttered door, while toward midafternoon as I shifted from buttock to buttock in front of Patuzzi's huge desk, translating papers for an international conference on the decline of opera, it was impossible not to notice a slight odor of dog feces rising from the small patch of ground where the creature was kept imprisoned. I mentioned this on the stairs one day to Giampaolo. His surprising reaction was to phone the local carabinieri immediately. They came out very promptly, confirmed that there was a potential health hazard, and warned the one-armed, fierce-eyebrowed Signor Negretti that he'd better clean up his dog's act.

Negretti came out onto the terrace with his two teenage boys and hosed down the grassy area below where the dog was some-times chained, sometimes free to roam for four or five yards in any direction. He hosed it for perhaps ten or fifteen minutes, directed a last squirt at the shambling, excited dog herself, then went indoors. After which all was left as presumably it always had been.

Animals. Did I mention in the opening pages somebody's bundling a dog into the back of a car? Quite a normal sight on Via Colombare. The car will be a well-worn, dull-green Fiat 128, the *contadino*'s car par excellence; the man will be wearing rubber boots and a straw hat with the name of a tractor company on its band. He will drive off with admirable caution, though without buckling his safety belt, if he has one. As the car passes you, muffled barking may be heard, or the thumping of the pointer's tail against the gas tank.

But perhaps a better way into the relationship between Italians and animals might be to consider the normal translation of the English word "pet." The Italian expression is *animale domestico*. *"Il cane è un animale domestico."*

Well, in English one might feasibly say to one's girlfriend, boyfriend, wife, husband, son, daughter, "What a pet you are!"— meaning what a delightful, cuddly bundle of fun, pleasure, and loyal friendship around the cozy hearth. And of course we have the fine word "petting," which I have so often tried to explain to puzzled students. But could one, in Italian, say to one's mate, *"Che animale domestico che sei"*? No, this would be unadvisable. For it would mean, first, that they were *merely* an animal, as distinguished from the more elevated, thinking, speaking, and shotgun-toting *Homo sapiens*, and second that he or she was submissive, knew his or her place, didn't bother anybody and barked only when supposed to. Even throwing in palliative adjectives—*"che bell'animale domestico . . . che animale domestico carino"*—would not help in the least, since these could only be perceived as irony, thus adding insult to injury.

In short, Italians think differently about their pets/*animali domestici*. In 99 percent of cases they keep them outside; they do not like them coming into their houses and would not dream of having them sleep, say, at the foot of their beds. The idea of one's child being licked all over by a dog, as I was as a boy, would be unthinkably horrible to the modern Veronese mother (perhaps very reasonably so). But there is also something obsessive and exaggerated in this aversion, something which may have to do with the fact that it wasn't so very long ago that many families in the country around Montecchio had goats in the kitchen and the cow stall opening onto the sitting room for warmth. Proximity to any but the most expensive "luxury" animals has become a sign of social backwardness. And hunting dogs like Vega are a mere utility. You don't want them prancing into the house with their wet paws and dirty backsides. You use them when you go off shooting so they can bring back the *uccellini*, the tiny birds, which you eat in your *taverna* in nostalgic revelry at the joys of the country life you have wisely left behind. Otherwise you keep them chained in the yard.

Outside our window, Vega barked, howled, moaned deep into the night. With that extraordinary insistence dogs sometimes have. Bark, bark, bark, bark, for hours on end. What were we to do about it?

"Poison the thing," a student suggested at once.

Poison. For weeks, months, it was to become an obsession. We noticed stories in the paper reporting dog poisonings. They seemed quite common. Almost the done thing. Somebody in a place called Bussolengo had killed more than twenty in a single evening. Well, we needn't go that far. And I read Sciascia's novel *A ciascuno il suo*, in which he mentions a whole Sicilian tradition of dog poisonings, a sort of low-order vendetta between rival huntsmen.

We considered rat poison. And bought some. We studied the dosages. Twenty or thirty pellets in a meatball should be enough. But what if a child were to pick it up? Occasionally the Negrettis had guests with small children who were left to ramble about the defecated garden area. A student whose father was a vet cheerfully suggested the easier solution of a sponge soaked in meat juice. Apparently the sponge expands enormously in the animal's gut, blocking intestines and eventually leading to death. He knew people who had found this method very effective. Well, we had a small sponge in the bathroom which overlooked Vega's little patch. Part of the Patuzzi heritage. Nothing would be easier.

We observed the animal's eating habits. She seemed perfectly used to having her food tossed at her from considerable distances. She was instinctively friendly, running to her master or his sons in the hope of a pat, which very occasionally, grudgingly, she got. Though sometimes it was kicks. On a sort of dry run, we tossed her a biscuit from the bathroom window. Immediately it was snapped up and appreciated.

"The only problem with the sponge," my knowledgeable student explained at another lesson, "is that the creature will die in unspeakable agony, and you'll have to hear her howling like mad.

Probably for a couple of days. Though of course it will be worth it in the end."

We couldn't do it. At night, startled from sleep by blood-curdling howls, we would feel that we could. I might go to the bathroom and squeeze the yellow sponge in my hand, feel how it contracted and expanded, sense how easy it would be to chuck it, laden with the weight of the meat juice, the three or four yards over the fence to the howling dog. But something prevented us. And we developed the alibi that it wasn't the animal's fault, it was the master's, and we would kill the master if only such things were feasible. As a poor substitute for serious action we took to phoning *casa Negretti* whenever the dog woke us. After a couple of nights they left the phone off the hook.

We talked to our neighbors about it. The Visentinis weren't badly affected, because they lived at the other side of the building and had installed elaborate double glazing. But the subject did allow for our first real contact with Vittorina. No sooner had we mentioned the dog than she was telling us how when her husband had been dying the previous July, he had been unable to sleep because of the creature and she had begged Rocco Negretti to do something about it, to no avail. They were *gentaccia*, filth, no fate was bad enough for them. She burst into tears, remembering her husband's suffering, and we were able to offer her coffee in our flat, where she amazed us by remarking that she had never been in here before. No, she and Lucilla had been good friends with Il Professore, but the hateful Maria Rosa was a city woman and believed herself above them. They had never been invited into the flat. Il Professore had always taken his coffee at Lucilla's. While Maria Rosa did the shopping.

Vittorina was in her late sixties, big-boned, only slightly overweight. With great dark rings about her eyes, she was obviously morose by nature, a lover of candlelit churches, superstition, mystery, and gossip. But when she laughed it was with sudden heartiness and enthusiasm, a sort of profound natural health. She would go and tell Lucilla, she said, what nice people we were, because her sister-in-law was mad not wanting us to use Il

Professore's parking place after Il Professore had treated her so badly.

This was good progress, and terribly interesting of course (should we ask Vittorina about the photo taken near Prague?), but it didn't solve the problem of Vega.

Until one Sunday we would wake at dawn to the celebratory crackle of gunfire. The hunting season had begun, the hunting season that litters the paths with spent cartridges and deposits as much lead on the national territory as all the Fiats, Alfa Romeos, and Mercedeses put together. And although we had never seen so much as a wild rabbit on our Montecchio walks, the surrounding hills echoed with sharp reports all morning. *Uccellini*, pigeons, purposely-bred pheasants were presumably tumbling from the sky. And Vega was quiet that night, having had some exercise at last.

STILE CIMITERO

AUGUST IS A BETTER MONTH than July in the Veneto. The days are still scorchingly hot, but after a series of dramatic thunderstorms bringing hailstones as big as marbles and prompting radio and newspaper discussions as to whether farmers really could ever have had all the crops they are claiming compensation for, the humidity finally fades like a bad dream; the days are dryer and clearer and the welcome dusk comes a bit earlier.

It's a good time to take walks. The countryside assumes its dusty green long-suffering summer look: mat colors under sizzling light. The vines are thicker now, their shoots knotting swiftly across the system of wires between one row of posts and the next, completely shading the ground below. You can walk beneath them under a panoply of leaves through vineyard after vineyard up the valley toward Mizzole, your hair brushing across berries that are just beginning to swell. In the scented green light a wealth of insect life goes about its business: you see extraordinary bright yellow spiders spinning their threads fast from tendril to tendril. And through the still air and intense heat, you gradually become aware of a great silent seething all around, urgent and secretive, as if the whole world were concentrated on growth, growth, growth. One tends to fall silent oneself crossing vineyards on hot summer days. The plants don't want to be disturbed. There is so much still to be done before September.

On the plain to the south the corn is already in and the *contadini* are burning the dusty stubble with a cavalier disregard for fire hazards. On the hill above us *il conte* (as most rich landowners seem to be known) loses an acre of woodland and there are whisperings of arson. Climbing a steep slope of stunted trees and scrub we find two men running around a large burned area trying to stamp down flames every time they flare up: here, there, behind them, in front. The smoke has a pleasant smell and is thin and lazy in the shimmering air. The men's task seems hopeless, but no, they say, they don't need help. We climb on and find the count's huge house, mansion rather: an austere facade of ocher stucco with travertine sills and plinths. Looking through the ironwork of the old gate we count six expensive cars. Rita reflects that Mussolini's roundup of iron for the war effort generally seems to have passed over the gates of the rich, while the *contadini* shelled out their saucepans. I feel we could do with another war effort to get rid of the thousands of miles of superfluous ironwork sprouting up in modern suburbia.

The radio begins to speak of drought, and in this our first year in Montecchio the regional government ordered us to stop watering our gardens. Weeks passed. The ban was not lifted. But there was little sign of deterioration in the swelling tomatoes, eggplants, and peppers that flourished in every vegetable patch. For the fat *vigile* entrusted with the business of enforcing the regulation, the same who had come to see if I was living where I was living, was not to be seen beyond six in the evening, while watering began more or less with the arrival of fresh air around midnight: old men and women pushing their hoses quietly between thick clods, the more arrogant new arrivals leaving it to their timers to turn on sprinkler systems under the stars. One thing the Italian politician perceives in a way his ingenuous English counterpart does not is that it is the enforcement of a law which is unpopular, not the law itself, which is patently a good thing and the right response to whatever problem it is supposed to be solving. Just as it is right for the Pope to insist on chastity, as long as one is left to do as one pleases. In the model anarchic society, to which Italy frequently approximates, there will be rules without end whose value will never be questioned. And under this excellent cover everybody will live as he sees fit.

In the minty night air the water hissed. The eggplants plumped out with their dark mauve of secret flesh. Practiced fingers tied up the pepper plants, and fat salad tomatoes were left to ripen on stone windowsills. Growth was almost audible.

So that at number 10, poor Vittorina was perhaps the only person in all Montecchio who out of some misguided sense of guilt or civic duty actually bothered to carry out her dishwater in buckets and chuck it over our vegetable patch. With the result that one would find strands of spaghetti draped over the *radicchio rosso*, or a few bones of codfish in among the parsley.

Giampaolo came out with a red colander, looked at the ground, frowned, went back in empty-handed.

Every condominium, of course, is galvanized by a sort of magnetic field of attractions and repulsions. Nowhere could these be more strongly and urgently felt at Via Colombare 10 than in attitudes to the large square communal garden to one side of the house. The truth is that the modern Italian has problems with his garden. He is not at ease with it yet as the Englishman is. Behind him he has centuries of a peasant culture, which ended, if it has ended, not a hundred years ago, but yesterday. For him the ground means crops, the vines, the towering corn plants, tobacco, fruit trees, tomatoes. Quite simply, he has this in his blood. And there are many who buy or build huge villas on the slopes just outside Montecchio, with a swimming pool on the terrace, gymnasium in the basement, and the most ornamental iron fence imaginable all around, and can then think of nothing to do with the garden but turn it into a vast cabbage and spinach patch, producing more than they could ever hope to eat or even give away. Out of a sort of nostalgia, one assumes, or inertia, or lack of imagination.

On the other hand, there are those who feel ashamed of their peasant roots and see the garden as a means of expressing their arrival in the stylish world of office jobs, high tech, and magazine-inspired domestic environments. In which case they attempt to reconstruct the traditional ornamental garden of the Italian aristocracy: dwarf cypresses, oleanders, religious statuettes, and tiny stone paths, spiced up perhaps with a variety of exotic plants that some garden center is passing off as fashionable and that haven't a hope of surviving the cold Veneto winter. Once everything is planted and growing, such people don't play in their gardens as an English family might. They tend them, brush them, and sweep them like some never-to-be-used front room, the way other people are forever cleaning cars they never take out of their garages. Until, with the somber smell of the cypresses and a curious stony stasis of upright trees and crisscross flagging, the status-symbol garden begins to look like a little cemetery without the graves (but waiting for those of its owners, perhaps). And house after house along Via Colombare, garden after garden, decorous little cemeteries alternate with vigorous pea and cabbage patches as each *capofamiglia* declares his particular response to the profound change that has taken place, the loss of that old obviousness that the land was for food you needed to survive.

Vegetable garden, cemetery; chained dogs in the first, a Siamese cat perhaps in the second; nervous animals and uncertain patches of green marooned by the lava flow from the city as it solidifies day by day in streets and wrought-iron fences. The tall tall fences of Montecchio, *la fortuna del fabbro*, the blacksmith's jackpot. Nowhere, nowhere does one find that happy, relaxed, cozy, ad hoc floweriness of the suburban English garden. It must be one of the only areas of domestic civilization where the British win hands down.

Lucilla and Vittorina were nostalgic for a peasant past. Understandably. They wanted those tomatoes and *peperoni*. Lettuce and *radicchio rosso* too. But Lucilla was fat and lazy. And a little ashamed. She drew the line at vines, for example, and was famous for having torn down with her own hands an attractive *filare* that Vittorina's husband had set up. What's more, if there was a vegetable patch, it must be away from the road, secluded from the casual glance of passersby. After all, the house itself was so stylish with its pretentious Californian eaves, *graffiato* finish, and big terrace balconies, it gave such an impression of having arrived; it would be a crime to disabuse the passerby with some humble salad crop.

So a thin strip of land away from the road and immediately beneath the wall of Negretti's house and terrace turned out to be the only place for productive cultivation. This annoyed Vittorina, who did the lion's share of the work in the garden and got some real sense of recreation from it. It annoyed her because the ground below Negretti's three-story windowless wall got no sunshine and little rain and was full of snails, indeed teeming with them. They bred in the unkempt clutter and cracked cement of Negretti's terrace and then slithered down three yards of damp brickwork in the night to stake out number 10's lettuce and peas. So Vittorina would far rather have had a sunny patch over toward the road, to feel the sun warm on her back in the early morning as she tied up her tomatoes. She didn't care about the impression this would give to the neighbors, as she didn't care about being seen carrying out her dirty dishwater; she had none of Lucilla's obsession with social status.

But a difference of opinion between Vittorina and Lucilla was easily resolved. Lucilla stamped her small, fat high-heeled foot, and aside from a dark muttering of a saint's name here and the Virgin's there, Vittorina inevitably succumbed. Along with her peasant's attachment to salad and vegetables, she also had the peasant's age-old submission to master and bad weather. With her never perfectly plucked mustache and fierce temper, Lucilla resembled both.

No, the real problem with the garden in Via Colombare was that of integrating the old ladies' earthy mix of nostalgia and shame with the younger Visentinis' more sophisticated, media-based, urban vision: an English lawn, shady trees, and , yes, a vegetable patch (because Giampaolo is a gourmet and fresh greens are tastier), but run along ecological, natural-food lines (because Giampaolo, like any modern man, is also something of a Green). Thus not only did Vittorina have to work the communal vegetable patch under the tall bare wall of Negretti's grim house, but to add to her troubles she wasn't allowed to poison the quite multitudinous snails. It all came out in the food, her younger neighbor scared her. We would all die of cancer.

And that was one battle Giampaolo won. Indeed, whenever Vittorina took up a position on something it was always clear she was going to lose. A bulky, heavy-breathing woman, she prayed a great deal, had masses said for her husband, visited the cemetery almost daily, and subscribed to such periodicals as *I miracoli di Sant'Antonio* and *La salvezza*. Her face had a morose wisdom which would occasionally light up in genuine friendliness. One suspected she was already resigned to losing the quarrels of this world, banking on the next. A pushover for the persuasive, courteous, and always well-informed Giampaolo.

However, since Giampaolo only rented his flat, whereas the others owned, when it came to getting trees or bushes for the garden proper, Lucilla insisted on choosing and locating them herself (Giampaolo was quick to disclaim responsibility). The result was one of the very saddest collections of dwarf cypresses and ornamental mutants imaginable, unhealthy things picked up in sales and planted apparently at random across two hundred square yards of dry lawn. A funereal tone was everywhere apparent, and indeed it occurred to us that Lucilla had probably never been into a garden that wasn't a cemetery. There were no gardens in her poverty-stricken youth, and most of her life had been spent operating an industrial cleaning business from a small suburban flat. Whereas the early death of her husband and various relatives had made her all too familiar with cemeteries.

To her credit, Lucilla was aware that something was wrong with the garden at number 10, aware that this gloomy assortment of dull evergreens was not really what she was after. In the hope of achieving some improbable rightness, she would thus, Giampaolo explained, move the trees about year after year, dig one up, shift it a yard or two this way, dig up another, swap it with yet another, put this one in the shade, move that one out of it, and so on and so forth, so that the weary plants became sadder and sadder while the business of mowing the lawn in Via Colombare now involved a dizzy weaving back and forth through the lost labor of Lucilla's search for harmony.

And of course the lawn had to be mowed regularly. Giampaolo was strict about this. Regularly and very low. Because it had to be an *English* lawn, as the Italians imagine English lawns to be, an extension, that is, of the meticulous formal elegance of the Visentinis' flat, licked cleaned from top to bottom day in day out with sacrificial anality. Yes, Giampaolo said at our first condominium meeting when my duties were outlined, the lawn had to be mowed twice or three times a week from spring through autumn and the cuttings had to be gathered with a rake and piled on a compost heap in the most hidden corner of the garden where shameful things like compost heaps are piled. It should be said here, in Giampaolo's defense, that most surrounding gardeners of the cemetery variety just had their grass taken away by the refuse men, and this was the easy solution that Lucilla, if not Vittorina, would undoubtedly have plumped for. But being a Green, Giampaolo rightly insisted that grass was a limited resource to be husbanded and utilized—along the snail-infested wall. . . .

Never has good neighborliness been more onerous, as, with the two ladies unable to handle the mower and no one willing to pay for a gardener, I was enlisted into the ritual twice-weekly mowing. And daily watering. For the lawn had to be watered assiduously throughout the hot summer, and most particularly it had to be watered at the front of the house where the terrace balconies of the two lower flats were only a yard or so above quite a few square yards of grass below, depriving the grass of water, but not light, since a low slanting sun shafted in of an evening to shrivel up the poor plants.

How we mowed and mowed that lawn. And how many hours I was to spend distractedly pointing a hose at those doomed patches of grass beneath the balconies, which were so important, of course, being among the most visible, through iron railings, from the dusty street. To make matters worse, it was assumed that, being English, I would naturally know a great deal about lawns, and my advice, as we settled in, would frequently be sought on dry patches, ring molds, moss, etc., as if such knowledge were carried in the genes. I thus got used to observing a genuine sense of disappointment when it was discovered that I knew nothing, but nothing, about lawns. And what's more (to my shame now, actually), showed every sign of not greatly caring.

Giampaolo: "What kind of fertilizer do you think we should put on the lawn toward the end of summer?"

Me, with a shake of the head: "The cheapest."

"Do you think we should leave the cut grass down this time, or rake it up?"

"Oh, let's leave it. Good idea." But my enthusiasm was too evident, and very soon it was understood that my opinions could be ignored, and that I wouldn't even mind if they were not solicited. Which was a relief. And to salve any conscience I might have, I reflected that at least I was doing my neighbors the favor of demonstrating the hollowness of national stereotypes.

LA STAGIONE È
FINITA

SOMETIMES WHEN I WASN'T actually called upon to participate in the garden, I would watch the others from the big window in our parlor. For ironically ours was the only flat with a good upper-story view of the garden. I thus observed that while the old ladies followed the seasons, Giampaolo went by the book. Or rather, it wasn't quite the seasons Lucilla and Vittorina followed, but the rigid set of proverbs and rules a thousand years of peasant culture offered them—some of which they themselves, having spent their adult lives in industrial cleaning, remembered only approximately. I recall in mid–September going out into the garden for a couple of tomatoes (just reward for all that mowing) to discover, to my amazement, that not only were there none left, but the plants themselves had gone, disappeared, been uprooted, the ground already forked over and raked.

"When Lucilla decides the season's over, she tears them up," Orietta Visentini told me. Her voice was still completely neutral, as it had been at all our early meetings. But now a half-smile played about the lips, suggesting the possibility of future confidences. "She's pulled up the peppers too, and the eggplants. It's the same every year."

"But they were still growing."

"Lucilla thought the season was over."

Lucilla was an extreme, indeed manic, case, but it has to be remembered that this is the country where if you go swimming any time after September, even if the temperature is in the sweltering upper nineties, you will be looked on with surprise. *La stagione è finita*. The season is over.

Giampaolo, on the contrary, to plant a row of peas, brought out the encyclopedia he was buying piecemeal and at considerable price. This would be on the weekend, since he had a regular office job. He laid the appropriate volume on a dry patch of ground and was careful not to touch it with earthy hands: if I happened to be around I would turn the pages for him and read. The spacing between one seed and another? Five centimeters. The depth of the hole? Three centimeters. Soil preparation? Brought up the last child of eight in Venice, he knew nothing of the earth, but being a modern man he believed that information could be had from books. We planted the peas together. We did everything the book said. Most never came up. And the few that did were eaten overnight by the rampant snails.

The ladies sniggered. As indeed Giampaolo sniggered when they tore up tomato plants that still had a good several pounds in them. Lucilla would stop you on the stairs: "Have Signor Giampaolo's carrots come up?" With that same half-smile around the corners of her lips, Orietta would say: "Now they've pulled up the pepper plants."

And yet, Giampaolo had considerable respect for the local peasant culture, because books teach this too. Parsley and spinach should be planted with a new moon, a lawn sown with a full moon, still wines bottled with a waning moon, etc., etc. And the old ladies in their turn had more than a sneaking admiration for anybody who could genuinely read a book and find something out. After all, it was

Giampaolo who fixed their boilers when they burst, and adjusted their cars and appliances, even if his peas never came up and the bulbs he planted didn't flower. In the garden, everybody watched everybody else in a delicious tension to see whose culture would prove the most effective. And in this respect the situation was typical of the small handkerchief of Italy I live in. There is such a collision of ancient ideas and new. Which will win? In a way it was not unlike Elisha and the worshipers of Baal waiting to see whose sacrifice would burst into flames.

And in the meantime we were all watched by old Lovato, our neighbor on the Via Colombare side, whose tiny garden bordered on our own. Bald, towering, broad-shouldered, Lovato was one of the old guard, a never-say-die pea-cabbage-tomato-and-pepper man, a retired farmer. His gaze, looking over the wall at our sad ornamental garden, was one of genuine puzzlement, turning to pity and just a hint of derision when his eye fell upon our miserable vegetable patch. In his own few poky square yards he produced a quite prodigious abundance of vegetables in the way only the small farmer knows how: working the ground furiously and using obscene amounts of fertilizer, weed killer, and pesticide. The snails must have felt sick if ever the faintest breeze blew from his direction.

Stolid, solid, and quite unashamed of a businesslike shamble of pots, canes, and cuttings all about him, Lovato watched. Through wire netting. For above the waist-high dividing wall, he had unaccountably erected a fence reaching up a good ten feet and lethally barbed on top, though sagging and rusting. I say "unaccountably" because intrusion from the direction of Via Colombare 10 was surely unlikely. But it was interesting that neither Giampaolo nor the old ladies found anything strange about his wanting to guard his property so determinedly. If an Englishman's house is his castle, an Italian's is his bunker. There is this obsession with self-defense: railings, remote-controlled gates, security cameras, bulletproof windows, armored front doors. No, from the Via Colombare point of view, Lovato's attitude was understandable. But it absolutely must not be at the expense of the ornamental quality of number 10's garden.

Lucilla and Vittorina had years ago asked Lovato to remove this *vergogna* (one is tempted to translate this as "eyesore," but literally the word means "shame," which is what they felt Lovato should feel). Lovato refused. Giampaolo more diplomatically referred to the fence as *anti-estetico*. Lovato played deaf. He would not take the thing down. At which Giampaolo suggested that the ladies buy a hedge which would grow up and cover it all. Yes, all three yards high of it, thus protecting the aesthetic qualities of number 10's cemetery. The hedge was duly planted. This apparently infuriated Lovato, who claimed it would eventually rob all light from his small patch, though it's possible he was equally concerned about losing his pensioner's view of our miserable garden (which must have provided considerable entertainment). He would go to court, he said. There was a law about blocking other people's light. Giampaolo politely remarked that his ramshackle garage of cinder block and corrugated iron located to one end of the fence had surely not been erected with the appropriate building permission. Since this was where Lovato's son-in-law kept the Lancia Prisma of which the whole family was rightly proud, it seemed unlikely they would be willing to pull it down just in order to embark on uncertain litigation against number 10. When Rita and I arrived in Via Colombare the hedge was a yard high with everything still to play for.

To straighten out your topography, then, we have the threatening hedge and nosy Lovato directly opposite the northern (and lateral) wall of the condominium, which includes our living-room window, where I sometimes stand beneath the elaborate dim chandelier to look out on the world. To my left (and west) as I look out is the long ironwork railing along Via Colombare, and to my right (never forgetting the mobile triffids in the garden between, of course) Negretti's tall windowless wall. And here's a curiosity. Negretti's wall has a cinema screen on it, a huge rectangle of white, for before number 10 was built the present garden area had been a cinema. Yes, rural Montecchio had once had a cinema, albeit tiny. Now, of course, the screen was no more than cracking white paint surrounded by broken brickwork where the cinema had been demolished and Negretti's wall reinforced. Not a little of Negretti's intransigence with his dog, we discovered, his almost relishing the disturbance she caused, was the result of his having wished to buy the cinema himself, only to be outbid by these two old ladies, who then ignored building regulations to stick their own *palazzina* rather too close to his. In revenge he refused to do anything about the unsightly wall, the yellowing screen, the broken bricks. Lucilla and Vittorina offered to go halves to have it stuccoed, but Negretti, like Lovato, refused. And the more they showed the wall bothered them, the more stubborn he would be. The ornamentality of number 10's garden was thus irretrievably compromised; for whereas Lovato's fence might one day be covered by that hedge, no ivy could really get a grip on the smooth white of the cinema screen. As for myself, wandering around in stifling heat, hose in hand, doing my bit for the lawn, the snail-sad lettuce, the scorched earth beneath the terraces, I would look up at the screen and wish with all my heart that the cinema could have remained.

IL PALO DELLA CUCCAGNA

Montecchio mornings, late September. Seven o'clock. The tiles under bare feet are beginning to feel more than pleasantly cool. You go through to the kitchen, heave up the heavy plastic roll-down shutter, all the rage in the late seventies, but spurned now in the general return to natural materials. You have to be careful not to pull too hard or the thing will roll away through the slit and into its little box above the French window, to be retrieved only after hours of fiddling. On the outside, the plastic is peppered with holes where the wind hurled big hailstones in an August storm.

You step out onto the balcony, air fresh and glass clear. Number 10 is exactly halfway along the street. In a lacquered morning light you see the Madonnina in her niche with fake flowers a hundred yards away to the right, the derelict bottle factory the same distance to the left. Opposite, above the houses, rise two more, rather nobler nineteenth-century mills, also derelict, one with an attractive design of little pillars and arches just beneath the cornice some six floors up. Both buildings have landmark status, their empty windows staring, innards gutted. And behind these again rises a low ridge of hills pushing south into the plain, with *Il Castello di Montecchio* on top: a square tower, a wall, a taller tower, a wall, a third tower the same height as the first—Austrian defenses. The Communist Party wants to turn it into a sports and community center. The Christian Democrats don't seem to be able to find the money, or the enthusiasm. At present, amid banks of blackberries going to waste, it's used only by the so-called *emarginati*: drug addicts, homosexuals, immigrants.

But what a splendid sight on a bright morning, with the larks still twittering high in the air, the most delicate fleecy clouds (*pecorelle,* the Italians call them, little sheep) curdling in milky blue above, and the light green horizontal flow of the ridge beautifully pointed up by the somber verticality of cypresses winding serpentine toward the sharp silhouette of the castle.

Down in the street, the old man who lives opposite slithers off his muddy bike. Giobatta Marini. Pushing eighty, hunched, flatfooted, fishing gear slung over his shoulder, he has his dawn catch in a plastic bag under his arm. His stout wife, who bore him all those Ping-Pong-playing children, comes out in apron and slippers to meet her patriarch and whisk away the fish. An early lizard creeps between railings along the wall. And leaning on the cool marble of the parapet, still in your pajamas, you breathe deeply, as your father used to whenever he got a chance to be out in the country. "How marvelous, what air!"

A boy in overalls with bedraggled hair and pasty face roars by on an ancient and deliberately unsilenced *motorino*. Leaving a cloud of oily blue behind. Well, okay. It's all part of the happy scene, not unpleasant really, and he does boast the name of Raffaello. At the end of the street he revs quite violently—a bit of frustration, unsatisfied libido, to burn up. Fair enough. He works at the mechanic's at the corner. But now he's turned the thing off, the cloud of exhaust has dispersed, and you can relax again, breathe in this beauty, and breathe deep: aah!

Until quite suddenly the whole marvelous morning is corrupted, tainted, transformed, by the most unpleasant smell.

It's sudden and overwhelming. One moment you didn't notice it, the next the whole picturesque scene—castle, fisherman, Madonnina—has become a deception, an enamel over something that reeks.

Words and smells don't go well together, but perhaps I could describe it as a corpse smell, a smell of something wrong, an abusive, acrid, clogging smell, and certainly a smell that one shouldn't be smelling at seven o'clock in the morning in a village in northern Italy. The chemical factory in the small industrial park is letting off the fumes from its storage tanks. Go in, close the door and all the other windows too. Look at the fine morning through the glass you really ought to clean. And get the espresso pot on to drown that stench.

The following morning, if the pressure is suddenly low and fine mercurial clouds are thickening over the *castello*, it could well be a chicken-dung smell rolling down from the factory farms that have taken over the surrounding hills as the *contadini* beat their long retreat. An all-pervading smell that may last half the morning.

And the next day, if we imagine a rare breeze is flowing from the north after rainfall, it will be the smell of intensive pig farming farther up the valley. Is this the worst? Or should pride of place go to the synthetic fabric factory to the south, whose methylated fumes, thank heaven, come only with the scirocco? But they're all bad. They all add to that constant threat of encroachment which typifies these villages. They all have to do with making money fast on territory that is cheap because it's being abandoned, territory that once provided a living, and little more. Unless perhaps a culture.

The evenings are more pleasurable. There are no particular smells. Your wineglasses are perched on the marble parapet of the balcony while from Patuzzi's abandoned armchair you watch huge moths whir about the streetlights hanging from wires which run zig-zag between the houses. The sound of Giampaolo's stubborn hose hisses from under the balconies. The old ladies call to each other up and down the stairs over the babble of their televisions: "Cillà! Rinà!" Tock-tock-tock goes the Marini tribe's Ping-Pong. And a blackbird whistles quite beautifully at twilight. Over a period of a couple of months we get to know his call. We stand on the balcony and whistle. There is a pause, perhaps a minute. To tease you. Then he whistles back. And again. And again. "Lest you should think he never could recapture . . ." But that was a thrush, of course. The blackbird whistles; we answer him. It's upsetting to discover later that he sings so well because Giobatta has blinded him. For on the mornings he doesn't go fishing, old Marini will take the creature out into the country in its tiny cage, to attract other birds to the muzzle of his shotgun.

Perhaps it shouldn't be upsetting. This kind of thing has always gone on. This is the old way. Why am I so squeamish? Yet whenever I whistle to the bird now I can't help imagining the moment of its blinding, and I both want and don't want to know how it was done.

Giobatta, of course, is short for Giovanni Battista. When a friend of mine recently took his child to be baptized and said, "Giovanni," the priest immediately came back, "Evangelista or Battista?" There was no other choice. You would have thought with his namesake ending up the way he did, Giobatta might have been a shade more mindful about taking sharp instruments to creatures.

Night falls. But the gently swinging lights keep the street quite bright. In the glow, little girls are playing something like hopscotch. There is no bedtime here. They dodge about their chalk squares and shrill and argue. Comes the sound of clashing gears and a car scatters them, driving recklessly fast in the narrow space. Their parents playing Ping-Pong under the pergola do not seem concerned. A red light goes on above the Madonnina. Or perhaps it is always on but only noticeable in the dark. From the window below we can hear the ladies giggling together over their television. Comes the portentous sound of the hour tones. A woman's voice announces that it is 10:04 precisely, then the strain of the tune introducing the evening news program. It is an endearing characteristic of Italian broadcasting that they are not overly concerned about starting programs on the hour.

One Sunday, after a morning of particularly unpleasant smells, we walked to Montecchio's industrial park to check the situation out. It lies just the other side of the cherry orchard behind the Madonnina. Sadly, the orchard is closed off by a ten-foot-high dry stone wall some hundreds of years old. One thus skirts around this barrier and goes by way of the bus terminus, where the driver is enjoying a few minutes in a bar before his return trip to Verona (terminuses always coincide with bars, which is as it should be). The road here is straight and narrow, with tall ivy-bitten walls either side. A first iron gate on the right leads into an avenue of cypresses and the cemetery. Then, after a large tarred area, which trucks could presumably park in, but never do, you turn into the industrial park.

And are immediately surprised. For what you see is: attractive villa, followed by long low prefab; then salubrious three-story *palazzina*, followed by grubby factory; then, green-stuccoed terrace with cascading geraniums, followed by woodyard; and again, lavishly funereal garden, chemical plant; gnomed patio with barbecue, printworks; and on and on: expensive house, business, expensive house, business, expensive house, business for three hundred yards. All the local *padroni* live here with their factories and factory smells. How can we complain when they get the worst of it? Circulars from the Communist Party will later explain that the land was more or less given away, allowing *imprenditori* to build cheap villas for themselves, their children, their grandchildren. "Not a single job more was created," they protest. Perhaps erroneously.

But as industrial areas go, and when the early-morning smell of lucrative enterprise has subsided, this is not an unpleasant place. Well-dressed families are eating ice cream on balconies. There's a sound of chatter and children. A fat man in fashionable tracksuit is clearing up his toasting forks. The chained guard dogs are asleep in the shade.

Then on our way home we stumbled upon *il palo della cuccagna*. In passing I might say that everything I have discovered in Montecchio I have stumbled on. It seems in keeping with the spirit of the place. And perhaps it was only because we saw them both on the same day that it occurred to me that this amusing celebration was not entirely unconnected with the mentality that produced the industrial park.

We had planned to walk back a different way so that we could lounge on the Roman stones by Laghetto Squarà for a while, something that was becoming a favorite pastime: just sitting and watching, in the heat, by the water, with the sound of the spring gurgling across pebbles from under the broken church door. But the banks of the *laghetto* were packed this afternoon. A hundred and more people were shouting and cheering. As we approached, the cheering grew louder and louder, then a great splash. And more cheers, or jeers, before somebody called a name on a megaphone.

We climbed up on a stone. Into a drain hole in the bank, the trunk of a fir tree, perhaps twenty yards long, had been fixed so that it stretched out horizontally just above the water, supported halfway by a spike driven into the lake bottom. A small red flag fluttered right at the end, where the pole was no more than four or five inches thick. On the bank, above the base of the trunk, stood a small gaggle of boys and men in swimming costume, shivering under towels. Beside them, on a high stool, sat the umpire.

The umpire calls out a name. The boy who serves me my *prosciutto crudo* in Brandoli's, the supermarket, lets himself down gingerly over the weedy stone onto the base of the pole, and begins to walk. All he has to do is reach the other end of the pole and grab the flag. This feat will transport him into the land of Cockaigne, i.e., he will get a reward. In the event, despite the thickness of the pole at its base, he manages no more than three yards.

Because the whole pole has been thickly greased with soap.

There are about fifteen contestants, and they go again and again in turns, slipping and slithering clownishly on the soap. If you refuse to go when it's your turn, you're out. And since the water rises right here from under the hills, it is not exactly warm. An older man, in his sixties perhaps, is shivering violently as he lifts his stomach onto the bank. A muscly exhibitionist clutches his crotch.

71

There's a clammy weed in his hair. At each attempt each contestant dissolves a little more of the soap, and then for four turns each is allowed to carry a handful of sand, which he spreads in front of his feet. Thus some kind of progress is made, pushing farther and farther toward the flag, amid the screams of girlfriends and mothers, and the chuckling of those men wise enough to appreciate that this is definitely a spectator sport.

It's interesting (and rather a shame) that no girls are competing.

At the end of the day (and we stay two hours and more), since it would be impossible to provide the winner with the real cockaigne of *palazzina* and family business beside, the prize, finally awarded to the lad who delivers bread from one of the village's bakeries, is 150,000 lire's worth of petrol from our local petrol pump. As a vision of plenty, it says much perhaps. Though this archaic festival is obviously timed to coincide with the harvest.

BEPI

ORIETTA VISENTINI SAYS that in twenty-odd years she has never really been accepted in Montecchio. For she was born in Peschiera, on the southern shores of Lake Garda, twenty-five miles away. People's friends here are their childhood friends, their family. Orietta sighs. They don't even know how to make friends, because they have never had to do so, and anyway, they can't imagine anybody being without his or her own circle.

What hope for me then?

Very little. I step off the bus outside the derelict bottle factory and walk down Via Colombare. I nod to people: to the grappa-scented car mechanic in his overalls whose work overflows onto the narrow street; to ancient becapped Giobatta, the hunter and fisher, but working on his vines today along a sagging fence; I nod again to the slightly mongoloid-looking woman in black who puts her father out on a chair by the doorstep in the morning, squashes his straw hat on his head, and brings him in in the evening (surprisingly, their dingy house, which opens directly onto the street, has an expensive aquarium in the window of a bare room with large table, wooden chairs, stone floor, and nothing else). I salute the portly heavy-jowled man in the light suit who finds climbing out of his Alfa 75 something of an effort, the more casual fellow who sells insurance in a Fiat 126, the stout vigorous woman who every morning takes a twig brush to sweep the dust from the road outside her house and push it over toward her neighbor's. My greetings, which after all follow the traditional Italian style and which all these people exchange with each other every time they cross paths— *Buon giorno, signora; buon giorno, signore*—are met at first with embarrassment, perhaps even suspicion, since clearly I am part of that world which encroaches; later with returned nods, muttered courtesies. And perhaps that is quite enough. Only in the greengrocer's does a loud voice reply: " 'ello, sir, 'ow are you!" And it is Bepi. My first friend in Montecchio.

I suppose Bepi fits into that class of Italians who are eager to know foreigners. One has to be careful not to be collected by these people. It's a group Giampaolo Visentini belongs to in a rather different, more sophisticated way. Not that these people have in any sense ceased to believe in the supremacy of Italian cooking, Italian wine, Italian style, etc., just that they are sensitive to a certain provincialism, eager to be associated with anything that lies outside their narrow circle. Perhaps they have been frustrated: Giampaolo by the stifling promotion procedures in the monolithic company he works for, Bepi by the obstacles put in the way of anybody without contacts who wishes to get a license for a lucrative shop. Both feel they have ideas bigger than the narrow mentality of the people around them. But, interestingly, they don't feel this provincialism could be overcome by going to Rome, as a man stifled in Barnsley might head for Birmingham or London. On the contrary, Rome would be even worse; the locals would already have staked the place out for themselves. No, they look to the fairness and openmindedness of the efficient nations farther north. Extraordinarily, they believe Britain to be such a nation. And can never understand what on earth I am doing here in Montecchio.

From behind his stone-topped counter, Bepi pumps my hand.
He is "very 'appy" to have an Englishman in his shop. He smiles
broadly. He's my own age or thereabouts, but physically a much
more impressive specimen: hugely solid, with thick shoulder-
length curly hair, and such a look of eagerness about him, such a
presence. Green green eyes. He sticks a couple of kiwis in my bag
and doesn't want to be paid for them. *Per carità!*

As I turn to go, the priest walks in, Don Guido. I am thus able
to witness the whole scene. In his black cassock, the priest stands
there sniffing the air, a short, droll old woman of a man. He sniffs
and sniffs, snub nose upturned, as the other customers go about with
their little plastic baskets picking up artichokes, peppers, and what-
have-you from the boxes around the wall. Then he lifts his
shoulders sharply up and down in a gesture of impatience. The
cassock has a shiny, worn look to it. "Something smells rotten in
here," he announces out loud and with almost a threat in his voice.

Quite unperturbed, giving or taking change, Bepi replies,
"Must be the carrion flesh of the last person to walk in." *Carogna* is a
common insult. At which the priest calmly proceeds with his
shopping.

I never managed to get to the bottom of this dispute between
our greengrocer and priest, a quarrel made attractive by the combination of intense animosity and total lack of consequence. And
perhaps that is the essence of the Latin quarrel, at least on this level.
It is almost enjoyed for its own sake. There is no feeling of any need
to make up or resolve things, because no harm is being done. The
priest came every day, ritual insults were exchanged, fruit and
vegetables selected, money handed over, and that was that.

In a place like Montecchio, the indigenous population are, as
Orietta had said, almost impenetrable. Because self-sufficient.
Thus, being a newcomer and peripheral to village life, one inevitably gets to know other peripherals, people who like yourself
have been washed up here, because at some particular moment this
was where the current flowed, and the place turned out to be convenient. Bepi had tried for years to get a license to open a supermarket—anywhere in the province of Verona would do—until

finally they allowed him to rent the downstairs of an unprepossessing old house on the outskirts of Montecchio—for a greengrocery.

Invited to dinner, he sits down, legs wide apart on his seat, his powerful body straining his clothes, and immediately, before I've even poured an *aperitivo*, announces: The man I call Father in the shop is not my father.

In a country where reserve and formality are usually excessive on these occasions, it is certainly a dramatic opening. And embarrassing. He proceeds to tell us that he is the illegitimate child of a woman whose family threw her out. Not wanting the child, she left him, Bepi, with a childless sister and her husband: the man he calls Father and who helps in the shop.

He then goes on to tell us how, poverty-stricken, the family sold their house in Rivoli and came to live in a meager flat in one of the downmarket residential areas of Verona. But he swore to buy back that house for the family to demonstrate that he was more than just an illegitimate child. And last year he finally did so.

If Bepi's abrupt, reductive autobiography is disconcerting, the obsession with family and home comes as no surprise. When an Italian leaves a place it's almost always with the intention of returning victorious and vindicated. Even if he believes that place to be hopelessly provincial.

How had he made his money? Bepi laughs. He taps a finger on his temple. All in here, he says, all in here. He tells the picaresque story of his entrepreneurial career. You know they're always saying Italian wine has no added sugar? Yes. And it's illegal to add sugar to wine in Italy? Yes. Well, I drove the truck that took the sugar to all the wine producers from Vicenza to Verona. At night, of course. There are no police about at night. They only work office hours. He grins, he is very pleased with himself. For this was an act of *furbizia*, of cunning, and it paid very well. Spent all the money setting up a restaurant with a friend, near the main road to the lake, a big restaurant, for coach parties and the like. The mistake was doing it with somebody else. The friend couldn't see reason. Didn't have it up here. Bepi taps his forehead again. They went bust. There followed two or three other restaurants, then finally the license for the shop. He had wanted a supermarket, but local shopkeepers always gang together and bother their political contacts to make sure no new licenses are given. This is common practice, they have the politicians in their pockets, or they *are* the politicians. But Bepi will beat them at their own game in the end. Yes, he will. Sooner or later he'll have the knife by the handle. . . .

As so often in conversations here, one notes this assumption of a fundamental lawlessness. The law is only one of the arms the individual uses in his essentially lawless struggle. Bepi talked at length about various court cases he was engaged in: with the phone company about stupidly high bills; with a neighbor about his (Bepi's) dog kennels; with INPS, the national insurance people, about unpaid contributions for the girls in his shop; and there were others too, which I forget now. Far from any desire to reform or change the situation, Bepi seemed pleased to have these various fights going on and not at all concerned he might lose them. As Negretti had seemed pleased when Visentini called the police about the stench of dog filth rising from his garden, as Lucilla was galvanized by her fight with Signora Marta. It is a bellicosity one finds hard to take at first, but which constant contact with other people, and above all the authorities, gradually tends to make more comprehensible, and even attractive. If there is an anarchical tradition here, there are certainly reasons for it.

Toward nine o'clock, his dinner barely over, Bepi simply falls asleep in the middle of a conversation on Patuzzi's cheap synthetic couch, one of the only modern items of furniture in the flat. The chandelier now has five small sixty-watt bulbs casting sharper shadows from the fancy moldings on the bookcase. But Bepi snores just the same. When we wake him he looks at his watch. *Diamine*, he has to drive twenty miles to Rivoli now to feed his dogs. Fifteen of them. Tomorrow he will be up at five to get to the vegetable market and pick up stuff for the shop, then in the evening he teaches a gym class at the abandoned church by Laghetto Squarà, which he rents from Don Guido (the source of their quarrel, perhaps?). Yes, he teaches gym on Mondays and Wednesdays, karate on Tuesdays and Thursdays. Do we want to come?

How can I say that after a day's teaching and translating I'm not sure if I'll have the energy?

L'UOMO
RINASCIMENTALE

WE GO OUT RUNNING with Bepi. He gathers about fifteen young people by the abandoned church beside the *laghetto*. Most of the group are girls, more than one with her eyes on Bepi. Off we trot out into the country, up the valley toward Mizzole. The evening air is cool. We run by the cherry orchards, leaves limp with a first suspicion of autumn. We run past the first long low poultry farm. The stench is unbelievable. And on an empty box by the side of the road, I read: BEST CANADIAN CHURKEY EGGS—SEALED CONTAINER—FOR INCUBATION FOLLOW INSTRUCTIONS.

Jogging (or "footing," as the Italians unaccountably call it) along tractor paths, we pass through a large vineyard, the purple fruit almost ripe around our ears. Here, beneath the dense foliage, Bepi stops for some exercises, barking out orders with an unmistakably authoritarian ring to his voice. *Flessioni!* And he's down on his stomach doing push-ups. *Addominali!* He's on his back doing sit-ups, hands behind his head, legs bent at the knee. *Dorsali!* Over on our stomachs again. Such a desire for leadership! He flogs us. Showing off his macho dynamism. It's endearing. The girls titter, most of them making only token efforts. Footing again, we pass through a delightful old wine-stuccoed farm. There's an ancient well in the garden with stone top and swallows mustering for departure on the roof of the barn. Panting now, we run on through the picturesque village of Mizzole with the golden onion dome on its church. Posters tell us about pollution from pig farming, courses in secretarial skills, the imminent grape festival, and the most recent deaths: Magnagatto Marta: *92 anni*, much missed by her family. Graffiti on the stone walls, however, are mainly directed against a group of southerners from Reggio Calabria who have formed a cooperative and plan to build themselves some *villette a schiera*—row houses (a brand-new fashion in Italy): *"Benvenuto a Reggio Mizzole"* has been scrawled over a road sign. Italians have a gift for graffiti. In the central square by the war memorial we read: "Long live the government, long live taxes, long live the south . . . or no?" Opposite, a sign over one of the village's two bars announces: "Real American Cocktails, by Gianni."

We arrive back puffing and panting. Bepi wants to do some more exercises, but I've had enough. Perhaps anyway he is only waiting to see which groupie will hang on the longest. A process of natural selection. Walking home, past the mill wheel, past a Roman arch, under which heavy trucks pass to two huge silage containers in a small yard, we reflect that if he votes at all, Bepi probably votes MSI, the not very reformed fascists.

Another evening we drop by the gym, where he is teaching karate to a mixed group of all ages. Italians take their sport very seriously. Black belt tight around his waist, Bepi barks out commands in what we presume is Japanese, his body squatting low, making the impressive ritual movements with concentration etched on his features. "All here," he tells us afterward, "all here," and he taps his forehead.

A few weeks later we are invited to the house Bepi has repurchased and is now renovating up in Rivoli. He drives us west through Verona and then strikes off north up the Valpolicella. It's *vendemmia* time, the grape harvest. The Alfettas and BMWs fret and fume behind tractors inching along with their cartloads of grapes; it's important that the fruit not get too knocked about, so they're taking the road as slow as they can. The air is heavy with an extremely pleasant drunken smell, an almost tangible sweet stickiness. Midges swarm in quite unbelievable numbers. Storms and clouds of them. These *vendemmia* days one finds oneself breathing midges the way the whale simply swallows his plankton as he swims along.

We arrive in Rivoli, perched high on the hills above the Adige, site of one of Napoleon's famous victories. Bepi turns his grocery van into a narrow track, bumping steeply down. At the end, the old peasant house that has focused his enterprising mind for so long is unprepossessing: a humble two-story rectangle divided into two small dwellings with chickens pecking about outside. Buying it back can have had only symbolic value. Especially since Bepi doesn't want to live here himself, and can't even get on with the ancient grandmother he has installed there. On our arrival they exchange fierce insults, much as he did with the priest.

The grounds are large, though, perhaps thirty or forty acres sloping steeply downward away from the house. Once laboriously terraced and cultivated, they are neglected now, like so much of this countryside. The vines are overgrown, the support walls crumbling, so that here and there a terrace has collapsed, showing how chalky-white the soil is beneath. Bepi takes us down to his dog kennels, a low concrete building a good fifty yards long and full of big black barking dogs. Our host apparently—he tells us himself—is the foremost breeder of Belgian shepherds in the Veneto, if not in Italy. His neighbor, despite being out of sight and earshot of the dogs, has started a court case about the kennels because he is resentful that Bepi outbid him for possession of the house. The same old story. Bepi thus stands accused of having built them without town planning permission. In typically belligerent fashion, Bepi has turned the case on its head, suing the local authorities for being so slow in granting permission that he was "forced" to go ahead without it in order to accommodate his business.

He releases a couple of dogs and lets them come with us. Disconcertingly, as we walk along, he barks at them in German. I ask him which language he prefers for his girlfriends. With touching honesty he tells us he hasn't yet found the language that girls respond to best. I assure him it is not English.

Before going in for lunch, he takes us up to a ridge at the edge of the property where we have a breathtaking view northward up the Valpolicella to the Alps, their rocky peaks barely visible for the haze. Deep deep below in the valley a huge irrigation canal leaves the River Adige and disappears into a tunnel under the hill. Disused marble quarries now converted into mushroom farms are dotted all about. The vista is vast, open, inspiring. I remark rather banally that it seems out of this world, *fuori del mondo*. To which, quite naturally, Bepi replies that, yes, UFOs ("oofoes," as the Italians call them) used to visit here quite often, but have now ceased to do so, ever since people became too violent. The Veneto, he says, along with parts of Russia, boasts the highest frequencies of UFO sightings in the world. He used to see the lights himself farther up the valley. I feel it isn't the moment to say that the Veneto also shares with Russia one of the highest consumptions of alcohol in the world.

Returning to the house we find Bepi's delightful "father," Vittorio, who has come out to the country for the day with his wife. Strong, squat, of great girth, and irrepressibly merry, Vittorio is just the kind of jolly chap one tends to see interviewed in the local paper after a UFO sighting. Now he presides over the big wooden table in the kitchen, where he has lined up five or six bottles of wine and seems intent on opening all of them at once. Meanwhile, his wife, Gina, buxom, retiring, and embarrassed about her poor Italian, has prepared the most wonderful lasagna from scratch. Oceans of it.

We sit down. Vittorio begins to describe the qualities of each of his bottles at considerable length. Since he speaks only dialect—unlike his wife, he isn't at all embarrassed about it—I can't understand. I pick up half of a jolly joke about a dog that only went for dead birds. "Don't let him come near me then" is the punch line. The word for "bird" in Italian also translates as "pecker."

Midday. The abundant lasagna. The labelless wine bottles. The smoke from an unnecessary fire in the huge limestone grate. Big thick steaks, which of course Bepi gets through a friend of a friend who would never give him anything but good stuff. Then *tiramisù*, again abundant, creamy, calorie-rich, cholesterol-rich, splendid. Alongside a treacly Recioto. And finally a score of different grappas to choose from after, or with, your espresso. Vittorio makes the grappa himself, with what's left after making the wine, flavoring it with such things as lemons, peaches, oranges, even coffee. The different brews are arrayed before us in the kind of tall, greasy, nameless bottles one expects to find in the garage with a couple of inches of brake fluid in the bottom. I try two or three and make a toast to the UFOs.

Going back in his greengrocer's van, Bepi tells me that what he'd like to do is study theology. The church and the Masons still hold on to many of the deepest secrets of this world; only the initiated will ever be allowed to know anything worth knowing. He has applied to join a lodge and is studying the Cabala in the evening when he can stay awake. Vaguely it occurs to me that this is all part of the Italian obsession with alternative power structures. And I wonder if Bepi isn't the closest I am ever likely to meet to a Renaissance man.

TROPPO GENTILE

To be earthquake-proof, modern Italian buildings are legally required to be constructed around a reinforced concrete frame. In the event of tremors the whole structure should thus shift as one unit, rather than crumbling into its separate parts. And indeed as one walks about the outskirts of Montecchio and on into the surrounding hills, builders are eagerly pouring cement into columns of roughly nailed planks, in a hurry to get things done before the November rains.

Concrete the columns and the beams, where shortly before were olive trees, concrete the roofs too of these new *palazzine* and row houses, and likewise concrete the floors, all wires and plumbing laid forever inaccessible in the cement. Gaunt frames take over a vineyard. Up go the walls between one beam and the next. The roof is then topped with terra-cotta, the living space inside tiled with ceramics: somber colors and smaller tiles in the seventies, brighter gloss-finish colors and much larger tiles in the eighties.

It makes for some rather curious acoustics. With no wood, you are saved the creaking board, the moaning stair. If you want to sneak in to check on a sleeping baby, or, God forbid, sneak out on wife or husband, there is no danger of the floor betraying you. In stockinged feet you are soundless. On the other hand, a hard object dropped on that ceramic-on-concrete floor, even a coin, will be heard in every room in the building, volume and intensity depending on the vicinity to a load-bearing beam or column. Leather soles clicking across the tiles will thus click across all the floors and ceilings of the condominium. A lavatory flushing in the dead of night is an explosion, an act of terrorism. And if you should take a drill to the wall and, after penetrating the plaster, happen upon one of those steel-reinforced columns, then all over the building, from *taverna* to *solaio*, it will seem that the eventuality for which the structure was designed is in full swing. The air vibrates. Sound waves oppress the ear. It is as if one were caught inside a guitar with some naughty Brobdingnagian child incessantly twanging the bass string.

We did experience a couple of small quakes in Via Colombare. The *palazzina* shuddered and sang. Patuzzi's wineglasses tinkled on their shelves. Apparently columns of trucks were passing in the night, or ships' engines starting up in the basement.

Lying down to sleep of an October evening, thankful that we can now close the windows against the TVs, accordions, and Ping-Pong of the velvety dark outside, we hear instead an unmistakable fierce trickling, coming, well, presumably from below us. At eleven-thirty every night. Trickle trickle trickle, dribble dribble, drop, drop, stop. We hold our breath. But there is no explosion of flushing, for unspoken condominium etiquette requires that the toilets—*tacciono*—fall silent after eleven o'clock. It's a special kind of intimacy this concrete brings.

Trying to sleep again after being waked by Vega in the early hours, I begin to hear footsteps going back and forth in our *solaio* under the roof above. This is alarming. Slow heavy footsteps, back and forth, back and forth, above our heads. Rita confirms it, they definitely come from our *solaio*, an empty attic. And in the dead of night one believes in *fantasmi*. Vega has been moaning rather than barking this evening, howling and wailing at the moon.

I get up, pull on a pair of trousers, then slippers against the cold tiles, and go out of the flat and up the stairs. Where I slip and fall on the highly polished marble. This particular flight to the roof is rarely used, but Lucilla waxes it regularly just the same. Everything must always be just so, a mausoleum odor. Cursing and rueful, I reach the iron door of the *solaio*, open it, and then remember I still haven't put a light bulb in. At which point the timed landing light goes out. I grope for the switch, but don't know where it is on this floor. So I go into the *solaio* blind.

I stare, waiting for my pupils to dilate, recognizing a smell of geranium cuttings and thick dust. A dark, softly shifting light, filtering from the attic's one window, finally enables me to see the shadows of untidily piled boxes, an ancient bed, a crucifix, a pair of bellows unaccountably left on the windowsill, and rows and rows of Il Professore's old climbing boots. None of them moving, thank God. I cock my head. No sound.

But back downstairs the footsteps go on and on above us.

Talking to Orietta, the quiet repository of all condominium gossip, we discover that Lucilla suffers from insomnia. The footsteps are hers; the ventriloquist building sends the sound where it will.

Orietta is loosening up. She is losing her suspicion of my Englishness. She recognizes the advantage of having other non-Montecchiesi to make friends with. Giampaolo, she tells us, has frequently complained about these footsteps. Getting up in the night, it seems, Lucilla will put on her fur coat, partly against the cold, partly because she likes her fur coat; she finds its luxury comforting, its moneyed smell reassuring. But since she is small and bought the coat long, she puts her heels on so as not to have it trail on the floor. And paces up and down.

Another night it is the squeal of heavy furniture being scraped above our heads. Bumps and banging. Thud, scrape, squeal. Yes, Lucilla tells us brightly on the stairs, she decided to rearrange the sitting room; do we want to come and see it?

Please would we come and see it?

Perhaps we would take a little drink with her? She has some Lacryma Christi.

Or perhaps we would like to have a piece of her *pastafrolla*?

Surely, if she isn't disturbing us, we would like to come and see her new curtains, eat her shortbread? Also, if we could explain something in the instruction book for her steam iron . . .

There is a scene in Fellini's recent film *La voce della luna* in which a local politician, fallen upon hard times, is seen returning to his dreary flat in an old *palazzotto* in some tiny town of the Po Valley. But every time he climbs the stairs and approaches his door, whether it be two in the afternoon or two in the morning, four ancient neighbors will appear at the door opposite and, like awful decaying sirens, try to lure him into their flat to share some old-fashioned dainty: a thimbleful of some sweet forgotten liqueur, a morsel of traditional crumbliness. Their faces are pictures of decrepit flattery and seduction. Close to obscenity. The furniture dingily glimpsed behind them is somber and coffin-inspired, with candlesticks in abundance, photographs of dead relatives on lace doilies. "Would a small glass of sherry be to your liking, your honor? Would a small slice of *pan di spagna*, councillor, be acceptable as our humble offering?" Their veiny hands are outstretched in supplication. Which is immediately perceived as a trap, as if a whole culture were refusing to lie down in its grave, but rising ghoulish to eat our contemporary flesh. Horrified and furious, the man manages to escape into his room, slams and bolts the door behind him. But already the four leathery faces are down by the keyhole. "Would your honor be so kind as to take a glass of brandy with some humble folk? . . . " They haunt his dreams. He sees their faces floating outside his window at night with the moon behind, luring him back into some archaic, provincial Italy of polished wood-work and thickly smoking candlewax, flattery, favors, back-stabbing.

Such, for me, were Lucilla's insistent invitations. So that one almost looked back with regret on her ravings from the balcony, her confiscation of the garbage can. Those days when one at least knew where one stood.

Barely has she got us inside her polished door—*troppo gentile,* too kind, Signor Tino (she never registered the name Tim)—than she is leaning out into the stairwell calling down to Vittorina. She has a direct intercom connection with Vittorina's flat, but prefers to call down the stairwell, if only to remind all residents in the condominium of her existence. "Rinà! Rinà! Come and have something to drink with *i signori inglesi.*" Is she calling up reinforcements? Or just increasing the size of her audience?

We walk in, and promptly slither on imitation-animal-skin rugs strewn over the usual lethally waxed floor. Lucilla is clearly nostalgic for her cleaning days. The year before we arrived she slipped on the rug in the entrance and broke her hip. But this has not deterred her. I all but come a cropper on the synthetic white hairy thing between low glass table and imitation-leather sofa. Vittorina, who has now appeared in a nightgown, hair thinner than ever, frowns with the air of one who is wiser than the person she is used to being bossed about by. And indeed, she doesn't even try to remove her mustache as Lucilla does. A vanity beneath her.

We are shown around the flat. The walls are simple whitewash, as in almost every Italian house. The furniture is what a local Veronese would laughingly describe as *stile Bovolone,* Bovolone being an industrial settlement twenty miles away in the foggy *bassa* where scores of busy companies produce clunky replicas of antique furniture. A Louis XIV dresser, bright and new, features prominently in the entranceway. There is a Renaissance chest in polished pine, and Lucilla's is the first home, aside from visits to Waltham Abbey and Hatfield House, where I have seen a bed with a canopy curtain affair over the headboard, here upholstered in electric nylon pink. The room is about ten by twelve.

Il Professore was a great man, she begins impulsively, having put little red glasses of *gingerino* in our hands. A great man. Of culture. She speaks in fierce dialect. I strain my ears to distinguish the words, my mind to understand. It is not unlike trying to make out a strange landscape through thick fog. Was that a house or a tree, a taillight or shop neon? And we are going so fast. My head starts to ache. Still, at the end of an hour or so of nonstop haranguing, I do manage to discern the following salient landmarks, if only because Lucilla goes around and around them so insistently, not unlike Pooh following his own tracks in the snow. Il Professore, i.e., Patuzzi, had written a will and put it in his deposit box in the bank (half of Montecchio seems to have a deposit box at the bank). He then died quite suddenly, of a heart attack, breathing his last on the ambulance stretcher right outside her door, *poveretto* (obligatory epithet for describing the dear departed). And what a fright for her! Anyway, the will had clearly stated that the wife would have use of the property only until her death, after which it would pass to her, Lucilla. Such an exquisite man, Il Professore. As had been agreed, of course. Because it was her money, her money had paid for the *palazzina*. She had worked her fingers to the bone all her life. So cultured. We would have admired him immensely. But no sooner had he passed away than Signora Marta and Maria Rosa were off to the bank, had opened the deposit box and promptly burned the will. For which they themselves would burn in hell. Whereas we would never meet anybody more *gentile*, more *generoso*, than Il Professore.

Lucilla's bosom began to heave, it wasn't clear whether out of love or anger or some dangerous blood-dark cocktail of the two. Then Maria Rosa had herself fallen ill, and become infirm. Lucilla had looked after her, as was her duty toward another "Christian," taking her meals, which she handed over at the door, whose threshold she was never to pass. Because that woman put on airs, while Il Professore, who might have had good reason to be haughty, was *dolcezza* itself. And when things got worse, Maria Rosa had come and more or less lived in her own, Lucilla's, flat; slept there for months, being nursed and helped to the toilet and so on. Until finally Lucilla could cope no more and the woman had had to go into a home. But toward the end of that period, in a fit of remorse, Maria Rosa had told Lucilla the story of the will and how it had been burned and had agreed to write a further will herself.

Lucilla fiddles under the flap of a rather oversized new Regency writing desk, bringing out a furry-gray piece of notepaper, which she then waves under our noses. *"Ecco, legga, legga, Signor Tino."* Her fingers are stubby and impressively bejeweled. I take the *documento* with due respect. Uncertain handwriting announces the last will and testament of Maria Rosa Griminelli. The whole of Via Colombare 10 belongs and always has belonged to Lucilla Zambon, who built it with her own money. There is a single indecipherable signature, no lawyer, only the beneficiary as a witness.

But Lucilla's hopes are pinned on that scrap of paper. She raises her voice. She is furious, defiant. Her bony teeth are in evidence. "The flat is mine, mine, mine." Though we are nice people and when she finally gets hold of the property, on Maria Rosa's death, she will allow us to stay, although she will have to ask us to buy it rather than rent. But we can discuss all this at a later date.

Would we like a *cioccolatino*, a San Pellegrino Bitter? Would we like to watch television with her of an evening? She would be grateful if we could adjust her set. There is a program on Tele Montecarlo with a man just like her beloved husband, here he is in this photograph. *Così bello!* Why did the men always die first? But she can never get a good picture on Tele Montecarlo. Signor Giampaolo has put up that new motorized aerial on the roof and it is sucking all the goodness from hers. Do I know anything about aerials? And could Rita perhaps phone her lawyer for her to have him explain something she can't understand, and tell him to hurry up with the case?

Lucilla talks on and on. There is simply no chink in her verbal armor, no hesitation into which one might thrust the dagger of a request to leave. Vittorina watches, silent, dark, with those sudden smiles when she catches your eye, smiles which say she understands your suffering, but this is Lucilla, this is how she is.

In desperation, we begin our long retreat. First simply getting to our feet, then edging out of the lounge and across the dining room with its dark dying plants, its sad canary, heading toward the entrance. Along a low wall are an array of those tiny twisted-glass Venetian ornaments, reminding me of my infancy in Blackpool, when we visited a Great-Aunt Esther who had rows upon rows of the things on a dresser.

Do we think she should ask for the *condono edilizio*, the "building pardon"? You see, she had this wall knocked down, that's why it is different from our flat, didn't we notice, between the entrance and the kitchen . . . so much more space. But without asking for a building permit . . . and now with this pardon . . .

Does she have the right lawyer? What do we think? Perhaps he isn't being tough enough. Surely the rent we are paying should go to her. How much are we paying? Il Professore only left the flat to his wife for use while she wanted to live there, but any rent should go to her, Lucilla. And of course in that home Maria Rosa is in, Signora Marta is putting pressure on her to sign another will leaving everything to her. But it wouldn't be right, because Rosa isn't capable of exercising free will now. She is senile. Though the doctors are all clearly *in complicità*, with what's being paid for her to be there. All Il Professore's fortune. The priest said . . .

Finally we make it to the hall. We are repeating *arrivederci*, *buona notte*, when I finally remember the purpose behind our visit, the subject I had originally come to broach. The nocturnal noises. We hope, I say, that we never, er, bother them, when we play our stereo, when we type late at night, when we have friends over. Noise carries so much in these buildings. One can hear everything. We wouldn't like . . . "But no, Signor Tino, no, no, no, *troppo gentile, troppo gentile*! We like to hear noise. We like to hear footsteps, laughter, banging. The more the merrier. We're two old ladies. It keeps us company. We feel less lonely. *Ma troppo gentile, ma che signore!*"

And somehow Signor Tino just can't bring himself to say what he wants to say. The way he can never quite make up his mind to poison that dog.

CONDONO

THE *CONDONO EDILIZIO* was first mooted in the early 1980s. The idea was to recognize that there are vast numbers of buildings in Italy which were put up without permission: villas and cottages in the north, whole blocks of flats down south. Since officially these buildings don't exist, they aren't paying the modest property tax (though they do of course receive electricity, water, postal service, etc., and residency certificates confidently assert that people do live in them and hence enjoy all the rights that go with officially living in a place). There are also, the new law would recognize, even greater numbers of buildings which have been altered in some way without permission: extended, restored, disfigured, rebuilt. Under the terms of the *condono*, the government would allow people to register these buildings or any changes made to them and thus get themselves *in regola*, as they say, paying in return only a fraction of the fine they would otherwise have to pay if prosecuted. For the government this would mean a considerable immediate income and the prospect of larger regular revenues in the future.

No sooner had the splendid idea been put forward than building began in earnest all over the peninsula. Of course, the law would refer only to buildings completed some months before it was initially drawn up. But if a building isn't registered it is not always easy to say exactly when it was built. And perhaps the government didn't really care, since finances were such (are always such) that the larger the injection of cash, the better.

The law was passed by decree, quite normal practice, but a decree has to be ratified by parliament within sixty days. The *condono* was not ratified. Which was curious, given the general enthusiasm. Some mischievous newspapers alleged that many of those MPs who voted against it were busy building their own illegal villas and eager to have them finished before the law was eventually passed, as they were sure it one day would be. But at the time, MPs had a secret vote in the Italian parliament, so it was impossible to tell who was involved

Along Via Colombare somebody knocked down a handsome old barn and began feverish work on a luxury extension, which pretty well amounted to a second house. Passing of the law was again delayed. Almost opposite the luxury extension, the woman who swept the road regularly with her twig broom began to lay the foundations of a two-car garage with terrace roof leading through French windows to the second floor of her house. Wielding her broom, she bustled about the old workers in their dungarees with their bottles of wine and Tupperware boxes full of cold pasta.

The law was now passed. But then the deadline for applications for the *condono* was waived on two or three occasions. To give a little respite. All over Italy the cement mixers rumbled; work went on apace. And I remember walking back along the more than usually dusty street one day to find in number 10's postbox one of those magazines that somehow always find their way to expatriates: *Investment International*, or some such title. They tell you how to send your children to English boarding schools, how to invest your money in offshore tax havens, how to prepare for the mental shock of return, how to let your Mayfair flat in your absence, etc. On this particular occasion a review of European stock markets remarked, of the Borsa di Milano, that one could do no better than invest in Italcementi, the state-controlled cement company. Cement in Italy, the article said, had miraculously outperformed all other kinds of stock, thanks to the vigor, the creativity, and the enterprising spirit of both manufacturers and building contractors. So much for the foreign perspective.

In Via Colombare we got a new fence to protect the really rather attractive beige-stuccoed, copper-drained three-bedroom extension which had replaced the old barn (beautiful, full of swallows' nests, but no longer functional). The fence was made of tall, spiky, brown-painted iron railings sunk into a marble-topped cement wall, and it ended in a sheltered, terra-cotta-tiled entrance-way complete with videocamera security. The tiny garden between fence and villa extension respected the cemetery style of dwarf cypresses and biblically inspired stucco statues. Opposite, the woman with the twig broom now swept her terrace of a morning, as well as the remaining half of the patio and a fair stretch of road outside.

But in the end this was a fairly innocuous form of anarchy. For around this time we took a week off to visit friends who live in the suburbs of Rome. Their house, a legal part of a new development, had simply been smothered by new building, much of it of the crudest variety, cinder blocks placed one on top of another with prefab roof, just enough to claim the *condono* and have the authorities accept the existence of a building which could then be developed in the future. Many houses were without utilities. Next door, the owner had converted the ground floor of his house into a body-repair shop, blocking the narrow road outside with dented cars. Our friends had called the local *vigile* about the noise, the smell of spray paint, the inconvenience, reminding him that this was a residential area. The *vigile* went to talk with the culprit and apparently took a bribe.

Italian stories. One hears them more or less daily.

Back in number 10, there were various reasons for asking for the *condono*. The *palazzina* was a yard or so too near Negretti's house. Then the *solaio*, for example, had tiled floors, whereas to remain in the tax bracket the house was in, they should have been left bare and "noninhabitable." The same was true of the garage and the *taverna*. One has a building inspected, is the trick, its tax bracket declared, and then one changes it at will: peeling shutters in the city center conceal luxury window fittings; pitted, flaking stucco fronts for polished parquet and granite and gold bathroom fittings. Everybody's at it. The humble facade, the lavish interior. Tall, broken-glass-topped walls. Secretiveness.

Eventually it was decided at condominium level (i.e., by Lucilla) that number 10 would not ask for the *condono*. Because in the end it wasn't free, was it? However small, the fine would still have to be paid. And why bother? Lucilla was indignant. Nobody had really done anything wrong, had they? Nobody had hurt anybody. Anyway, the chances of the authorities ever catching you were infinitesimal; otherwise they would never have introduced the *condono* in the first place. And it was so dangerous to draw attention to yourself. Once they had your name in black and white, heaven knows what they might find out.

Lucilla was right. Some years later an income tax *condono* was passed by decree. People would "reconstruct their tax careers," paying a modest fine. Thus the government would know how much tax to expect from such people in the future. But almost nobody applied for the pardon, since the very fact that the government had introduced it was an admission of its inability or unwillingness to catch anyone. Parliament then voted out the decree after the sixty days. This meant that while over the previous two months it had officially been the law, it was now considered never to have been the law at all. Upon which a few zealous magistrates attempted to prosecute those guilty few who had somewhat hastily confessed to their tax crimes in the hope of getting *in regola*. A lesson for the rest of us if ever there was one.

DISCRETO, VALIDO, RELATIVO

If Lucilla's most common expression was the flattering and subservient *troppo gentile, troppo gentile*, a social tick she had presumably picked up in her deprived girlhood of floor-scrubbing and straightforward begging, Giampaolo Visentini's most characteristic utterances were always built around the three words *discreto*, *valido*, *relativo*.

Imagine you are sitting in the Visentinis' tastefully and above all cautiously furnished sitting room. You are drinking excellent *prosecco* which Giampaolo bottled himself, which he has put in the refrigerator three or four days before your planned evening get-together (in the back of the refrigerator, not the door, since that would involve its getting knocked around too much). Upon your arrival and acceptance of the offered treat, he has carried the bottle from kitchen through dining room to sitting room with the concentration of a bomb disposal expert shifting primed Semtex, has released the detonating cork ever so gently to prevent explosion, then tilted the bottle painstakingly slowly over an attractive pottery carafe bearing the name of some Sardinian seaside town—all this because it's so desperately important to avoid disturbing the sediment which is both the hallmark and curse of home-bottled wines. Giampaolo watches intently as he pours, brow knitted, long pale fingers strong and steady, his whole attitude conveying the slightly glazed worshipful concentration of the devotee. The contents froth out, the carafe fills, the sediment, which would have given the wine an unpleasant acidy taste, remains safely in the bottle, and—*ecco fatto*, done it! Being bourgeois, it might be said, is never an easy way out in Italy.

Of course, if this is your first evening with the Visentinis, if this is the first time you have drunk home-bottled *prosecco*, the whole elaborate rigmarole will seem nothing short of ridiculous. You can barely hold back a giggle. The caricatures are true, you're thinking. These Latins are obsessive about food and wine. What's going to change your mind is when you actually taste the *prosecco*.

And here at last it is. Loving as ever, but more relaxed now, Giampaolo pours from the carafe into tall slim glasses. *"Salute."* You raise a crystal stem. The cold sharp taste stings the lips, demands attention. It's desperately dry, cutting like a knife through the sweetness of whatever goodies are being handed out. And as it fills your mouth, you become aware of wanting to hold it there. Bubbles froth on the palate. You are drinking something special.

So there you are, perched on geometrically arranged chairs about a rug of soberly colored squares and rectangles surrounded by polished tiles, chinking your tall glass with your host's. The Visentinis' daughter is there too: Lara, named after the heroine in *Dr. Zhivago*. A strapping twelve-year-old, she giggles merrily when Rita cracks a joke. I'm making compliments about the wine, asking if it is the same that we will be bottling together in the spring. There are the makings of a pleasant evening.

But Giampaolo is so solemn. And, perhaps not wishing to discuss wine with a layman, he launches into serious conversation. He's telling you about some new law. For he likes to talk about politics. Concerning drunk driving, for example. Yes, the new law on drunk driving has been drawn up *discretamente* (i.e., quite well, with intelligence if not flair) and is in fact for the most part *valido* (sound, functional), but all of this is *relativo* (of only secondary importance), since the instruments for enforcing the law are not available, or if they are nobody has any intention of using them. He smiles, as if having performed a conjuring trick, takes a sparkling sip of *prosecco*, picks up another piece of *pastafrolla*.

And the formula, you discover as the evening progresses, can be applied to almost any area of life upon which Giampaolo cares to reflect. The Italian system of *autostrade*, he is telling you now, is definitely *discreto*, road surfaces and markings are always *valido*, but all this tends to be *relativo*, since with the exorbitant price of gasoline and the very high tolls, one would need to be rich indeed before one could use the roads with regularity.

Another long sip of this extraordinary wine.

Likewise, efficiency in Italian companies, such as his own, is certainly *discreto*, the managerial class indubitably *valido*, but again these pluses are rendered *relativo* by a public sector which simply sucks blood from the rest of the economy.

And so, if you encourage him, he will go on all evening: the constitution, the electoral system, the TV networks: *discreto*, *valido*, *relativo*. It is a curious and, I believe, curiously Italian stalemate, in which ineradicable national pride (and why not?) exists side by side with a sense of cynicism (equally justifiable) and, at the end of the day, resignation. The judicial system has been "conceived *discretamente bene*," and the constitution in this regard is undoubtedly *valido*, in that it establishes the total independence of the judiciary. But whatever the institutional makeup, it is inevitably only *relativo* given the endemic corruption that always allows the mafiosi to get off scot-free.

The mental pattern propogates itself like someone cutting pastry (or *pastafrolla*) with a die, or pouring wine into tall glasses. There is no question of simply showing anger or outrage for all the things that make the country a less attractive place to live than it might so easily be. The blunt analysis and sleeve-rolling gaucheness which form the typical reaction of, for example, the English inevitably carry the subtext that something could and should be done, and quickly: reform the poll tax, cut inflation, dump Thatcher, etc., etc. English people usually believe such things to be possible, or at least imaginable. But the Italian knows that nothing can or will be done in his country, and that if it is done it certainly will not be done quickly. This is his experience. After all, with all the shifting coalitions and merry-go-round of prime ministers, most people here haven't seen a real change of government in their lifetime. Thus an Italian's satisfaction, when he talks about politics, will lie in feeling that he has analyzed the situation accurately, appreciated its ironies, seen the pros and the cons, absorbed the subtleties, and above all gone beyond the crude simplicity of foreigners who talk in ingenuous terms about changing things.

Discreto, *valido*, *relativo*—none of them are particularly complimentary or pejorative terms. They are the cool words of the astute analyst, the man who looks at the whole show from a distance, then goes about his business as he would have done anyway, regardless, but happy to have had the chance to illustrate his powers of observation. In the final analysis: "*La legge non mi tange* (The law doesn't concern me).''

Fortunately there is Orietta's gossip to brighten up the evening. Lucilla has apparently called on the priest, Don Guido, to be a witness in the case she is bringing against Signora Marta. He has agreed. Which is interesting. And did we know that Lucilla has a fancy man? Simone, an ex-carabiniere. Yes, he comes three or four evenings a week. The daughter giggles and begins to explain about the vacuum cleaner. Lucilla has what must be a prewar vacuum cleaner, but recently she has been borrowing Orietta's (Vittorina doesn't have one), claiming that her own is broken. Whereas in fact Lara, the daughter, saw Simone, the carabiniere fancy man, bumping down the stairs with the thing only a week ago.

To mend it? To use it? Can't he afford one?

Anyway, this is becoming a problem, Orietta says, since there's so much dust about these days with all the building going on in the street. She needs to use the thing herself two or three times a day.

Everybody nods gravely.

Orietta is small, doll-like, and clearly perfectly attuned to sedentary domestic life. She doesn't have a job, but every corner of the room shows evidence of her tireless cleaning. Only the other morning I watched her diligently polishing inch after inch of the long marble balustrade of the terrace balcony. There was concentration on her face, satisfaction, the devotion of the acolyte cleaning the altar. Not unlike her husband's expression while pouring his *prosecco*. Later we will discover that when Giampaolo wanted to accept a more dynamic job in a much smaller company, Orietta forbade him. It wasn't safe.

She is also scared of earthquakes.

And of every possible disease. Thus, as so often with Italian acquaintances, we are not far into our first evening with the Visentinis before Orietta is discussing her blood pressure. Which is a mite high. She shouldn't have more than two cups of coffee a day. Also she occasionally gets attacks of tachycardia. She is appalled to discover that I don't even know my own blood pressure. As far as I know it has never been taken. Her face shows genuine concern. Apparently we are touching on a real cultural difference here.

Orietta explains that after she felt somewhat faint a few days ago the doctor arranged for her to have an exhaustive series of blood and urine tests, together with an electrocardiogram and a heart scan. She has thus been getting up early every morning to get to the hospital, wait in all the queues, fill in all the forms, and fix all the appointments. She remembers last time she had a blood test her bilirubin was way outside the norms indicated on the test sheet, whereas cholesterol was thankfully low.

I remark that I have never, to my knowledge, had a blood test. I don't even know my group.

Lara had a rash a few weeks ago on face and chest. Although this cleared up almost immediately, she too was sent off for complete blood and urine tests, including tests for such things as syphilis. It appeared that her *trigliceridi* were rather low.

I can't decide if this is surprisingly intimate or rather frightening, or both. And I remember our landlady, Signora Marta, fiddling with her keys at the gate that first day, talking about her gynecological problems.

With the gravity of a Houyhnhnm, Giampaolo takes this opportunity to reflect that on the whole public hospitals in Verona function *discretamente bene*, when compared with hospitals in other areas of Italy, and of course the idea behind the health system as it was initially conceived is indubitably *valido*. However, it has to be admitted that the apparent success of the local system is *del tutto relativo*, since if all the people who presently go private were to turn to the public system, it would break down in a matter of days.

Lucilla, for example, and Vittorina.

"Really? They go private? But they're not particularly well off, are they?"

Giampaolo explains that the old women go to a local health service doctor whom they tip generously. When they have any tests to do, he always tells them to go to a private clinic, of which he, as it so happens, is a director. And they pay a lot of money. And say, *troppo gentile, dottore, troppo gentile*.

We thus discover that it is not so much, or by no means only, the upper middle class and the important executive who go private in Italy. Above all it is the ignorant, the workers and peasant class who have tucked something away in their deposit box or in a few government bonds. They can't believe the public system can work, and then, of course, it's a status symbol to say I am going to my private gynecologist, my private cardiologist, my private pediatrician. From whom, more often than not, they will get no receipt.

Rita tells me a joke her mother made up when her father, Adelmo, kept going to the hospital for tests upon tests upon tests. It goes like this. What does a German do in the morning? He jumps out of bed, grabs a cup of coffee, and rushes off to work. What does an American do in the morning? He climbs out of bed, sips a cup of coffee, reads the paper for ten minutes, and strolls off to work. What does an Italian do?

Long pause. Puzzlement of the Visentinis in their spic-and-span sitting room.

Urinates in a bottle and sets off to the hospital!

Only Lara truly thinks this is funny. The others have a sort of pained smile. Health is so important. Not for nothing did we say *Salute* when we raised those glasses.

And Orietta touches her face. Do we think she should have her mole removed? This little one in the dimple on her cheek. She's afraid it might be growing. No, it's not very visible, because she powders it. Her doctor said to leave well enough alone, but she went for a second opinion and that doctor said to have a biopsy done. At a private clinic, Giampaolo adds.

Idly, Lara picks up the remote control and the television flicks on. With its usual brutality, the news is showing yet another Mafia killing. Corruption on a more impressive scale. The scene is always the same: the car caught at the traffic lights, riddled with bullets, the corpses in a heap on the front seats, perhaps an arm thrown out of the shattered window, blood trickling down onto the asphalt, spotlights all around for the TV cameras. They have shot General Dalla Chiesa, chief of police in Sicily.

Giampaolo plays with the controls of his motorized aerial on the roof to enable us to get a better view. Weeping relatives are being asked how they feel.

We finish our *prosecco* and go upstairs. Leaning out over the balcony to get some fresh air, we are lucky enough to witness the departure of Simone, the ex-carabiniere. He's solid, sixtyish, thick head of bristling gray hair, and he has a package under his arm. Too small to be a vacuum cleaner, though. He fiddles for the keys to his Fiat 128 parked a hair's breadth from our iron fence. Lucilla appears on her balcony, barely ten feet away across the facade of the building, though she hasn't noticed us. In the swinging light of the overhead streetlight we can see she is heavily made up, dressed to the nines, wearing higher-than-usual heels, decidedly Felliniesque. She leans over the parapet and begins to whisper enticingly: "Simone, Simone *caro*, when will you phone? Simone, when are you coming to dinner again?" One imagines him glimpsing her long teeth as he slides down into his car with the heavy sigh of one who has overeaten. *Ciao, bella*, he calls. She stands watching after him, pensive, huge breasts uplifted. It's sad to think of this woman being taken for a ride by her doctor. But then, as Rita remarks, she probably paid no tax in the good old days of the cleaning company, so it all works out in the end.

For the next few weeks I practice *discreto*, *valido*, and *relativo* on any and every subject that comes up.

UNA BUSTARELLA

THEY HAD SHOT GENERAL DALLA CHIESA, the man who had defeated terrorism, the man the government had appointed to defeat the Mafia. About the same time a very close friend of mine paid his first bribe to a state official. These two facts are not perhaps entirely unrelated.

It's a complicated story, perhaps a little bit of a digression, but I'd like to tell it all the same because it shows how even the ingenuous foreigner who arrives here, as one arrives most places, more or less by chance can so easily run up against the dark side of Italy.

This was an extremely close friend of mine. Like me he had arrived in Italy some time before, like me he lived in a little village not far from a sizable town, like me he had slaved for a while with private lessons and commercial translations until good fortune had landed him one of the much-sought-after jobs teaching English at the university, a position offering a decent, steady income for work that is pleasant and not overly taxing. He was delighted. Now he could relax a little. No more the breathless hurry to get from one lesson to the next, only to find the student had canceled. No more the embarrassment of having to insist that patently rich people deign to pay one with a certain regularity. No more the smell of the correction fluid in the early hours while laboring over translations on the recycling of waste sludge in marble sawmills, the unsurpassable tourist attractions of the nearby town. He was home and dry.

But the contract they made him sign at the university was a strange one. Although to all intents and purposes an employee, in the sense that he had a timetable and certain well-established duties, he was in fact officially a free lance, the university retaining 18 percent of his income as tax (had he not had *residenza* they would have retained 20 percent), but paying no health contributions and requiring him to declare the money on a free-lance basis.

Now, since this friend of mine had a VAT number, which he used for his translations, he went to the university accounting office to ask what exactly his tax situation might be. Complicated, they said, and went into great detail. Which he didn't entirely understand. Italian tax law might well be written in hieroglyphics, for all the average citizen can understand of it. Never mind a foreigner. Rather than on actual income, everything seems to depend on the category of worker you are (artisan, lawyer, doctor, plumber, farmer, shopkeeper . . .) and the nature of the work you do (regular, casual, occasional, for one client, for various, etc., etc.), with different rules applying for each different category, different tax brackets, different deductions, different percentages for national insurance, and so on and so forth. So that at the end of the explanation, which might also have been described with the much-used Italian substantive *mistificazione*, my sensible friend demanded to know the bottom line: could he retain his VAT number, do a few translations, and do the job at the university without paying VAT on it.

They said yes. And made him sign something. The usual *documento*. They also said that even if he did want to charge VAT on the job, they wouldn't pay it, but would deduct it from his salary.

Had any of the other thirty or so *lettori*, readers, opted for this alternative? he asked.

And was told, none. Because it wasn't necessary.

But being a cautious lad, my friend also had an accountant. And went to see him. To clear the matter up. The accountant, however, could do nothing more than offer a second equally mystifying "explanation" which simply defied comprehension, perhaps because, as the accountant readily admitted, the law in many areas was not only unclear, but frankly contradictory. It also changed with great regularity, and often government decrees, which were officially law, were not ratified by parliament and thus not only ceased to be law but were deemed never to have been law in the first place. Basically my friend could do what he wanted. Since everybody else at the university was doing precisely that, my friend took this wise advice. He worked, he got paid, and, at least in this regard, he was happy.

Four years later he received a small white card in his mailbox. From the VAT office. He was required to present himself with great urgency, indeed before a date already past, for the printed card had taken more than a week to travel the four miles from the center of town to his modest flat in the outlying village.

He got on his moped and rushed into town, found the VAT office, showed his card at reception, and was directed along a maze of corridors to a huge office whose walls were lined from floor to ceiling, door to door, with box files bulging with tax declarations. It quickly became apparent that the four mustached men behind four gunmetal desks were sorting through the VAT declarations of four years before.

My friend was breathing heavily, because he had made it just in time. Like most public offices in Italy, this one was open only in the morning, since, unlike employees in the private sector, civil servants enjoy a thirty-six hour week, six mornings, six hours a day. It was now ten to one.

He handed his card to an older, weary, dusty, bespectacled man behind a huge dusty heap of papers colored the kind of garish pink and yellow that forms can be. In parentheses, I find it is curious how coloring forms does nothing to make them more attractive. Rather, the colors themselves become, by association, somewhat frightening: those tissue blues, washed-out mauves.

He apologized for the delay, but the mail had been slow. The man said the date was a formality and of no relevance. He then proceeded to look for the English teacher's VAT return out of the thousands, perhaps hundreds of thousands, which not only lined the walls, but were arrayed in great barriers of box files between the desks.

When the document was finally found, it emerged that while my friend had been wise perhaps to realize he needed an accountant, he had been unlucky in his choice. For the accountant had made a mistake. In the declaration of four years before, he had mentioned the university income and stated that it was exempted from VAT, but without indicating the code that would explain this exemption. The dusty old man now wanted my friend to tell him which code it was, so that he could write it in the space and the completed form be filed away and forgotten.

In passing, it's worth pointing out here that had the accountant filled in that space with any code, even a nonexistent one, there would most likely have been no problem. For Italian tax inspection appears to be mainly involved in finding contradictory statements within any given declaration. Only very rarely do inspectors go out of their offices to see if the life-style of the taxpayer bears any resemblance to his declaration. Thus it is common and frequently repeated wisdom (in the bars in Montecchio, for example) that it is far better to make no declaration at all than an incomplete or even minimally incorrect one. A line made all the more attractive by the fact that in this case one doesn't have to worry about an accountant. When Franco Pazienza, a millionaire entrepreneur, was arrested in connection with the collapse of the Banco Ambrosiano and the death of director Roberto Calvi (hanged under Blackfriars Bridge), it emerged that he had never made a tax declaration in his life, nor even bothered with a tax code. He had thus never run up against the kind of problems experienced by my friend. And the same could probably be said of one or two people within striking distance of Via Colombare.

But the story that follows will offer a certain justification for that apparently antisocial kind of behavior.

For my friend now made a terrible mistake. Lulled into a false sense of security by the bland innocuousness of this man with dust in his wrinkles and along the rims of his spectacles and peppering his anyway gray mustache, he said, truthfully, that he didn't know what code it might be. The man kindly suggested that he go away, consult his accountant, and return with this information inside a week or two. But here the young foreigner was quite criminally ingenuous, a born victim. He didn't want, he said, to have to return over such a small matter, nor to have to go and consult his accountant. It took him more than half an hour every time he came into town. Surely if he told the old man the nature of the work, he in turn could produce the code; they could then write it down and all would be over.

On the desk there was a little carousel of rubber stamps of all shapes and sizes, some adjustable, some not. The old man tapped the thing with his finger and it began to turn, squeaking slightly. Perhaps this was a warning.

Unheeded. My friend told him the nature of the work. Indeed of all his work. As a person who has nothing to fear from investigation and authority.

The older man became more interested, licked the dust off his lips, said he couldn't say offhand what code that would be; they would have to go and talk to a colleague.

The maze of passages again, gray carpets, fluorescent light. Indeed, apart from the occasional crucifix hanging under the heating pipes near the ceiling, this could perfectly well be an unemployment office in some quiet London suburb. But it isn't.

In another gloomy but more private office the colleague is of an entirely different variety. He is young, sanguine, peremptory, and dust-free, despite the tomes and papers on his desk.

Such work, he pronounces, after hearing the story, should not have been exempt from VAT. There is no question of there being a code.

But my friend has a document provided for him by the university accountants, whom he consulted precisely over this question.

Already he appreciates what a mistake he has made. But it is too late.

A document from the university? The younger man is scornful. No accountant worth his salt would be working at the university, getting only a million and a half a month. Would he? How could they advise him? In any event my friend, as a resident and contributor, is personally responsible for paying his taxes regardless of any advice received—even, the man adds triumphantly, if such incorrect advice were to come from this very office.

The dusty man has stayed to listen. Warming his hands over the radiator, he looks out over the window at a building identical to the one the three of them are in, five, six stories, white concrete, regular square windows. In every room all the typewriters are supplied by Olivetti, as they should be.

"And you're still working at the university?" The sanguine inspector has assumed an interrogator's tone.

Yes.

So that this has been going on for four years?

Yes.

During which time your remuneration has been what?

My friend tells him. The other man's fingers are extraordinarily rapid on the keyboard of a calculator. "You have evaded VAT for around nine million lire," he says.

But as the English teacher gasps, makes to protest, the inspector has suddenly become friendly. "However, we should see this document you mentioned and your contract before we go into detail. Why don't you bring them in?"

He smiles, goes to pick up his coat. Is it because he's realized that it is time for him to go home for lunch? Or is there some other reason?

"When?"

"Oh, when you like. But don't forget."

Leaving the building, my friend reflects that this kind of vagueness is more disconcerting than comforting. As was the unexpectedly chummy smile on the young man's previously severe face. Extremely anxious as he is, he wants the matter settled at once, not left hanging over his head. And so he rushes things. When perhaps he might have been wiser to do what Orietta would no doubt have advised: had his blood pressure checked, wait till it had fallen.

In any event, he calls his accountant immediately, from a phone box outside the tax office, and tells him the story. At no point does the accountant apologize for his original mistake. If his client wishes, he says, he will go and talk to the tax office about it himself, but perhaps before he does so, it would be better if my friend got the document in question and the contract, took it to the inspectors, stressed his ingenuousness, and insisted on his good faith. He has not, after all, pocketed any money in VAT and then avoided paying it to the state, as perhaps a shopkeeper might. He has merely omitted to charge the client VAT on top of the regular price, always assuming he was in fact supposed to do so. In this way he has not profited from the situation at all. Nor will the state have lost through the university's having detracted from their own VAT payments any monies supposedly paid to him.

My friend, however, is losing his nerve. He positively flaunts his anxiety by returning to the tax office with his documents the very next day. First there's the dusty man again, then the sanguine man, the one dryly polite, apologetic, apparently innocuous, the other tougher, dismissive, immediately assuming the attitude of one who is fed up with hearing cock-and-bull stories.

Allora?

Here is the document.

The younger man looks at it; the older is window-gazing again. The document quotes three or four different laws, sections, paragraphs, amendments—convincing pomposity.

"Incompetenti" is the comment, and the VAT man opens a tome on his desk, finds a page, begins to read rapidly out loud from

one of the laws cited. My friend, who is actually a whiz at translating complex commercial insurance documents, can't quite follow it. Somehow it all depends on whether his nonuniversity jobs are *continuativi* (regular) or *saltuari* (occasional). He earns, he says, about ten million a year from translations from a variety of clients, some new, some old, but he would be hard pressed to say if this added up to *continuativo* or *saltuario*. The words surely require more precise definition.

The sanguine man undergoes one of his mystifying changes of behavior. He smiles, he is relaxed. *"Sì, Sì, sono d' accordo,"* he agrees. And adds: "Five in ten people would probably feel you were in the right."

"After all, given that I've made nothing out of it, no one can deny I'm in good faith."

"D'accordo, d'accordo."

The dusty man turns from the window to watch. My friend is smiling, seeing lights at the end of the tunnel. The accountant seems to have advised him well.

Then the younger man lifts a hand to his face, touches his cheek, and says very politely: "Though good faith is no defense under law, only a mitigating circumstance."

"But . . . "

"And my interpretation remains that you should have been paying VAT, that you have evaded VAT for a sum of approximately nine million lire, and that you are thus subject to repayment of that sum, plus further payment of a fine."

Flabbergasted, my friend can barely get out: "How much?"

"Fines are usually equal to the amount evaded. A further nine million, with some reduction if you pay immediately, of course."

A total of eighteen million lire, or about eight thousand pounds. With his back to the window now the older man doesn't bat a dusty eyelid.

"But only a moment ago you said interpretation could go either way."

"Naturally you could appeal against this, and the judgment could indeed go either way. Which would clarify the law most usefully in situations of this kind. In the meantime you would be obliged to pay thirty-three percent of monies due as a first installment. You would also lose any possible reduction for immediate payment."

My friend and the inspector are of about the same age and build. They stare at each other across the desk. One in disbelief, the other almost quizzical. And at last my friend makes his first smart move, even though his original idea is merely to gain time. He explains that some of his colleagues have recently fought and won a case to be recognized as employees of the university, not free-lance workers; this means that the job cannot be considered subject to VAT. And recognition was retrospective. It would cover this period.

The sanguine man caresses his chin, narrows his eyes. He reminds my friend that in Italy the decision of a court does not establish precedence. It merely offers one interpretation of the existing law. The verdict in favor of his colleagues, if such a verdict exists, thus refers exclusively to those who fought the case, not to him. A second judge could perfectly well decide differently in his case. His status thus remains the same, and as far as he, the inspector, is concerned, VAT has been evaded to the tune of nine million. As an employee of the government he has a duty to collect evaded taxes and to punish those who evade them.

For the first time my friend lies, and this is another step forward. "But I have begun my own case too," he says. He is trembling.

"Ah?"

"So at present, in a way, everything is *sub judice*."

There is a long hard pause, much eye contact. The dusty man pouts, coughs dryly. Finally the younger inspector politely invites my friend to come back once again, this time with a copy both of the sentence of the case won by his colleagues and of his lawyer's presentation of his own case to the Tribunale di Lavoro.

Which, of course, he hasn't got. Looking back at the building as he leaves, my friend remembers *The Castle*, the courtrooms of *The*

Trial. Immediately he phones his accountant. The avuncular man, in yet another cluttered office complete with crucifix, is kind and genuinely concerned. He hadn't initially wanted to go and speak to the tax people personally, since *"finora io e te abbiamo sempre collaborato in modo amichevole,"* i.e., "so far you have paid me under the table and I haven't given you a receipt for my services or in any way indicated in my books that you are a client of mine." However, at this point he agrees it is time he went to talk to these people. Yes, he knows who it must be.

A nail-biting week. During which, to pass the time, and then because once there's an itch you have to scratch it, my friend goes to the university accounting office and again inquires, as if merely to reassure himself, about his tax position. Again he hears, as he did four years ago, that there is no need for him to pay VAT on his university income. He then tells the accountant, a forty-year-old man with the dress style of someone determined to stay young, an expensive mixture of Armani, Gianfranco Ferrè, and Benetton, that the VAT office thinks otherwise and is at this very moment asking him to pay a heavy fine. To which the other man replies with great promptness that he can in no way be held responsible for the advice he gives. A brief slanging match follows, since this is one person, my friend feels, he can give a piece of his very worried mind to with impunity. As always Christ is looking on from his own particular cross. Plastic in this case.

Finally the accountant phones. He has talked to the VAT people. Could my friend come into his office. They can't discuss it on the telephone.

And in the office he says: "They want a Christmas present."

"Prego?"

"Una bustarella." A little envelope. A bribe.

"Did they say so?"

"God forbid."

So how does he know?

He knows. And this burly accountant with thick bushy eyebrows now proceeds with nostalgic revelry to launch into the story of the very first time he offered a bribe. Oh, twenty years ago.

He simply became so exasperated with the obtuseness of the official he was dealing with that he said, "Okay, how much do you want?" and then fell silent, stunned by his own rashness. What if he had read the signals wrong? But he hadn't.

Later he learned the trick of dropping an envelope on the floor and asking the other if he had dropped it there. Another important indicator was if the official invited you out for a coffee.

It occurs to me, writing this down, that this sort of breathtaking breaking of cover—the dropping of the envelope, the invitation to coffee—is not unlike one's first declaration of attraction to a possible lover; there's sudden intimacy and self-exposure. It's exhilarating.

And, my friend tells me, his accountant was indeed exhilarated. In this case, the man began to explain, he had understood that they wanted a bribe, because otherwise they would have already proceeded to fill in the document requiring him to pay the fine. After which there could be no turning back, the matter would be officially registered. And had my friend really evaded so much VAT, they would almost certainly have proceeded with the matter and nailed him. As it was, appreciating he was merely a victim of circumstance, they were inclined to let him off the hook in return for a small Christmas present.

"How much?"

Two days later the accountant phones to say the matter in question would cost 800,000 lire. My friend should come to his office in a couple of days' time to say whether he intends to pay.

My friend is still very English. Though less than he was a month ago. In the past week he has joined a group of colleagues bringing a case against the university to be recognized as employees. So he now has a lawyer. An attractive young woman six months pregnant. And finding the idea of paying a bribe somewhat offensive, the kind of awful initiation into a different way of life, a different state of mind that theft or adultery might be, he phones this lawyer to discuss the problem. She is polite and patient, listening to the complex story. Until he gets to the bit about the little envelope, at which she suddenly becomes frantic. "*Per l'amore di Dio* we're talking on the phone." Anyway, she will consult her accountant and ring back.

Which she duly does. Indeed, it's surprising how kind and helpful and civilized everybody is being. On the phone she's calm, matter-of-fact: "The manner," she says—and my friend has written her circumlocutions down because he finds them so amusing—"in which your accountant has chosen to resolve the particular difficulties in which, through no fault of your own, you find yourself, although perhaps not immediately attractive, and you do have my sympathy here, is nevertheless not so mistaken as you appear to think. If you follow his advice to the letter, I am sure you will be able to arrive at a *soluzione felice* without my help."

But another anxious week has definitely Italianized my friend that little bit more. For rather than simply shelling out the 800,000, as it now seems he will have to, he points out to his accountant that since the VAT office's complaint is based only on that one declaration of four years ago, they could perfectly well pull out the next declarations one by one, year by year, and have him over a barrel for the same amount again.

The accountant accepts this. It is agreed the 800,000 will be paid only if the VAT office can dig up the other declarations and allow the accountant to change them; otherwise the sum must be renegotiated. The VAT men, whom my friend never saw again, and whose names he does not know, are likewise reasonable. No, they can't dig out the other declarations; yes, they do appreciate the problem this represents; they will bring their request down to 400,000.

Pride satisfied, my friend pays.

"And a hundred thousand for me for negotiating the deal," the accountant says, with still no apology for his initial mistake. And no receipt.

Before leaving the office, in the state of exhilaration that every initiation, every surrender of self brings once one has decided to go through with it, my friend asks the accountant: "But it's so little. Why would anyone corrupt himself for so little?"

"No accountant worth his salt," the burly man explains, "would work in the VAT office. How much can they be getting— two million a month? They have to supplement it. A hundred thousand from you, half a million from me, it all adds up. And the rules are a lot simpler than the written ones." Reflectively, as if this has occurred to him for the first time, he adds: "There's only one person I know of in the VAT office who won't take something sometime. Lucky it wasn't he who picked up your problem."

My friend walks out into the bright street with the feeling of one waking up from a nightmare. In the end he's only lost 250-odd quid. Not much to pay for a significant experience.

UNA
SCAMPAGNATA

Y<small>ET WHEN ONE DOES WAKE UP</small> from such occasional nightmares, when one turns off the TV with its bullet-ridden cars and improbable corpses (eight in a single village in Sicily the very morning I write this), when one closes the newspapers with their intricate political scandals from top to toe of the peninsula, it will often seem that one is living in paradise.

There is no smell on the balcony this Montecchio morning. Perhaps because it is Sunday. The late-October air has that look of water in a wineglass, so that one expects, on walking out of the front door, to step into a magic world. And magic it is. Old Marini's blackbird whistles brightly, perhaps remembering how fine the trees were on such sweet mornings, the sharp silhouettes of the hills, the nobly etched cypresses dark against the glowing gold of autumn cherry leaves.

We wait in the street for the old ladies to return from mass, then set off with them, Orietta, Giampaolo, and Lara on a *scampagnata*, a long walk up into the hills. We are going to see Lucilla's daughter, Marisa, who is not in fact her daughter, Lucilla now confides, but the child of a sister conceived and born adulterously while the husband was in prison and handed over to Lucilla at just a few weeks old to make the husband's release less turbulent. Lucilla's own and only child died at eighteen months, *poveretto*. From the long story she tells us about his illness it becomes clear that Lucilla quite probably provoked his death herself by applying scalding poultices to his entire body in an attempt to overcome some banal influenza. Shortly afterward, a miscarriage led to her having *la totale* at only twenty. *La totale* is the grim Italian expression for a hysterectomy. Once again one reflects that while people from the Veneto are generally reserved and formal, nevertheless when they get onto the subject of their health there is simply nothing, nothing, they will not tell to the most casual acquaintance, from varicose veins to mastectomy, prostatitis to mere constipation. And indeed, it's not long before Rita, Vittorina, and Orietta are discussing various tisanes, or herb concoctions, which help to keep one regular. Vittorina has a plastic bag to put in camomile plants as she walks along. A new shop, it appears, is to open next to Bepi's, and the girl is an excellent herbalist. She even has a mix for flatulence.

I remember how rigorously my own parents avoided discussion of such complaints. That was the English *omertà* perhaps, our own peculiar conspiracy of secrecy. Orietta is tackling an overabundant period now. Much confabulation.

To try Giampaolo on the subject, I remark that the other day the parent of a friend of ours informed us on the very first meeting that her husband had only one testicle. Giampaolo neither laughs nor winces, but with polite interest inquires, "Tuberculosis, or war wound?"

We pass the Madonnina, at the end of the street, dead Christ on her lap, then a second tiny Madonna behind glass where the road leaving the village forks. *O Gesù salvaci!*—someone has attached a popular sticker to the wall just above. And how benign they are, these plaster guardians of dangerous junctions in their faded blue robes and dusty halos, one hand inevitably raised in blessing. The glass has been polished. The Madonna is composed, wistful. A hundred yards farther up the street, someone is still putting chrysanthemums in a stone vase to mark the spot where a boy was killed on his *motorino* in the summer.

We climb steeply out of Montecchio to Olivè, where so many parents send their children to the convent school, because there are never any strikes and the church is more efficient than the state. There is building work going on in what was recently an orchard, but the cement mixers are silent on Sunday. To the left a fine old farmhouse has been restored with a warm beige stucco that has a honey look to it in the now yellow morning light. The white chairs and tables on the terrace outside, the patently movable dwarf trees and statues arranged in geometric design, offer, in what was once a farmyard, a last testimony to urban invasion. From here on, *stile cimitero* gives way definitively to flourishing vegetable patches. Olivè is solidly indigenous.

A woman is attacking clothes with a soap stick at an outside sink. With every new fence a fierce dog barks. There's no sidewalk, and parked up against the walls the cheaper Fiats predominate, with the occasional tractor. Weathered old men in trilbies and Sunday best descend to Montecchio for the second mass, lighting cigarettes.

Then the asphalt gives way to dirt track. The road turns sharply left by a noble gate and goes into a steep cutting between high stone walls where a beautifully arched old bridge crosses above. With ivies hanging thick from the parapet, capers sprouting from the walls in vigorous tufts, the dusty road almost white, and the sky ever more deeply blue above, the scene seems made for one of those tiny paintings by Sisley or Pissarro that you find tucked away in the corners of rooms dedicated to grander canvases, paintings which convey such a sense of a single moment in a single place it is as if time had been made palpable. Even now when I pass that turn in the road I always remember it as it was that morning. It made such a picture.

Lucilla is volubly discussing Il Professore again. How often they used to come on walks like this! How cultured he was! How polite! Vittorina shakes her head, pouting silently, as if to tell us Lucilla is inventing. Clearly we are never going to get to the bottom of this. "In my will," the fat woman puffs, "I've left everything to Marisa and Leone, but only on the understanding that they continue the case against Signora Marta." She shakes her fist. Odd, I think, how despite her loathing she continues to refer to the woman so politely as Signora Marta. As if cowed by her urban credentials.

It's a long walk. We meet the main road climbing the side of the valley, but since it goes up in a series of tight bends, we merely cross it, following a little path that strikes up steeply from one hairpin to the next. The old ladies are surprisingly energetic, Lucilla amazingly managing perfectly well in high heels on the chalky-white soil of the path. She has a posh coat on, though not her fur, plus a frilly blouse, a pearl necklace. Her bright makeup, one fears, will soon begin to melt.

Vittorina is plainer, but stalwart, peasant-solid with broad-brimmed straw hat, constantly bending down for her camomile. Orietta trails behind, already tired, limp. She hopes she won't have an attack of tachycardia. Giampaolo has that fine proud upright urban gait so admirable in Italian men. He wears a fashionable jacket, good walking shoes. Every Latin black hair is in place on his polished head. Lara is chattering about her homework. At twelve, she has been set by her Italian teacher an essay entitled *'La verità nella filosofia, nella matematica e nella fisica.'* It's mind-boggling. But not so tricky perhaps, as *la verità* in the VAT office.

We are crossing another bend in the road when there is a sudden swishing sound, followed by grunts, heavy breathing. Turning around, it's to discover a pack of young and not so young men standing on the pedals of their sparkling racing bikes as they attack what seems an impossible slope. To a man they are fully fitted out with the cycling shoes, the elastic knee-length pants, the fluorescent sweat shirts, the caps. Not one without the perfect gear. A mobile love affair with sports equipment. One can do little but gasp with admiration at the energy with which they attack this slope.

"Not for someone with my blood pressure," Orietta shakes her head.

"Or sloth," says her daughter. Giampaolo maintains his reserve. Mentally I rehearse: as a sport, *valido*; the design of the bikes, *discreto*; but pleasure rendered *relativo* by the fact that by the time you get back you're fit for nothing but bath and bed.

Comes a sudden cry of *"Pista, pista!"* Make room! Out of the way! And from around the corner where the muscled backsides of the cyclists have just disappeared flies a girl on wooden skis. The skis have small wheels at each end. The girl wobbles precariously, gives a heave on one of her ski poles, and vanishes down the road—getting in vital practice for the season.

In sharp contrast to these healthy activities and all the talks of herbs and remedies, we now pass a cypress in a small clearing whose trunk is bristling with used syringes stabbed into the bark. Nobody has anything to say about this sad rejection of the usual social rituals. The old ladies shake their heads in incomprehension. Orietta worries that if the point of a discarded syringe should pierce the sole of her shoes, it could give her AIDS. But Giampaolo knows that the virus lives for only fifteen minutes outside the body. And we're back on safe ground discussing the reliability of the information they give us and whether the state should bow to Vatican pressure not to advise people to use condoms.

We trek on. The land, like that around Rivoli, is semi-abandoned. Elaborate stone terracing, now overgrown and ill-kept, reminds you that only fifteen, twenty years ago these hills were worked intensively. But not even the expensive blandishments of the Common Agricultural Policy have been able to keep the peasants at work up here. Now the only productive aspect of the landscape is the olive trees, their fantastically gnarled fairy-tale trunks and curious leaves, at once dull green and bright silver, adding a further touch of magic to the landscape, an autumn play of stark twisted southern evergreen against paling breaks of deciduous copse. More prosaically, whenever the contours allow for it, there will be a long low prefab factory farm for chickens or turkeys. Approaching, you hear the sinister hum of electricity, then a busy clucking that explodes into excitement, or protest perhaps, as the birds sense your passing.

A couple of hours later, when we reach the top of the ridge

above the village, the whole fantastic landscape to the north opens up before us. Range after range of hills rise one after another to blue mountains. The panorama is vast, hugely open, intensely exhilarating. We stop and gaze. Two rapid reports from a shotgun, then two more, tell us hunters are about, though we have seen not a single wild animal along the walk, heard not a rustle. Bang bang go the guns. Presumably aimed at some fluttering *uccellino*. *Poveretto*, says Vittorina, who enjoys cooking them so much. And having absorbed the view, we press on toward the little village of Cancello.

When Lucilla retired she sold her cleaning company to a bigger one, but Marisa and husband Leone still work on in a management role. With the decent incomes these two no doubt deserve, they have built themselves a house up in the hills. They would have liked to be nearer Montecchio, but unusually for Italians they chose not to accept the offer of the flat immediately below Lucilla's. It is to this perversity that the Visentinis owe their good fortune in occupying flat two.

At first sight, Marisa and Leone's *villetta* looks like an English bungalow, for local zoning forbade them to build over a certain height. However, the attic is *abitabile*—livable—and opens onto a most attractive terrace cut in the roof. The ground floor is spacious and luxurious: tiles, parquet, rugs, two bathrooms, three bedrooms. But this wasn't enough for Marisa and Leone. Unable to build upward, they decided to go down. The hills are limestone and easily cut. So there is a basement dug into the rock, comprising a garage for the Mercedes and then a huge *taverna* with absolutely all mod conveniences: TV, well-stocked bar, second dishwasher, fireplace of medieval castle proportions (including spit), etc., etc. And still it wasn't enough. For below that again, two floors beneath the rosemary, chives, and minty grass of the hillside above, is the cellar. With bare rock walls, it is clammy, cool, and abundantly stocked with wines labeled and labelless, alongside a variety of hams, salamis, and sausages suspended from hooks in the ceiling.

Stiff Giampaolo is most impressed by it all. *Validissimo*, this idea of a second basement beneath the first. The temperature is just perfect. And the wine selection is certainly *discreto*. Whatever the inevitable relativity of the situation may be, he chooses not to mention it in deference to our host.

We climb back up to the tavern. In bright and fashionable halogen lighting hidden in the false ceiling over the bar, I find myself surrounded by antlers, boars' heads, stuffed grouse, and the like. And fleetingly I wonder what the same kind of people in England would aspire to. Perhaps the sort of show house I blundered into in South Wales on holiday last year: a simplified, wood-frame copy of some grand Victorian original, with quaint furnishings, imitation Laura Ashley curtains, glass-covered bookshelves boasting leather-bound editions (surely fake) of Shakespeare and Dickens, and very sophisticated naughty underwear laid out on pink-silk-lookalike counterpane in the master bedroom.

But Leone and Marisa do nothing to hide their humble origins. They speak a broad dialect which I can't always follow. They have no cultural pretensions. If the floor is paved with a warm red *cotto*, it is because they like it. Likewise the designer tiles in the bathroom. They happen to like them. They have the money. And they are incorrigibly jolly as they serve us the usual abundant Sunday lunch of a pasta dish (*al pesto*), followed by various boiled meats and fatty red, quite delicious, *cotechino* with polenta and salad. Then the inevitable *tiramisù*. And cheeses. A piece of Parmesan to sweeten the mouth? A piece of seasoned Piave? Or would you like some sheep's cheese? And now fruit, of course: *uva moscata*, kiwis . . .

We are sitting around a table designed for thirty-odd. There are photographs of big parties on the wall. But Leone's booming voice and merry stories make up for the lack of numbers. The wines come and go in the usual sequence, as they must: a Bardolino *novello* for the *aperitivo*, sharp and fresh from the vines, a smooth Barbera to bring out the flavor of the meat, a blood-red sickly Recioto for the sweet. And now a glass of grappa appears beside your coffee. There's giggling, backslapping. Even Vittorina is lighthearted, despite, at one point, some low-voiced conversation with Marisa about a Madonna who has been seen to cry recently in a church at Cologna Veneta. "What about some chestnuts?" booms the incorrigible

Leone. "Chestnuts, chestnuts." He's gathered them himself in some wood farther north. Italians have always been off gathering or picking something for themselves. The chestnuts are placed over the grate on a sort of frying pan with holes, then wrapped in cloth in a basket and handed around. No salt. That would push the pressure up terribly. But another cork is pulled. It's all hugely pleasant and at the same time far far far too much.

"*Troppo, troppo gentile,*" Lucilla says at the door, appearing to forget that this is the girl she brought up as her daughter. *Troppo gentile.* Buxom Marisa in Sunday best winks at the others. Leone goes down to get the Mercedes.

But surprisingly, the seventy-year-old ladies are all for walking back. They don't want to be taken in the car. So we set out in midafternoon in an atmosphere of dazed merriment and with a great deal of extra ballast to work off.

There is a lot more traffic about now as people return from their Sunday lunch in the surrounding trattorias. But not everybody is going straight back to Verona. Here and there, as we cross the road to follow the path, we find cars have pulled off the tarmac to park in the fields, and while mother and children walk about looking for mushrooms, flowers, and herbs, *papà* sits in the driver's seat listening to the radio and nervously cracking his knuckles. Or alternatively, *papà* does go off walking with his wife and children, but all the while holding a tiny transistor radio to his ear, cracking his knuckles against his thighs. An elderly and very well-to-do couple stroll by: distinguished, snooty almost, arm in formal arm, mohair coats, traditional hats. But the man has his radio at his ear. And he is biting the corner of his lips.

They are listening to the local football game. Across fields and slopes, it comes from behind, in front, above, below you—the sound of a nasal voice commenting on play with the very same pomposity Lara is presumably supposed to bring to *La verità nella filosofia, nella matematica e nella fisica.* I overhear something like "The dynamic oscillation of midfield deployment with interchangeable roles in zone configuration is indubitably sound when considered from an exclusively tactical perspective, but perhaps the precariously semi-advanced position of the two center backs which this inevitably entails is not entirely suitable to the psychological tension in which players understandably, though it must be agreed regrettably, approach a game that could prove the watershed of this intriguing championship." It's bewildering, and I for one certainly haven't the faintest idea what it means. But people are listening intently enough. After all, this is the place where the choice of referees for next week's games is announced together with political scandals and spiraling national debt on TV news headlines. The little radios hiss and crackle between the olives. Sunday afternoon. Verona is losing. Faces are long and severe.

We press on. Then, in the twilight of this beautiful day, hurrying down the hill paths, Lucilla begins to sing. She sings a sickly hymn tune: *"Tu scendi dalle stelle, o re del cie-e-elo!"* Then, more merrily, a grating old pop tune: *"Ciao ciao bambina, un bacio ancora . . . "* She is very loud, with a cracked, witch's voice, and completely tone-deaf. The others join in, if only to drown out Lucilla. Then Rita and Giampaolo launch into some of the famous songs of the Alpini, the Italian mountain regiment. They are all World War I songs from when the regiment won a notable victory, turning back the Germans in the mountains. With very great loss of life. There's a sort of spirited mournfulness to tune and words that reminds one of traditional Welsh singing. And the occasional refrain tells all: "That long train that went to the frontier . . . " "On the bridge at Bassano, we'll hold hands." "Don't get yourself killed, soldier." "They are shelling Cortina." "Ta-pum, ta-pum, ta-pum."

Italian friends tell me these old songs are corny, and yet I always find them desperately moving: the young men marching into the mountains, ill-equipped, to death and glory, for undoubtedly a certain sad glory is to be had in such situations: "But if I fall among flowers," they sing, "I don't care if I die." "Ta-pum, ta-pum, ta-pum," go the guns. It always brings tears to my eyes. I must be hopelessly sentimental. And I can't listen anymore. So I fall back a few paces to walk beside Orietta, who immediately asks me if I think it's wise of them to let Lara do so much volleyball. She's such a big girl already. Isn't there a danger she might get thick ankles, muscular legs. . . .

We're still walking when night falls, though Montecchio isn't far below us now, the castle sharp against the glow of Verona behind. The radios have fallen silent. Ghostly among the hills, long thin lines of light flicker on. For the chickens it's always fluorescent daytime. They produce more. I take Lucilla's arm as we negotiate our way along the last stretch of dirt track. She tucks my hand tight under her elbow. And so back home, after what must surely have been our most successful day as a condominium.

To hear, through the fence, from a hovering Lovato, the momentous news that Il Professore's wife, Maria Rosa, died today. During our *scampagnata*. The battle for the inheritance of Via Colombare 10, flat four, opens in earnest.

UN PANINO DUE . . .

My first months at Via Colombare I bought my bread at Tosi's, a shop which is little more than a hole in the wall but still manages to sell every possible foodstuff in just ten square yards. There's a cash desk at the door, the wooden shelving is chockablock, the floor is made of old stone conglomerate, the cheapest, and behind a cluttered deli at the back, old Tosi himself, bald head threatened by salamis above, cuts squares of pizza in the half-dark and counts out bread rolls from bins. He always counts them out aloud. *"Otto panini Mantovani, per favore,"* you say, and he begins: *"Un panino, due panini, tre panini, quattro panini . . ."* Before we learn his name, we always refer to him as *Un panino due.*

When he's tucked your rolls into a brown paper bag, this lean old man scribbles something with a practiced shopkeeper's smile and you turn to the wife at the desk to pay. They don't have a proper electronic cash register, which means they're declaring a very low turnover, since above something fairly pathetic, VAT-approved cash registers have recently become obligatory. The signora doesn't have a head for sums and invariably gives you less change than she should. Meanwhile, Tosi is already counting out the next customer's rolls: *"Un panino, due panini . . . "* He has recently built a small estate of four *palazzine*, sixteen flats in all, opposite the gas pump. They go for more than a million a square yard. A fortune. On the hill behind us he is building two much larger villas surrounded by elaborate iron fences for himself and his family. Rumor has it that in the hungrier years of the war he would give people bread in return for land. Certainly he now owns large areas of hillside, and is eagerly courted by the local building contractors. But for all his wealth, however gained, old Tosi continues to count out panini: *un panino, due panini . . .* And you say to his wife, *"Mi scusi*, Signora Tosi, you haven't given me enough change." *"O davvero?"* she says. "I am sorry."

So when Bepi expands his greengrocery, adding a bread and deli counter, I'm happy to switch there. Which means I walk past Tosi's shop now, my plastic bag in my hand. Perhaps the old man has come out of his cave for a moment to stand on the steps beside the ancient enameled blue sign that says, OLIO D'OLIVA, OLIO DI SEMI, ZUCCHERO . . . He has a soiled white shopkeeper's coat, arms folded. And to show that my betrayal is of no concern, he makes a point of smiling his scrubbed shopkeeper's smile from around a long hooked nose. For his old customers will never betray him. Old Marini and his wife will never betray him, never go to a shop run by a parvenu like Bepi. Lucilla and Vittorina will never betray him. They're in there. Despite the fact that everything is more expensive. *Troppo gentile, troppo gentile*, Lucilla says to Signora Tosi, not counting her change at the door.

Bepi is sorting through piles of paper as he takes your money at the till. Scores and scores of loose scraps of paper: green paper, yellow paper, blue paper, printed, typed, scribbled. "What are they?" I ask him. *"Scartoffie,"* he says: rubbish. And he laughs his barrel-chested laugh. In fact, they are all delivery receipts and invoices from suppliers: a farmer who brings goat's cheeses in jars of oil, an importer who sends him Swedish salmon, a processor who prepares olives and red peppers, again in oil. It's a serious deli.

Bepi has a blunt pencil behind his ear in thick hair. I ask him if he does his accounts himself. He says yes. I ask him how he can possibly manage this with his gym, his karate, his dogs, his court cases, his occult studies, the house he is renovating. Of course he can't, he says. But then if he can't, they certainly never will, will they? We both know who "they" are. "And if they bother you?" "I'll prosecute them," he says, "for harassment." And he means it.

Rather than giving you too little change, Bepi usually rounds your bill down. "Five thousand two hundred and fifty? Oh, just give me five thousand." He has an electronic cash register, but doesn't always open it. After all, I'm a friend. The government, one might mention, agreed to pay shopkeepers a percentage of the cost of introducing approved electronic cash registers. Mainly produced by Olivetti.

Mopeds whiz round the bend in the road as I leave the shop. One towing a bicycle. Outside Tosi's shop there are now four or five youngsters sitting on the steps behind their bikes eating oily squares of pizza out of sheets of paper. I walk to the other end of the village to pick up my *Arena*, and outside the newsstand there are other youths perched on more mopeds; these ones drinking Coca-Cola and eating potato chips. Moreno, the tiny half-wit in deerstalker cap, is trying to talk to them, and they are gently making fun. Going past the church there are yet more youths, yet more mopeds, hanging around in the gardens there. They hang around till late in the evening, summer or winter. Generally they are well behaved. I don't get the impression they booze at all, but occasionally a phone box, *the* phone box, will get damaged—or a road sign. And they catch colds, of course. Because it's mid-October now.

Giampaolo protests at the first local council meeting I go to. Kids are hanging around all over the place vandalizing things and freezing their feet because there are no facilities in Montecchio, no green spaces and nothing for people to do. Actually, Giampaolo is not really very worried about this, since for the moment his daughter always returns at a reasonable hour; but word has gotten about that the cherry orchard behind the Madonnina at the end of Via Colombare is not to become a public park and recreation area, as originally promised in the plan for the village, but a cooperative housing estate. Which will mean tripling the traffic along our narrow street.

Giampaolo is well-spoken, polite, but forthright. A modern, liberal man. There are cries of *"Sì, giustissimo!"* But the Christian Democrat leader in Montecchio, who is also the weasely fellow in charge of the post office, calmly dismisses him. There is volleyball some evenings in the school gym, and the church lays on meetings for young people one or two nights a week. The reason kids are out on the street vandalizing things is that they are not being brought up with traditional Christian values in good strong families (murmuring of approval from the older contingent). And it is calumny, he says, to suggest that the party is in the pockets of the building contractors.

The Christian Democrats' local office is in an old church on one of the main corners of the village. They poll around 70 percent of the Montecchio vote. The Veneto in general has a higher Christian Democrat vote than anywhere else in Italy, including Sicily. The old church has a small tree growing on its unkempt roof. Below, on the gray wall above the flood-overflow ditch which runs alongside, someone has spray-painted: FOREIGNERS OUT OF THE VENETO.

Only two hundred yards away, the Communist Party headquarters is a dark poky place on the main street opposite Pasticceria Maggia. On a handpainted wooden board above the door the hammer and sickle are fading fast. Through the windows old men can be glimpsed at a bare wooden table on which stands a labelless two-liter bottle of wine.

The very same men are also to be seen some mornings sitting under straw hats on a bedraggled couch under a fig tree against the sagging wire fence that surrounds their allotments. The two-liter bottle, however, from behind which they look out over lines of enormous cabbages, is doubtless a fresh one. Youths roar by on their mopeds, confabulate in knots at street corners. After dark, when their parents could not see even if they drove right by, they kiss.

A modest crop of unmarried mothers patrol the streets with their baby carriages, and in general have the sympathy of the population.

The very attractive *barista* in Pasticceria Maggia is such a case. Her child is eight years old, and perhaps aptly called Luna. The *barista* serves the people coming out of church. Out of church and into the bar in their Sunday best, which means furs for the women now the cooler air gives them an excuse. There's a parade feeling about it all. From one institution to another: the host, the brioche.

The church has the largest parking lot in the village, aside from the supermarket's, which nobody uses. A capacity of around a hundred cars. It is full Saturday evening for the mass for those who want to dash off skiing first thing Sunday morning, or those who'll be so long in the discotheque tonight they don't expect to make it tomorrow. And it is full again Sunday morning for the mass for those who want to show off clothes and well-dressed children and get a cappuccino afterward in the bar and buy attractively wrapped trays of pastries for visits to relatives. Some of these people drive from only three or four hundred yards away.

The church parking lot is also full for funerals and weddings. A bride and groom come out. They have married in their late twenties after being boyfriend and girlfriend since puberty. A photographer is waiting on the steps. But the groom is already lighting a cigarette. Anyway, the real photos will be taken later in an ornamental park the other side of Verona where there is a lake and stone nymphs. The photographer will fade one face over the other against a pre-prepared full moon behind floating in the water. For the moment, though, everyone is rushing out of church to try to get his car out of the park before the crush. Since it's a wedding, they all honk.

Yes, it was certainly wise of the local government to provide such ample parking space, such a large area of asphalt in the middle of the village. But when there are first communions to be celebrated, even this space is unable to contain the flood of traffic and enthusiasm. The cars tuck in by the emergency overflow dike and down the embankment as far as the supermarket. The spiffily dressed relatives step out of black BMWs. Clean, *per bene*, as they say here: healthy, wealthy, right-thinking people. There is something almost Victorian about the overdressed children, the fussing mothers. Certainly they all know their catechism well enough, as one child after another is accepted into the community. And after the ceremony's over, it's off to a restaurant, where a table has been reserved for twenty. The expensive festivities will go on all afternoon, and the children will be given their golden chains and crucifixes and signet rings.

On his election poster, a local Christian Democrat uses a picture of himself and his wife standing with family and friends around a beautifully laid table with white embroidered tablecloth, tall glasses of bubbly, large slices of *panettone*. There is no message or slogan, just the candidate's name; but we can feel reasonably sure that this man supports all the best local aspirations, is the very avant-garde of the bourgeoisie perhaps.

The Christian Democrats' annual festival is called *La festa dell'amicizia*, the Festival of Friendship: good friends, good contacts, an aura of universal love and piety. With a subtle shift of emphasis, the Communists called theirs *La festa dell'unità*, the Festival of Unity. Conjuring up images of rump solidarity, a last stand. In the event, both festivals mean barbecued food and wine, dancing in front of a noisy band (the same one, quite probably), and lines of booths where trivial skills are rewarded with soft toys. If you go to the one you may as well go to the other too. As everybody does, in fact. Because both are a lot of fun.

My wife goes to see the priest who preaches to the faithful week in week out: Don Guido, the small, bespectacled, faintly squinting character who smelled something rotten in Bepi's shop. He sits behind his large desk in modern *canonica* next to the new red brick church which he himself had built.

What can he do to help?

Rita (for her sins perhaps?) is translating into Italian an American book about the papacy. The book quotes extensively in English from various encyclicals. Does Don Guido by any chance have copies of these encyclicals in Italian? She ought to use the originals, not translate them back herself. And she knows encyclicals are automatically sent out to all priests.

Don Guido has his black cassock on, loose about the shoulders, tight about the stomach. He makes a gesture, at once sly and resigned, of raising his hands, palms upward. Yes, he gets all the encyclicals. And when they arrive he files them away—in the wastebasket. He smiles. That's how it is. A modern priest doesn't have time for encyclicals, he has to deal with real life as it is.

While he is smiling, Rita notices something odd about the desk. Under the glass top he just raised his hands from to make his ironic gesture are row upon row of tiny photographs. Photographs of faces. Passport-size. And they are turned so as to look not at the desk's usual occupant but the other way, toward the supplicant, the interviewee. Rita recognizes a face and draws a breath. They are Montecchio's recent dead staring up from the priest's glass-topped desk. *"Riflettete,"* says a little piece of card he has propped up: "Think about it."

Turning to leave, she sees there is a photocopier in one corner. A notice says: "Copies are free, but contributions are not refused."

A popular private midwife in the village has the same line. Her prenatal examinations are free, but if people want to give her something . . . Women ask other women how much they should give. Not less than fifty thousand a checkup.

Perhaps inevitably the figure of the priest attracts all kind of stories, some probably apocryphal, some not. It is rumored that late one night, Don Guido, famous for his careless driving, had to call on a farmer to get a tractor to pull him out of a ditch. And in his car was an adolescent boy who had no cause to be there. Others maintain he has had more than one girl around the village. Recently, the *canonica* was robbed and poor Don Guido bound, beaten, gagged. All the same, he did not report the matter to the police. Why not? Because his son was involved, wasn't he?

Or so the rumor goes. But one quickly gets the impression that this is merely the kind of thing people like to say about the village priests. The combination of celibate status and social prominence is too inviting for the fablemonger. And then it's important for the congregation that the priest be a wholesome sinner like themselves. Just as it is important for them that the men in the tax office take bribes. . . . Certainly I have never met anyone who pretended to be shocked.

One evening in Via Colombare, Giampaolo adds a new element to the Don Guido dossier by confirming that the priest has made something of a mission of going to preach to the prostitutes who hang around on the sheepskin seats of their white Mercedeses near the station in Verona. Giampaolo admires him for this and feels he is *valido* as a priest and *discreto* as a preacher. The *relativo* aspect would appear to be that Giampaolo sees the church as one of the conservative elements that keeps the local mentality so provincial. "After all, prostitutes do have a social function," he reminds us very seriously.

More prosaically, Don Guido keeps rabbits (also white and furry) behind the church, and hens and ducks too. When he meets children in the street he pulls boiled sweets from his pocket and tousles their hair. Then invites them to come and see his rabbits.

For Lucilla, Don Guido is a great religious intellectual, a kind generous man, another person she can endlessly find *troppo gentile*. Especially now he has agreed to testify how she nursed Maria Rosa those years after Il Professore died. A major point in her favor when it comes to authenticating the scribbled will.

Vittorina pays Don Guido to say masses for her dead husband. She likes to light candles at twilight and mutter her rosary in the fat, waxy smoke. She buys any number of the religious publications displayed near the door. Miracles upon miracles of the saints.

Orietta is thankful to Don Guido because when, in confession, she told him she used contraceptives, he told her to act according to conscience. It was between her and God. There is concern and disbelief, over another excellent bottle of Giampaolo's *prosecco*, when I point out that this is one of the main precepts of Protestantism.

But Don Guido is a little less Protestant when he goes to talk to Maria Grazia, the busty herbal specialist next to Bepi's who can advise such efficacious tisane. Her shop is officially a *sanitaria*, a sort of drugstore, but without the pharmaceutical side. It sells baby equipment, basic orthopedic aids, elastic stockings, corsets, maternity bras, bandages . . . and condoms. Don Guido complains that being the fine churchwoman she is, she shouldn't be selling contraceptives. Maria Grazia thus has the unenviable problem of trying to reconcile genuine religious devotion with social conscience and commercial flair. She goes on selling her condoms. And, what's more, at less than the manufacturer's list price. When the representative comes around, he tells her the local druggist has complained. He knows she is undercutting him on the price. He sent a spy to buy some. The representative says she will have to comply with the list price or he won't bring them. But Maria Grazia continues to sell at the lower price to people she knows. Because it is ridiculous that a condom should cost twice or three times as much in Italy as it does in other parts of Europe.

Does the Pope's strong stand on contraceptives have anything to do with Don Guido's complaints? Or is he a good friend of the druggist's? In any event we discover that Maria Grazia rushed into marriage as a result of an unwanted pregnancy. She had meant to be a doctor.

The Dr. Scholl's sandals representative also tells Maria Grazia that the druggist has complained about her undercutting him. It is *concorrenza sleale*, unfair competition. She must comply.

A *Corriere della Sera* article shows that Italian shopkeepers have the highest margins in Europe.

Maria Grazia tells us that when she opened her shop, the first *sanitaria* in Montecchio, she couldn't understand why so many old women would come in asking for large, sterilized sponge gloves, right-handed. Later she realized it was because they did not want to touch themselves "in that place" when they took their bidets.

When a tax inspector comes to see if Maria Grazia uses her electronic cash register and gives receipts that correspond to the price paid, you can always tell, she says, because they hang around a few minutes, looking a bit lost, then choose the cheapest item in the shop, the herbal chewing gum she has on the counter, for example. She gives the man his receipt and promptly phones a couple of other shopkeepers to pass on the message. If they haven't already called her. But not the druggist. Who is opening his own herb section now.

The inspector then goes on to *Un panino due*'s and asks him if he has the *pane comune* whose price is fixed by the government and used to determine the rate of inflation. A baker is obliged by law to have this bread. So the old man pulls out the one bag he bakes a day just in case the inspector comes. The government has fixed the price too low, and anyway nobody asks for the stuff. Maria Grazia says it has no bran in it and makes you constipated.

Speaking about health, I ask Giampaolo jokingly if he doesn't suffer from tachycardia like his wife. He drinks so much coffee. Perfectly poker-faced, he says no, he suffers from extrasystole. He is having a series of tests done at the hospital. I have to consult my dictionary later to discover that extrasystole simply means he sometimes misses a beat.

Orietta meanwhile has been missing more than one beat recently, because they have changed the garbage collection system. In the past a man came down Via Colombare on a bicycle affair behind a huge bin. He emptied the street's garbage into it, then pedaled off to unload the lot into a truck. There was something very Dickensian about it. But now they have introduced the *cassonetto*, a very large fiberglass container on wheels with lids opening on top and fluorescent reflectors on the side. There's one every twenty or so houses. You take out your garbage and next day the truck comes by, lifts the container with automatic arms, and tips it up into its press. A jet of hot water washes the fiberglass inside, then it is lowered back into place again.

All of which seems marvelously efficient to me. The best garbage service I have ever seen. The truck passes regularly three times a week.

But the woman at number 8, wails Orietta, keeps moving the wheeled *cassonetto* so that it's always opposite our flat. And when it gets full, the lid won't close anymore. The smell could bring germs and disease and death!

Emptying her own rubbish, Orietta heaves the heavy container with rubber-gloved hands back toward number 8. Emptying hers, the mongol-looking woman at number 8 rolls it back toward number 10. Back and forth. Back and forth.

Don Guido drives by in his battered car to bless a house restored without a building permit. He will also do exorcisms and disinfestations. On San Biagio's Day he blesses the village's children so that they won't get sore throats. Just this week, though, he has installed the first two blacks to arrive in Montecchio in one of the flats the church keeps for the poor. A gesture of true charity in racist Veneto.

WE SAY NO TO A MULTIRACIAL SOCIETY appears on a wall by Laghetto Squarà near the flat. Other graffiti complain about pollution from chicken factory farms. A truck from Germany has parked behind, come to pick up the things that stink so much in the chemical plant, whose owner is prominent in Don Guido's congregation. . . .

And so one could go on and on. Rambling back and forth through Montecchio, dodging the fast cars and wobbling bicycles. For everything links to everything else: the priest, the *sanitaria*, Bepi, the political parties, the *cassonetto*, the mopeds, and the huddles of youths in the night. . . .

There is no one characteristic which makes Montecchio Montecchio, Italy Italy, or the Italians Italian. And yet, as in any place, the slow accumulation of details does gradually form a sort of mesh or matrix. There is this constant entangling, as though in the weaving of a tapestry, or net. And the more entangled and connected it all is, the more inevitable it comes to seem. It takes on the weight, the impenetrability, of a dense contingent world. Yes, you tell yourself, it had to be so, because this is what this place is like. The barber believes himself a faith healer, but never gives you a receipt. You open an account at the bank and ask what the interest rate is, but instead of telling you they ask, what interest rate do you want, what do you do, who is your employer? Health is desperately,

desperately important, but the air is laden with industrial smells every morning. Everybody likes the Pope, and racism thrives. But of course. What did you expect? This is Montecchio. And perhaps the best test of initiation is whether, on being presented with some new element, you immediately have a sense of its belonging here, of its being a new manifestation of the same matrix, rather than just another alien fact, another surprise.

On a mild autumn morning you see a young woman in a seal fur climb out of a sky-blue Fiat Panda and start to fight with her remote-control driveway gate, which won't open. And you understand why she has a fur and why she has a Panda and why she paid more for her coat than her car. You also understand why she has a huge iron remote-control gate outside a modest house. You even have a fairly good idea why it's not working. She salutes you with a friendly smile. She's nice. You help her. She curses in dialect. Finally the thing starts rolling and she drives off the few hundred yards to church.

Then toward the end of October, as *I morti*, the Day of the Dead, approaches, flowers appear in one of the village's back streets decorating a little stone plaque in a wall, behind which a chained dog laps water from an old bidet. You hadn't noticed the plaque until the flower appeared. It says: QUI, SOTTO PIOMBO NEMICO, CADDERO DUE PATRIOTI—Here died two patriots, slain by enemy lead. And you think of the old men in the Communists' office behind their two-liter bottles, of Lucilla begging on the streets of Vicenza, and Tosi counting out his bread rolls for acres of land: *"Un panino, due . . ."*

I MORTI

To put your car in the garage under Via Colombare 10, you inch along a crazy-paved drive on the opposite side of the *palazzina* to the garden, then down a steep ramp behind the building and sharp sharp left into the garage. Among the many early-morning sounds, as I sit at my desk translating sales forecasts for marble granulates, comes the roaring of a small motor, tackling the ramp from the garage. Suddenly the roar dies, and instead there's a sharp whine, then a puttering, almost immediately beneath my window. Then the whole noisy business repeats itself.

I don't normally go out onto the back balcony above the ramp. I don't go out because directly opposite, across Negretti's garden where Vega tugs at her chain, is a thin, tall, crooked house like something from a children's book—the witch's house: flaking stucco, battered shutters, grubby lace curtains awry. And at the window exactly on a level with mine, an old old woman with long face, skin shrunken onto her cheekbones, and black shawl pulled tight about her hair is constantly looking out, so that if I step onto the balcony my eyes inevitably meet hers. Upon which a ghost, very definitely a ghost, of a smile will cross her face. My salute is hollow. The experience is not unlike seeing Don Guido's photographs of the recently dead. And in fact today is All Saints' Day, or as the Italians more commonly call it, *I morti*, the dead.

But the unusual sound of this car—roar, whine, putter putter putter, roar, whine, putter putter putter—is too intriguing, and I head for the balcony, studiously avoiding that ancient gaze.

It is the first time in the four months since we came to Via Colombare that Lucilla has got her car out. From above I can just see that the backseat of the tiny Fiat is full of flowers. She has a fair few cemeteries to visit today.

If she can get the car up the ramp.

On the flat patch at the bottom outside the garage she revs it furiously. With the choke full out, the air turns Fiat blue. The engine is racing. And out comes the clutch with a jerk. The car shoots up the ramp. But at the top she must turn sharply right to fit in between the railings and the wall of the house. Racing up so fast, she loses her nerve and hits the brake. The car stalls and comes whining back down the ramp, careering about dangerously close to the outer wall that shores up the garden, coming to rest askew on the patch at the bottom. Immediately she turns on the engine again, putter putter putter, and is presumably getting up courage for the next attack.

After watching the show through two or three times, I go down to help. The car isn't warm enough, she explains. I nod in agreement. Would she like me to try? *Troppo gentile, Signor Tino, troppo gentile!* Though the car is not old, the white paintwork is dull and cracked. Giampaolo has explained to me this is because she uses some old industrial cleaning fluids she has to wash it. Lucilla's approach to cleaning is nothing if not radical. Only a few days ago we saw her wash out the canary cage by simply holding it under the garden tap. With the canary inside. Flapping about terrified.

The Fiat 126 is a minuscule car. Lucilla has the problem of reconciling the physical needs resulting from short legs and great girth. If she moves the seat too far back she can't touch the pedals; if she moves it too far forward she is squashed against the steering wheel. I telescope myself to about half my normal height and climb in. There is a fresh smell of chrysanthemums: flowers for her dead husband, flowers for her dead child, flowers for her dead brother, Vittorina's husband, flowers for Il Professore, flowers for Maria Rosa. I waggle the gearshift. In the center of the driving wheel she has stuck a crucifix; in the well of the speedometer, completely obscuring it, a Madonna.

When I've got the thing out on the street, like a teacher giving a good boy a reward she says she's been meaning to tell me that if I want to, I can start using Il Professore's place in the garage now; yes, I can tuck in between the heap of firewood for *taverna* evenings and the pillars with their memorials of the dead. I am duly grateful. Vittorina arrives in a very somber black coat with velvety tassels and the two elderly women set off on their lugubrious rounds.

How the Italians love their dead! *I cari morticelli*, the dear deadikins! Shortly after lunch, out of curiosity, we wander along to the cemetery, which lies just to one side of the industrial park. As when there is a first communion at the church, the small cemetery parking lot is full and scores of vehicles have overflowed into the villas and factories of the industrial park, and even out onto the main road to Mizzole. It's a public holiday. Some cars have out-of-town plates from as far away as Tuscany, Piedmont. For it is important to visit your dead, however far afield they may be. And it is important to do so today, on this Day of the Dead. For one must have a sense of occasion, of formality, of rhythm. November is the dead time of the year; the leaves are falling, the soil is cold and bare; one visits one's dead. Giampaolo, for example, has taken his twin-carburetor Giulietta to Venice to get a boat out to the island cemetery where his father is buried. Lucilla will even now be terrorizing traffic on the road to Vicenza, Vittorina muttering her rosary beside her. One thus fulfills a duty, which is also a natural thing, not a burden, and then it is over. The fact that everybody else is doing the same duty at the same time certainly makes it more attractive.

The cemetery is rectangular and has tall walls, perhaps twenty feet high, like a little citadel. The crowd flows in from the parking lot, from the main road, from the pedestrian approach along an avenue of cypresses, and enters through the one big gate. Inside, there are white stone paths and more cypresses. The local authorities have cleaned everything up for the occasion. It's a job they've discovered the immigrants can do. The porticoes around the perimeter wall have been thoroughly swept. The marble is clean. Heading off directly to their loved ones' graves, people are dressed more or less as they were for first communions, weddings, and funerals: formally rather than somberly. And they are all holding chrysanthemums. Which have doubled in price this week.

The English, of course, bury or burn their dead and then largely forget them, at least after a few years. The main thing is to have them out of harm's way. But the Italians, like other Catholic nations, I presume, behave differently. When I tell Orietta how my own father was cremated and his ashes scattered in the Thames from a plastic box whose color and design seemed more suitable for the sale of ice cream, she is appalled, as if some awful sacrilege had been committed. But then he was a Protestant clergyman.

The fact is that Italians intend to remain on intimate terms with their dead for quite a while, and not merely by remembering loved ones as they were or placing framed photographs on mantelpiece or dresser. No, they want to sit by a grave and feel that there is a real whole body right there beneath them with whom they can somehow communicate. Setting up this privileged state of affairs in a busy modern world where space, and likewise health, is at a premium naturally requires some careful organization, as immediately becomes apparent on entering a cemetery.

It is interesting, in this regard, how devotion and bureaucracy go hand in hand. On walking through the somber iron gates past hooded statues and beneath the confidently engraved RESURRECTURIS, you find yourself in a fairly small space with graves in the ground before you and graves, or burial niches, in the walls around you. The niches are six high, the coffins being slotted into the honeycomb wall like drawers in a dresser. And the graves in the ground don't look quite like English graves either. There are none of those leaning tombstones, that tufty look, that precariousness of stone and affections sinking lopsided into the clay, so gothic and so romantic. Here, on the contrary, everything is neat, rigidly perpendicular, brushed clean, the atmosphere of some quiet, tidy courtyard in a government building after hours.

Almost at once you notice that the graves in the ground are of two kinds: one where the covering tombstone is full-length and more, one where it is smaller. Where the stone is full-length, what you have is not a single grave with a single coffin six feet below in the earth and stones, but a cement vault in which as many as four coffins are stacked on shelves right up to the surface, which is then sealed over by cement. These are usually owned by families. After thirty years, a coffin can, if more space is required, be lifted up, the bones removed, and a new coffin with a fresh corpse introduced in its place. Obviously this makes for some interesting family politics.

Where the tombstone is smaller, we have something closer to the Anglo-Saxon tradition: a coffin in the cold ground. But even here the organization is rather different. The graves are not dug individually. A long trench is opened up with an excavator. Starting from one end, a coffin is placed on the bottom of the trench and covered with earth. The earth is then shored up with planks to prevent it from falling into the trench, which awaits the next occupant. This gives the whole process a rather industrial feel. But this is not a problem, since the Italians are more ritualistic about death than romantic. And ritual is by no means alien to mechanics.

The trench fills up. When all the coffins have been down there ten years or more, they are then all dug up together and the bones removed, and the space is once again available for the freshly dead. This obviously has immense advantages over the Anglo-Saxon system of leaving people in the ground more or less forever. It also suggests that a grave is there for as long as it suits the living to go and visit it, not out of some eternal respect to the individual's remains. Cemeteries are a social phenomenon.

However, the practical considerations are more complicated than they may seem, and the authorities must be careful. If the same earth is used over and over, it becomes too rich and greasy, as a result of which rainwater ceases to drain away properly and the third or fourth round of corpses will not get enough air to decompose on schedule. One imagines that this makes their eventual exhumation rather unpleasant, not to say unhealthy. In order to avoid this state of affairs, sand and gravel are thus constantly added to the recycled soil to allow air and worms to pass through. If you are interested, the *Arena* will always keep you up to date on developments.

The cement vaults cost money. They are family-owned, and the recycling of spaces is under family control. The graves in the earth are free, and considered much inferior, if only because they suggest that the family did not have enough money or respect to purchase a cement version. On one such grave we find a headstone clearly designed to head off complaints from indignant in-laws. "He wanted to be buried in the earth," the wife has had engraved on white marble, "and I did as he asked."

Naturally, since these graves are not paid for, the families of the dead have no control over their recycling. The authorities merely inform relatives some months before they plan to exhume the plot. Relatives then have the choice of having the bones boxed and placed in a very small burial niche at a small expense, or having them added to the cemetery's communal ossuary. If the relatives have moved, died, or otherwise disappeared, it's the ossuary by default.

Thus for some people the Day of the Dead will hold a sad surprise. They come to find their loved ones and discover the grave is gone. The letter never arrived. Perhaps it was lost in the mail. Bureaucracy is bureaucracy in the end. Things can go wrong. They scuttle this way and that about the cemetery, wondering if perhaps they haven't forgotten where Father was: then tears, protests, the search for whoever can be held responsible.

An equivalent problem for the very rich might be to have the remains of their dear departed stolen from the expensive family vault. Then a few days later comes the request for a ransom. It happens occasionally. The rich are inevitably churchgoers here. Indeed, it's an interesting party game to ask people if they know of any rich, famous businessman or celebrity who is not a practicing

Catholic. When the head of the Ferruzzi family refused to pay a few billion lire for the corpse of his dead father-in-law, the kidnappers sent a message to the newspapers, denouncing the industrialist for his shameful lack of respect.

But a more mundane unpleasantness that might occur in Montecchio's cemetery on the Day of the Dead has to do with the *loculi*, the niches in the wall into which coffins are slid. Colloquially, these are known as *fornetti*, little ovens. Since there is no earth to cover the coffins, they have to have a metal lining inside and are sealed so as to be airtight. The corpse thus burns itself up under its own steam, as it were.

But the unpleasantness has to do with flowers. Each *loculo* has its little metal ring for a vase. You remove the vase, chuck the old flowers, put in the fresh ones, and put the vase back. But for the upper rows of *loculi* you'll need a small stepladder to get up to the vase. Stepladders are provided, though you may have to wait. Worse still, you may find, especially on the Day of the Dead, that holders of the bottom *loculi* (notoriously wealthier) have invaded the floor space with an extravagance of flowers. This means it will be difficult for you to site your ladder. You move the flowers. The person who placed them there returns and complains. Arguments are not unusual. Voices echo around the stone walls. The *Arena* prints a story about a group of old men who came to blows in Verona's *cimitero monumentale*.

"*Non fortunae, sed labor,*" claims pompous gold lettering in black marble referring to the exploits of some local entrepreneur. As with the graves in the ground there is a hierarchy with the *loculi*. You can have the cheaper variety where you are pushed feet-first into a long deep niche, or the more expensive version where you are introduced sideways and have a whole two yards of facade space. Which lends itself well to declarations of undying love or long lists of achievements, grandiose claims: "*Industria ed onestà,*" boasts another marble slab. The more preposterous dead. But for the most part the stones are simple: the name, the dates, a photograph, a tiny red light or *lumino*. These lights were once candles, but are electric now. All the *loculi* and indeed the graves are wired up. It's part of the package. The electricity company sends the bill and gives warning before cutting you off.

We walk about. There's a buzz of low voices, the clipping of heels along the porticoes where flowers abound, the scraping of stepladders. A subdued murmuring echoes back and forth between the high walls, the graves. The word *poveretto* can occasionally be heard. It is very civilized. Sober, but not gloomy. There are smiles, exclamations, perhaps some tears where a knot of well-dressed folk are visiting the more recently deceased. The day is bright, the flowers attractive, likewise the sun on clean stones. People come, pay their respects, go. Old attachments are at once acknowledged, distanced, given structure. There's a sort of serenity about it, which is charming in its way.

We find Il Professore's *loculo*: Umberto Patuzzi. The photograph is recognizable, though one had almost expected to see him standing beside one of his road signs—to where? Purgatory? Paradise? With his little backpack. Instead he is wearing a collar and tie like the people walking along the gravel paths around him. And he, or perhaps Maria Rosa, resisted the temptation to put in a photo of a much younger man. He looks his sixty-something years. Whereas Lucilla has already chosen her grave snapshot, and shown it to us. A flirty, well-built young woman of thirty years before. "They feel sorrier for you," she explains.

Beside Il Professore's small slab is a square of blank cement: the freshly inserted Maria Rosa, as yet without her stone. It's disgusting, Lucilla tells us that evening, that Signora Marta, being the niece and closest relative, hasn't even ordered a stone yet. It simply makes it clearer than ever that she never cared for the woman, she just wanted her money. Well, she'll never get it. Nor her flat. Never, never, never! After her day dutifully carrying flowers around, Lucilla is burning with rage again. "Because the flat is mine, mine, mine," she shrieks, giving me a key to the garage at last.

And indeed our position in Via Colombare appears to be getting more precarious. Following Maria Rosa's death, Signora Marta produced a will apparently written in the last days of the old woman's life. It leaves all the property to her, and she is eager to sell the flat as soon as she has the title deed in her name. Fortunately, Lucilla has produced her will too and is contesting Marta's, saying the signature must have been assisted and is thus invalid. Indeed, she is now accusing Marta of corruption and fraud, and her lawyer has asked for the opinion of a handwriting expert. But Lucilla wants to sell too if she wins. Either way, we lose.

And we begin to get telephone calls. The woman with the twig broom and the garage extension doesn't want to be nosy, but is the flat for sale? And who owns it exactly? Her nephew will soon be finishing university, etc., etc. For a couple of weeks we get one or even two such calls a day. So-and-so has mentioned to so-and-so that Via Colombare 10 may be for sale, and since their daughter is shortly to be married . . .

From over his wall, where he is digging the ground to let the frost in, Lovato watches. He hangs around, and when I'm out there doing some condominium duty, he motions to me to show he wants to speak. Is the flat for sale? His daughter and son-in-law are cramped living with them. There's only one garage for two families, and if . . .

Thus it occurs to us at last that when all those people came out onto the street that first day we arrived, it wasn't just because they wanted to enjoy the spectacle of Lucilla's raving. No, they all have designs on our flat. Pretty well every family in the street. If it becomes available they want to be able to buy it. For the dream of so many of these people is not only to remain at home, but to have their children and grandchildren remain at home too. They would do anything to stay in the same village and as near as possible to all their relatives from birth until death; and afterward too, the attraction of the vault as opposed to the grave in the earth being precisely that proximity: *papà* at the bottom, then *mamma*, the brothers, the sisters, the children, and all the long slow recycling afterward.

Most of them seem to manage it—to stay at home, that is. The local paper tells us that some 70 percent of residents in Montecchio were born and bred here (the figure is disturbingly close to the Christian Democrat vote). For myself, I can never decide whether this indicates a sad lack of any sense of adventure or the true flowering of wisdom. The way I can never decide if the formal atmosphere of annual cemetery visits is the height of civilization or merely a suffocating cultural inertia. In any event, the effect on house prices in a place where the population has long outstripped new building will be obvious enough.

Lucilla's lawyer is bullish. So Lucilla asks us if we would mind prospective buyers coming in to look at the flat. She can thus have a contract drawn up even before the place is actually hers. This is nerve-racking. We suggest she might do better to show them her own flat, which after all is the mirror image of ours, and, frankly, rather better furnished. She responds well to flattery. *Troppo gentile, Signor Tino.* And people gaggle around the head of the stairs being shown into her flat. Lucilla's is always the loudest voice. The words *valido* and *discreto* are heard, perhaps in unconscious imitation of Giampaolo. Viewers study the fittings, practiced hands swing the front door to and fro to feel the weight. Clearly, it will need reinforcing, another security lock perhaps, but overall . . .

I point out to Lucilla that we might want to buy the flat ourselves and that she did once say she would be happy for us to do so. Then from a legal point of view, as sitting tenants we surely have the right of first refusal. She is polite but uneasy. For selling also means doing a selected person or a selected family a favor. But yes, she says, if we are really interested, of course we can buy. She hesitates, then names the kind of price that chased us out of London in the first place.

On the phone, Marta quite bluntly asks us if Lucilla is showing any signs of falling ill. Her blood pressure must be so high, with her being overweight and always shouting. Then this business of turning the thing into a criminal fraud case is crazy and very ugly. Just an opportunity for the lawyers to get rich. Our rent isn't even covering her legal costs now. Do we realize that? *Mi scusi?* Well, yes, if she wins she might sell it to us, but actually she's rather changing her mind and probably won't sell at all now. Her sister's daughter has a boyfriend, and they are planning to marry in three or four years' time, and . . .

In three or four years' time. . . . I'm bewildered how far ahead these Italians can plan their love lives. And it occurs to me there must be some intimate link between being able to choose your death photo before you're even ill, or decide which relative your corpse will replace in the family vault, and this ability to plan your marriage for some date that sounds to me like science fiction. Life is so carefully controlled here in the Veneto, so attractively wrapped up: cappuccino till ten, then espresso; *aperitivo* after twelve; your pasta, your meat, your *dolce* in bright packaging; light white wine, strong red wine, *prosecco*; baptism, first communion, marriage, funeral; *loculo, lumino*, exhumation.

Driving up into the hills of an evening, to a trattoria, one looks back down into the valley and sees the cemetery: a neat rectangle of glimmering red pinpoints in the night, the electricity board keeping the sacred lights burning in perpetuity. Or at least till your ten years are up.

STATALI, DIPENDENTI, AUTONOMI . . .

Aɴᴏᴛʜᴇʀ ᴡᴀʏ ᴏғ wrapping up your life in Italy is to become a *statale*, a government employee, a civil servant. Of course, every nation has its own way of dividing itself up. The English have their classes, the Irish their religious denominations, the Americans their racial origins. In Italy, apart from the drastic north-south divide, one of the most deeply felt group distinctions is that of the *statali* and the *non-statali*: the government workers and the rest. Basically, as the rest of the population sees it, the *statali* enjoy a network of privileges so fantastic and far-reaching as to establish them as a class apart, something almost approaching "party status" as it was until recently in the Eastern Bloc. To truly understand your neighbors, then, you must appreciate their position in this regard.

The privileges of the *statali* (as perceived, of course, by *non-statali*) may be listed as follows: they are not obliged to work; they are not even obliged to turn up at work with anything more than token regularity; midmorning and midafternoon they can take a long coffee break in the nearest bar and combine it with a spot of shopping, or with filling in their pools coupon in their favorite *tabaccheria*; they enjoy shorter hours than the private sector, which means they have more time for moonlighting; they can get cheap holidays in hotels and camps reserved exclusively for them; they can get very low interest mortgages directly from their employers while they are given higher interest rates on savings at the bank; they have quite unbelievable maternity and paternity rights; they have a better health insurance plan; they have the right (so important for an Italian) to be transferred to their home area after a number of years' work elsewhere; they enjoy the most extraordinary pension arrangements, which often allow them to retire well before they're forty on a decent index-linked income; but above all—and it's worth all the rest put together—they are absolutely and utterly unfirable whatever they do, wherever they do it, whenever and how often, it doesn't matter, they simply cannot be fired. They have arrived.

In the protected world the *statali* live in, some of their exploits have become quite legendary. Given that managers in government offices are for the most part unable or unwilling to discipline their staff, when things get out of hand the police or carabinieri will, once in the bluest of moons, arrive in force to check up on who is there and who isn't, perhaps prosecute a few dozen absentees. Thus the *Arena* tells us how in one administrative office the carabinieri came across an expensive fur coat on the back of a chair, but no person in that chair. The employee in question had clocked in and then disappeared, as she did every morning, returning briefly in the afternoon to clock out. The following morning the carabinieri followed her, to discover that she was working as a call girl in a flat directly opposite her office.

Stories like this strike a very deep chord. Naturally, the immediate reaction is one of disdain, of self-righteousness. *"Maria santissima,"* Lucilla says, clapping her hands, "when you think how hard I worked all my life, Signor Tino." But there is also profound admiration. How smart of her to have fooled the state like that for so many years. And they haven't even put her in prison or anything.

How *furba* (sly, shrewd) she's been. Then look at the fur coat she put over her chair. "Pure sable, Signor Tino!" What a smack in the face that was. Good taste too. Perhaps I should have been a *statale*.

And at a deeper level still, people think: If that is how the state wastes its money, mismanages its affairs, then why should I be paying my taxes? The truth is that the *non-statale* has a psychological need for the *statale*. They are two sides to a coin that is common currency here. For just as the chaos and corruption of the south justify the peccadilloes of the north, so the lazy, absentee *statale* (who notoriously *is* a southerner, or so northerners will tell you) justifies the tax evasion of the *non-statale*.

Always assuming he is in position to evade tax. For though the *non-statali*, the private sector, will present a united front in their disdain for *statali*, they themselves split into quite distinct factions when it comes to taxes. Leaving aside all the many nuances, there are basically two groups of *non-statali*: the *dipendenti*, or employees, and the *autonomi*, the self-employed; and there is as much animosity between these two groups as between both of them and the *statali*, if not more. Indeed, the *dipendenti* and the *statali*, with their taxes deducted at source, may often form a united front against the *autonomi*, since they are convinced, and not without good reason, that the *autonomo* pays next to nothing in taxes and what's more earns a great deal more than either of them do. Everywhere jealousy is the key.

Three classic conversations result. The *autonomo* (perhaps our shopkeeper Bepi) meets the *dipendente* (let's say office worker Giampaolo) and they complain about the *statale* (somebody in the post office for example), his benefits, his proverbial laziness and rudeness, his constant presence in the pasticceria, his twenty-day sick leave over a sore thumb, Italy's hopeless inefficiency in the public sector which is preventing it from becoming a truly important player on the European scene, etc., etc.

Or the *statale* (Lovato's son-in-law, for example, with his Lancia Prisma in the illegal prefab garage) meets the *dipendente* (Giampaolo again) and they complain about the quite shameless acquisitiveness of the *autonomo*: never a receipt when you pay for your cappuccino, when you have the plumber in, when you see your heart specialist about your extrasystole. These people are unscrupulous. They steal from the community. We all have to pay more because they pay so little. It has to stop.

And when the *statale* meets the *autonomo*? Well, there's caution, obviously, but a certain mutual respect too, an air of self-congratulation even, as of two people who have made the right decisions in life. And why are these miserable *dipendenti* always complaining? If they're not happy they should change their jobs. Or if the name of a mutual friend comes up, perhaps the word *poveretto* will be used, as of one who is lost, beyond hope. For it is generally agreed that the *dipendente* of a private company has the roughest deal. With his rigid hours, his limited opportunities for moonlighting, his difficulty justifying sick leave, his slavery to the market, his taxes always deducted, and his comparatively low salary, the *dipendente* is undoubtedly the loser.

Hence there is nothing the likes of *dipendente* Giampaolo can do but assume the rather stony moral high ground and talk about the citizen of the future and a society where everybody will one day have a sense of civic responsibility. This Giampaolo does with great dog-in-the-manger frequency. And England, for example, is much admired because there the social contract between government and people is truly *valido* and the level of fiscal honesty (yes, Italians talk that way) is *discreto*, even if all this is rendered *relativo* by gloomy weather, bad food, and a general lack of taste. Never does Giampaolo like to distinguish himself more from the provincial, narrow-minded aspects of Italy than when talking about *dipendenti*, *autonomi*, and *evasione*, as if his own fully paid-up taxes were some sort of avant-garde internationalist creed, a measure of moral stature rather than mere misfortune. Though in the *taverna*, one evening toward Christmas, barbecuing trout from Montecchio's fish farm and drinking rather more than he usually would (because *novello* is no good after December), we do get him to reminisce with obvious nostalgia about the good old days before a withholding tax was introduced (in the mid-seventies), the days when you declared next to nothing and nobody could do anything about it. So from his high ground, in the time machine of the *taverna*, the condominium *dipendente* will turn a wistful wine-soaked eye back on the cities of the plain. Which were, and for others still are, so much more fun.

One is tempted at this point to proceed to the rather grand reflection that while the English have their lower classes, their middle classes, and their upper classes, the Italians in turn have their *dipendenti*, their *statali*, their *autonomi*, so very deeply are these distinctions felt here, so bitter are the resentments, so sweet the triumphs. But the analogy could be nothing more than superficial. For this is not a hereditary system (a railway union request that jobs be made hereditary was recently turned down), nor a family affair. On the contrary, father and son can all too easily be turned against each other. Old farmer Lovato, for example, with his years of hard autonomous (though mainly tax-free) work on the soil, obviously feels not a little contempt for his wimpy son-in-law from the same background who has bagged a prize *statale* job as cook in a nursery school: just five mornings a week, plus all school holidays and the endless benefits, a day off to give blood, a day off for a union meeting, a day off for a urine test . . . The young *statale* pulls the Prisma out of the garage and cleans it meticulously beside his father-in-law's hard-worked cabbage patch. Or sits in the window opposite our living room, building an elaborate nativity scene to grace the church porch a month hence. While old Lovato digs and eyes our flat. . . .

Then there is more mobility between these groups than one would expect to find in a class structure. A *dipendente*, given the chance, or an *autonomo*, should his business take a dive, might well decide to become a *statale*. And a *statale*, on retiring at some ludicrously early age (*i pensionati baby*, they call them), might well become an *autonomo*, though he is unlikely, it must be pointed out, to want to become a *dipendente*.

Orietta, for example, a woman who has turned worrying into a fine art, who quakes when the ground trembles in Calabria, shivers when it snows in the Val d'Aosta, would very much like Giampaolo to become a *statale*, because then his job would be safe beyond any market logic for ever and ever and she could look forward to middle and old age with serenity in the full knowledge that the family will be able to pay for a well-placed *loculo* at the end of the day. And Orietta is by no means the only wife pushing her husband in this direction. The search for security is an obsession here far beyond anything I ever came into contact with in England or the States. I imagine it is linked to postwar insecurity, to the rapidity of economic change, the survival of a peasant culture forever seeking protection from bad weather. And presumably it's not unconnected to those frequent visits to the hospital for blood and urine tests, and then in a different way to the entrenched conservatism that surrounds all local customs and traditions here. Which is rather attractive. In any event, the more people despise the state, the more, nevertheless, they appear to wish to depend upon it, to become *statali*. As one dear southerner, Pasquale, self-declared anarchist and evening-school teacher, explained to me: "During the year the state cradles us, and in the summer holiday they just rock us to sleep."

CONCORSI

Bᴜᴛ ʜᴏᴡ ᴄᴀɴ Giampaolo become a *statale*? By doing a *concorso*. The reader may be getting weary of so many Italian words, but this is one that quite definitely defies straightforward translation. My dictionary, for example, offers a whole range of meanings: "a throng of people," "a coincidence," "a competitive exam," "complicity in a crime," etc. All of these, I fear, are appropriate.

The idea is as follows. A *statale*'s job is a very comfortable spot, a meal ticket for life. This the state tacitly acknowledges. Indeed, the government has deliberately allowed this situation to develop in order to ingratiate itself with the population. But given the unfairness inherent in the fact that these jobs cannot be available for quite everyone, it becomes absolutely crucial that their allocation be seen to be fair. No favoritism must operate. Only merit will be considered. Merest merit.

Thus the local railway station cannot, for example, simply put an advertisement in a local employment office saying it needs three cleaning women and then give out the jobs on a first-come-first-served basis. Because then the stationmaster might take on friends, or friends of friends—as a favor. Worse still, in the south the Mafia would get control of things. So no, the railway has to hold a *concorso*, a public exam, and this must be announced at national level. Because again it would be unfair to exclude people from the south, even though they may, of course, after a couple of years, request transfer back home, thus contributing to overmanning there while reopening the vacancy in the north.

Our "competitive exam" is thus announced in the papers and on posters inside and outside public buildings. Our "throng of people" applies. Perhaps a thousand. Sometimes twenty thouand. Everybody wants to be a caretaker, a receptionist. "Fifty Clerks Taken On to Process Applications for Garbage Collectors" might be the typical headline of some small article in *Corriere della Sera*. It is never clear how these selecting clerks were themselves selected. Whether there has been a *pre-concorso*, or what. It is as well, one suspects, not to inquire too far into the matter.

But what qualifies a person to be a garbage collector? Well, a certain level of intelligence, a certain mental attitude; so a written exam. Then a certain level of reliability, a certain personality; so an interview. But above all, health, of course, and so a medical examination.

Which is where we come to the *concorso* as "coincidence" or "complicity in a crime," or both.

The story I have in mind is Giampaolo's, a splendid Italian tale which I think sums up more or less everything that need be said about *dipendenti*, *statali*, and *concorsi*. In one of the departments of Giampaolo's company works a highly skilled young technician who is very clever at his job. So clever that under the table the company is paying him more than his fellow workers to keep him. This lad's father is a Christian Democrat, has always held his membership card, and the son too is a member of the party and lends a technical hand with party activities, setting up the dais at *La festa dell'amicizia* and suchlike.

After a few years at the company, the young technician

marries. Both his own family and his wife's feel that the couple would be much more secure if he had a job as a *statale*. There are threats of recession. The state is the only organization which will never fire you. Even if it means taking a cut in salary, security and peace of mind are the overriding concerns. And there will be the months of paid paternity leave when they have a child.

So the talented young man decides to take part in a *concorso* to become a bus driver. And he goes along with his father to talk to his local Christian Democrat councillor. It is time the councillor did something for a family which has always voted for the party and always been ready to help out. Otherwise what reason is there for being members? *D'accordo*, agrees the councillor, *va bene*. Which is as much as to say: Will do.

But our young technician is a conscientious, honest boy, with a sense of loyalty. He goes and warns his foreman that he will be leaving the company in six months or so, thus giving them time to train up someone else. Because he has applied to be a bus driver, he explains. And, yes, he knows hundreds of people have applied, but he is sure he will be selected because he has spoken to Christian Democrat councillor X who knows Y who is on the committee.

The foreman promptly buttonholes the managing director. This boy is the cleverest and most efficient we've ever had, he says; it will be a major setback if we lose him. The managing director, who is a Christian Democrat and a friend of the same local councillor (here's our *concorso* as "coincidence," though not such a great one perhaps), phones the said councillor. "What is this, stealing our workers? It takes years to train someone to that level. How can a private company even begin to compete with the state with all the ridiculous benefits you're offering? I'm sorry, but this isn't right. You've got to keep him from being selected."

This places the councillor in a delicate position. The written exam and the interview have already been done, he explains. The boy is already through. He apologizes profusely. "I can't change those now, I'm afraid. If only I'd known." Until at the last moment he has a brainwave: "There's still the medical, though."

And we arrive at "complicity in a crime."

The doctor is looking at an X-ray. "Don't you get any pain just above the pelvis sometimes?" The confident young technician says no, he never does. "Really? Try and remember. In the small of the back. A dull ache?" "No, never." The doctor frowns, hangs the X-ray up on the viewing screen. "Come and look at this. Here, you see, too much space between these lower vertebrae. Quite a common malformation, nothing to worry about in the normal way of things." He is shaking his head. "But I'm afraid it would soon result in disk hernia if you started driving a bus six hours a day."

And incredibly everybody is happy: the doctor is happy because having done the councillor a favor he is now owed a favor in return, he has a card to play for the future; the councillor is happy because he has ingratiated himself with both young technician and managing director, and they will see him as the right man to vote for, their own personal access to power; the managing director is happy because he has kept his worker and demonstrated his ability to wield influence; the skilled young man is happy because he never really wanted to be a bus driver anyway.

Only the families of the young couple are left with a lingering feeling of regret, of wistfulness for that safe haven. A *dipendente*'s life is not an enviable one—he depends, as the very word suggests, on the whims of the market, the whims of his employer—and they had wanted the best for their children.

Whenever this story is told, by myself, by Giampaolo, people burst out laughing. The kind of laughter which greets jokes that confirm a caricature. Yes, how they enjoy this harmless breach in the general *omertà*. And where could you get a story like that if everything was done in an honest, open way? According to merit. Or even if everything was done on a straightforward and acknowledged basis of nepotism and favoritism. No, it is the superimposition of the bureaucratic and apparently fair over the private and determinedly unfair, the public umbrella, we might say, over the personal intrigue, which breeds so many such stories, and which creates such a delicious tension in so many areas of Italian life. The rules are only a veneer, and indifferently glued on at that; like the Pope's diktats, or the catechism—no more than the thinnest coat of paint. While in the soft old wood beneath, the jolly worms honeycomb past each other in the dark. Busy and alive.

Curiously enough, I got confirmation of Giampaolo's story one December evening traveling back from town on the bus. It was rush hour, the bus was packed, so I went ahead to stand at the front behind the driver and watch the black countryside flinging by, the starkly twisted shapes of the bare vines against the twilight, the pinpoints of light rising up the hills to the north. In Borgo Venezia, another driver got on and came to stand beside his colleague. Barely a foot away from me, they talked about the most recent *concorso* for maintenance jobs in the garage. The new arrival had heard from someone in the know that these jobs were to be divided up equally on the basis of the local strength of the political parties; three people chosen by the Christian Democrats, one by the Socialists, one by the Communists. This made it unlikely that a friend of his would get in.

The speaker made no attempt to lower his voice to prevent me from hearing. Nor did he show any sign of outrage or even unease that in this case a *concorso* was more a question of complicity than an exam. He might have been talking about a patch of dull weather, or the difficulty of finding fresh tortellini in the late afternoon, some irritating contingency. His colleague at the wheel drove on at great speed between the cement walls beside the flood ditches, stabbing at brake and accelerator as we hurtled through the narrow stretch where, if a bus or truck comes the other way, there is no room.

I moved back down the bus to the door. Two old women were knowledgeably comparing their blood sedimentation speeds as exhibited on the familiar health service printouts. A group of fourteen-year-olds discussed whether horsemeat was nicer than beef, whether polenta was better with melted cheese or without. Then they argued about what kind of car their favorite soccer stars drive. I climbed off. A bulldozer had been having a go at the old factory at one end of Via Colombare. A notice announced the construction of a complex of flats and shops. Reassuringly the Madonnina was still in her place at the other end of the street, promising to protect us. Electric light gleamed on the more tangible security of iron railings. Simone's car was outside the gate at number

10, come for an abundant dinner: codfish, polenta, Valpolicella. An electricity bill addressed to Patuzzi was in the mailbox. The *cassonetto* had been pushed down toward number 8. Vega was barking, the TVs were on, and all was apparently well with the world.

MUSSULMANI

ONE OF THE SHARPEST IMAGES winter conjures up here is that of dry sticks. It will be hard, perhaps, to sing the beauties of dry sticks, but I shall try.

Maybe the fact that these sticks are seen against a blue sky is the first thing that need be said. For after the autumn rains, much of winter in the Veneto is dry, bright, and very blue: a crusty colorless cold ground under brilliant sunshine.

The leaves finally fall in late November. They fall from the vines, leaving strong, gnarled shapes behind. They fall from the fruit trees, the peach and cherry orchards. There is no wind, and the thin dark branches are perfectly still against the heavens with an almost shiny blackness of polished bark. Often, tin cans and strips of plastic have been tied among the twigs—to scare the birds when there was fruit. Now they look like decorations for a ragmen's ball. Along the edges of the fields, or winding along by ditches and streams, the

fiercely cropped plane trees take on the despondent monumentality
of surviving columns from some ruined portico.

In the smaller farms on the hill slopes above, the rows of vines
are often supported by the cherry trees. A horizontal wooden slat is
strapped to the tree; four or five wires are stretched from one slat to
the next, one tree to the next, and the vines, twisting and splintery,
cling on between. When winter comes and the luxuriant summer
foliage of vines and cherry leaf is gone, the rude peasant mechanics
of these slats and wires are left stark in the bright light, like the
tangled rigging of some beached clipper. There are the complex
twists and turns of natural growth, branches and twigs curving back
on each other, then the sharp man-made angles of sawn wood, and
the graceful physics of sagging wire swooping from slat to slat, to
end in small unused coils around the last cherry bough. All of which
is seen against the terraced climb of the hill, the silver green of olives
higher up and the somber vertical dark of the cypresses.

Everywhere the _contadini_ are cutting sticks. They prune the
vines, moving slowly along the rows, arms constantly raised with
knife and secateurs. It must be tiring work. They bring out the year's
now reddish-brown tendrils, hardening into sticks, and burn them
in low bonfires in the fields. At the bottom of the hill, along the
ditches, they cut the young branches from the knobbly heads of the
plane trees and tie them into bundles such as old women carry in
fairy tales, then leave them to soak in streams or big water tanks sunk
in the ground. Kept pliable, they will do for tying up next year's
vine shoots.

And they prune the fruit trees and the olives, sawing off whole
branches, dragging away huge tangles of wood in their tractor
trailers to be cut up for firewood on the power saw in the farmyard.
As we walk, the hills echo monotonously with the squeal of steel
disks slicing through wood. There is something mournful about it, a
lament for the lost summer, for last year's growth.

They cut longer sticks from poplars and birch trees, poles ten
feet long perhaps, and these they strip and leave standing in clumps
in their farmyard, to serve as fenceposts and railings, vine supports,

shafts for pitchfork or shovel. Tall, leaning at an angle against a barn whose two main beams are themselves resting on the cleft branches of two ancient cherry trees, the birch wood is a smooth blue-gray in winter sunlight. The walls of the barn are old packing cases, boards, strips of corrugated iron, an assortment of planks which once served other purposes, a sheet of pink plastic, an iron bar. On the other side of the building, a cable is taut between the tarpaulin roof and a concrete post driven into the hill. Unlike the thriving cemetery, the scene here shows only token observance of such notions as perpendicularity. Why doesn't the thing fall down? you wonder. Why doesn't it blow away? I stand and stare: the winter branches, the canes and cut sticks poking at the sky, the beams resting on the cherry tree, the tracery of crisscrossing wires; such a tangle of man and nature, the antique and the provisional, the old seasonal rhythms and the shamelessly makeshift. When the leaves are gone it's so clear.

We are at the farm, not far from Via Colombare, where we pick up our eggs. A big German shepherd strains at the end of a chain which slides along a wire strung from barn to cowshed. Sixty-plus, the farmer's wife is in her slippers and dark woolen stockings. She speaks good Italian and is bright and witty. Her husband is in the office, she laughs, and her thumb indicates the cowshed, which forms one side of the L of the house. We go in to chat for a moment. In fact, there are two farmers here, brothers, pushing seventy. Their lease runs out in a few years and then the land will most probably cease to be a farm and the builders will move in. A builder bought the place some years ago and is pulling all the strings he can to get permission to put houses here. Sooner or later some contact he has, some favor he has done for priest or politician, will prove the winning card. For although the regional plan designates the land as agricultural "in perpetuity," no one has any illusions. After all, the surveyors are already marking out the orchard at the bottom of Via Colombare.

The cowshed is ancient, dark, with swallows' nests in the beams and soiled ropes knotted to iron rings in the stone wall, plastic sheeting over the windows. The smell of the eight cows standing in their straw and shit is overpowering. Here they stand and sit all year. They are never let out. The terraced land with its fruit trees, vines, and strips of wheat or maize is not suitable for grazing. The men go out to mow grass for feed in summer, and in winter there is the hay in the ramshackle barn. They have one milking machine, and the two urns they fill stand in a little stream behind the shed to await collection. Perhaps this sort of arrangement explains why in summer the milk here sometimes goes off almost as soon as one has bought it.

Giuliano and Girolamo, they're called. They wear dirty blue dungarees and brown felt hats. They speak in such fierce and garbled dialect that it is difficult to latch on to single words. One is merely left with a general impression of what has been said. Which may or may not be correct. Girolamo, the younger, but obviously the boss, is gritty and sarcastic. He likes to mock our city clothes and easy life. He scratches behind his ears, slaps a cow's thigh, smiles the smile of the old fox. Ailing and very bent, Giuliano is sweeter, though virtually toothless. He has just had his prostate removed—his *prospera*, he amusingly calls it—and there are the usual detailed inquiries after health, all the more so because before the operation Rita recommended him to her brother, who is a urologist at the hospital. Although this recommendation didn't improve Giuliano's lot in any significant way, a human contact is considered very important. It is a favor we have done them. Perhaps this is why they have agreed to sell us their eggs despite having an arrangement under which they're supposed to deliver them all to a local shop. Or maybe they say that to everyone.

Giuliano frequently carries a spade or hoe or just a pole around with him so he can lean on it. He is pleased I am English, because it gives him an opportunity to reminisce about his prisoner-of-war years in Scotland and Wales, which seem to have been very happy ones. He lived with local farming people and they sent him out in the fields every day to do more or less what he does here: weed vegetables, cut grass. He settled in well. But when the war was over they gave him only twenty-four hours to decide whether to stay or return. And he would have stayed but for the thought of pasta. The thought of a plate of pasta put him on the boat back to Italy. I wonder if his toothless grin is meant to indicate that he appreciates what a caricature he is offering. Girolamo, on the other hand, returned from forced labor in a German factory, near dead with starvation. Even a plate of Scottish potatoes would have been good enough for him. He scorns his brother's sentimentality.

Because now Giuliano is complaining that the Ministry of Defense has stopped sending him his Christmas card. Every year after the war he used to get a Christmas card from the British government. Until that "Tatchair" came to power. She stopped it. Margaret's cuts, we discover, struck deep all over the continent. But it would be unkind, one reflects, to speculate out loud on what would have happened to a farm like this had she ever got her way over the Common Agricultural Policy.

It's funny. These old farming people seem both suspicious of us and at the same time eager to take a break and have a chat. Occasionally they invite us in for a glass of something. The big nameless bottle containing a strong dry wine stands in the middle of a long scrubbed wooden table. The floor is bare stone, the walls powdery whitewash. There are straight-backed chairs and no armchair or sofa, but a huge color television stands in one corner and two grandchildren are watching. It's curious how impervious everybody is to the Roman accent of all the announcers.

Since it's Sunday, the conversation—not at my prompting, I can assure you—gets onto religion. Rita explains we don't go to church. The farmer's wife says brightly that their son-in-law doesn't go either, but that he is not a Jew. This is a little disconcerting, until we appreciate that all she means is that he is a believer, but he doesn't go regularly, just at Christmas and Easter: that is, the only imaginable nonbeliever in her universe is Jewish, and her son-in-law isn't. Nor, she clearly assumes, are we. Her warm smile suggests an indulgent subtext: you young people are understandably a bit lazy and selfish, but later you will go to mass every week just as we do.

Rita, however, has an infuriating habit of being honest in conversations like this. "That's not exactly the situation," she says.

"You must be Protestants," says the well-traveled Giuliano, perhaps remembering bare Presbyterian pews in war-torn Galloway, comrades carving images of the Madonna.

"Not exactly," Rita says again.

"What then?" Girolamo is scratching vigorously behind his ear, smiling his mocking foxy smile. Every Sunday morning, as we make for the pasticceria, we see him and Giuliano heading off to mass, awkward in their old smoke-blue suits and dark ties.

"Nothing," I finally join in. "We are nothing. We don't go and that's that."

"But you must be something. Everybody has some religion."

Girolamo turns out to have a conversational manner not unlike his German shepherd's way of straining threateningly back and forth on its chain. He begins to mock us. Everybody has some master, even if it's only money. What am I living for? I must be living for something, and that is my religion. So what is it? He sounds disconcertingly like sermons I used to listen to twenty-five years ago. But one feels it would be churlish and above all pointless to launch into an argument. For of course we both know what we know: his world of sticks and pruning, mine of town and translations.

"You must have some religion," he insists, as if having cornered his prey. And he drains his wine belligerently.

I can't think what to say.

"We're *mussulmani*, Muslims." Rita solves the momentary embarrassment and raises a laugh from everybody. Though Girolamo continues to eye us darkly. Going back out into the farmyard, trying to change the subject, I ask him if he ever lets the dog loose from its chain. To which the old man casually replies with a common expression, *"Non è mica un cristiano"*—He's not a Christian, is he? Similarly when you rebuke a naughty child you might say, "So, are you a Christian, or a beast?" For these are the only two categories of living creatures the old idiom allows: Christians and beasts. Apart from the Jews, that is. I almost forgot.

And when the world is going from bad to worse you can say, *"Non c'è più religione."* There's no religion left anymore. As if that were the problem. And you repeat it, shaking your head: *"Non c'è più religione."* It's something Lucilla, with all her Madonnas and crucifixes and sacred hearts, has been saying a lot of late. Because Marta's lawyer has managed to have the hearing over the presumed forgery of her will postponed for another three months. For the moment things appear to be going swimmingly for these parvenu *mussulmani.*

LA TREDICESIMA

Winter in Verona means chestnuts toasting over coal braziers in Piazza Erbe; it means the crowded market for Santa Lucia where suspicious-looking gypsy folk sell every kind of candy, nougat, and dried fruit from brash mobile caravans. It means shops and supermarkets full of huge, colorfully packaged *panettoni* with special offers on Johnnie Walker and local brandies.

In Montecchio, winter means steam on the windows of the pasticceria, swollen watercourses, mist rising thick from Laghetto Squarà on frosty mornings, polyethylene bags over oleander bushes and lemon trees, and Christmas decorations on the big cedar in the main square.

In Via Colombare, winter means the stout woman with the twig broom sweeping away the leaves almost before they have fallen. It means old Lovato digging his square handkerchief of vegetable garden down almost three feet to let the frost right in. It means the genuine mink of the woman whose husband drives the

Alfa 75 and the fake mink of the mongol-looking woman opposite who cleans offices in town.

At number 10, winter means sweeping and mopping the stairs with the same monotonous regularity with which we watered the garden in summer. It means freezing to death because the roguish builder who put up this place installed tiny, inefficient radiators. It means a plastic Christmas tree appearing on the first landing and schlocky red-and-gold decorations pinned to the satin-finish wooden front doors. At night it means Vega wailing to the cold stars as she paces the frostbound soil outside, and the constant whine of Lucilla's central heating pump.

Although each household has its own separate heating system, the boilers are not located in the flats but all together down in a tiny cellar; and Lucilla's is mounted at the outer wall against one of those reinforced concrete pillars. Thus every time her systems starts up, the building hums. And she keeps it on all night.

Giampaolo goes upstairs to complain. As for everything else in Italy, there is a law about when you can and can't turn on your central heating. It was brought in after one of the oil crises. You can't turn on before November 1 and you must turn off after the end of March. During the day you can't turn on before six in the morning and you must turn off after eleven in the evening. And between six and eleven you can't have it on more than a total of twelve hours.

Naturally, like the emergency provision about watering gardens, this law is generally ignored, except perhaps by the stingy owners of large blocks of flats where the rent collected is supposed to cover the cost of heating. Giampaolo, however, hopes to use the rules to play on Lucilla's fears of authority and persuade her to stop bothering us with the sound of her pump every night.

It is typical perhaps of a *dipendente*, an encyclopedia reader, and a modern man to appeal to the law. And Giampaolo does seem to know them all, how far they are *valido* and how far their value is *relativo*. I can hear him talking politely and persuasively to her at her door, right outside our own. But on this occasion Lucilla isn't impressed. Because her health is at stake. She has been coughing a lot. Then she is dieting, which makes her cold and constipated despite all the herb teas she is trying. When Giampaolo, polite as ever, backs down, she tells him he is *troppo gentile* and asks if he would like to come in and drink a glass of something with her. She is having trouble getting Telepace, the Vatican channel, on her TV. . . .

Winter. I sit at Patuzzi's great desk, where he must have leafed through many a sunny brochure on similarly bleak days, fantasizing the ever more exotic road signs he could pose beside. The temperature is well below freezing, but the breath of the cadaverous woman opposite barely steams her windowpane as she stares out with infinite patience. To one side, between her house and ours, a tangle of branches reaches up into the sky. It's the one tree in Negretti's garden. And on those branches are what I at first in my ignorance imagine to be oranges: beautiful big round abundant fruit hanging by invisible threads from a tracery of leafless black twigs above. In the staring twilight, they start to glow, reminding me of Marvell's lines: "He hangs in shades the orange bright, / Like golden lamps in a green night."

But we're not in the Bermudas, despite Patuzzi's ghost. And the evening isn't green, but gray, a blue smoky gray. And of course these aren't oranges at all, but *cachi*, a very soft fruit with a peel like a plum's, only thicker, and inside a lush pulp with a tremendously sensual texture and sticky sweet taste. They are the only fruit I know of that I've never seen in a London greengrocery. They are too delicate to travel. Even Bepi doesn't like stocking them, because they ruin so easily. Negretti lets most of his fall to the ground in a blackening orange mush over dead leaves before telling his sons to go out and pick the last few. Then, one-handed as he is, he does a little pruning with a chain saw. Twigs and branches fly. The old woman with her shawl watches impassively till evening deepens. Then she leans out and draws her decrepit shutters to, turning to give me a last wan smile before they close. It seems unlikely that her house has any central heating at all.

Vittorina comes out of her Christmas-decorated door to find me mopping the stairs. For it is our turn. She is obviously disturbed to find me rather than my wife doing this menial work. Is Rita ill? If I had told her, she would have taken our turn. "No, she's fine, but she has a rush translation job," I explain. Clearly it is not sufficient explanation. Vittorina looks troubled; cleaning the stairs just isn't a man's job. Her husband, Giosuè, for example, whose grave she is off to visit, never cleaned the stairs. I tell her how often I wish I'd been born into the world and values of fifty years before. She takes this perfectly seriously. And maybe it does have a little sniff of seriousness about it. For if there's one thing I hate it's cleaning these marble stairs, and reflecting how carefully Orietta and Giampaolo will look at them afterward, how they notice if you don't get your mop into the corners or if you sweep dust under doormats. I have heard them criticizing Vittorina's performance. There's something that spells death for me in obsessive cleaning. The cemetery is a clean place. Could it be the English let their cemeteries get untidy so that they won't remind us of death so much?

Giampaolo walks in with a carpenter holding a huge polished shelf about eight feet long and almost three inches thick. They apologize for muddying my stairs, but Giampaolo is paying for the carpenter's time. Then Lucilla comes out onto the stairs above. "Rinà! Rinà!" she calls. I tell her Vittorina is out taking flowers to Giosuè. Lucilla asks if I would come up to her flat and help her with the yellow pages. She can't remember the name of her dressmaker and would I read out all the ones in the phone book. I lay down my mop.

For some reason everybody is having something made. Perhaps it's because with the world outside being so icy and damp, winter naturally becomes a time for home improvements. Giampaolo is changing the focus of his sitting room, the position of his TV. Instead of having it on a raised platform in the far corner he has invited the same carpenter who previously did that job to relocate his impressive set alongside a row of equally impressive encyclopedia volumes on one of two huge specially made shelves which pin directly into the wall with no visible brackets. The whole plan is undertaken with the utmost seriousness. An electrical outlet will be moved to directly behind the TV so that no wires need be visible.

At the same time, Vittorina, in the flat opposite, is getting another carpenter in the village to replace her kitchen furniture. There are long consultations as to the height and depth of cupboards, the position of the lights, the need to replace the refrigerator so as to have one the right width for the new cupboards, etc., etc. People here seem to enjoy this so much more than just going to a store and buying the ready-made thing. Over the years they establish a relationship with their carpenter and then during dinner-table or *taverna* conversation they will boast that he is the best in the *provincia* and they would give you his name and number if only he wasn't so busy he'd never have time to fit somebody new in. They talk about *il mio falegname di fiducia*, my trusted carpenter; and quite probably they have an electrician *di fiducia* too, and a bricklayer *di fiducia*, and a tailor or dressmaker *di fiducia*, and undoubtedly a butcher. Indeed, the Veronese rarely seem happier than when talking about their somebody *di fiducia*. A social status is implied, the status of the person who doesn't just buy what the market offers, nor stoops, as the Englishman might, to do-it-yourself, but discusses and creates together with his craftsman. It's the status, almost, of the patron.

But as in any relationship, there are drawbacks. The most common being that the somebody *di fiducia* is too busy. And the reason he is too busy is not just the enormous demand there is here to have everything done and made privately, but that the somebody *di fiducia* is actually a *statale* working on the side in his spare time. Our postman, for example, is frequently to be seen about the village busily engaged in illegal masonry or installing radio-controlled gates and garage doors. A man from the health clinic is troweling on stucco. And this sort of situation can lead to a quite schizophrenic attitude on the part of the client, one moment praising the skill of his carpenter or mason or gardener *di fiducia*, and the next berating these *statali* and all their privileges and craftiness. Still, at least when the man gets his early retirement, he will have more time for your domestic projects.

Inspired by the general enthusiasm, we have found a carpenter ourselves and are getting him to make a bed for us to replace the uncomfortable medieval thing which always makes me feel I'm sleeping in the central panel of a triptych of tortures. Recommended by a student, our *falegname di fiducia* is young and enthusiastic, talks Green politics more intelligently than most, rapidly produces an attractive design for a simple bed with bay oak surround, quotes us a price that is a good 30 percent below anything in the shops, and then disappears. He is so busy that we won't see the bed for another six months and more. It's the price you pay, Orietta says sagely, for using a good carpenter. But it's worth waiting.

I go up the stairs I have just mopped to help Lucilla rediscover her dressmaker. She had her kitchen furniture remade only a year or so ago. On a walnut tabletop she has a pink *gingerino* waiting for me. "Now, Signor Tino"—and with simpering and obviously relished embarrassment, shifting her tubby bulk from one slippered foot to another, she explains. She has to have her bras made for her specially. Yes. Otherwise they are not comfortable. You know? Normally she would ask her dressmaker *di fiducia*, but the woman is too busy (this sad admission indicates that the client's importance is only *relativo*); so she went and asked somebody else, but has now forgotten the name. Seeing that the bras were due to be ready this week, perhaps I can find the name for her in the yellow pages, assuming it's there, since of course she didn't use the yellow pages herself to find this person, but got a friend to give her the name of her *sarta di fiducia*. And the friend is off on holiday.

I look up *Sartorie per donna*. It turns out there are about twenty in Verona. I ask Lucilla if she remembers the name of the street. Only that it was in the center. But they all seem to be in the center, more or less. We arrive at a name she thinks she recognizes: Riccadonna. I dial the number for her and hand her the phone. She has her synthetic pink dressing gown on, fluffy little-girl slippers, a glimpse of varicose ankles. Her hair is in a sort of plastic cap, covering curlers, one assumes. Perhaps Simone is coming tonight. When she gets through, she puts on the most extraordinarily servile, obsequious voice: "*Buon giorno, buon giorno*, I am Zambon, the signora of the seven bras, are you the dressmaker I ordered from?"

It is the number seven that somehow renders it so magically incongruous—seven seas, seven seals, seven bras.

The second place we try asks for specifications, which Lucilla duly gives, but I am not familiar with cup sizes. On the third, remarkably, we hit the jackpot. The seven bras are ready and waiting. I write down the name and address on the notepad in her kitchen. As I do so I notice out of the corner of my eye a covered birdcage next to the garbage can on the balcony. Lucilla has cleaned out her canary, *poveretto*, once too often.

"Troppo bravo," she tells me at the door, as if I had been responsible for finding the right name. She is clearly pleased that Vittorina was out. She likes to have men do things for her. And she says if only I could afford to buy the flat when she becomes our landlady she would be very happy indeed to have us stay.

Giampaolo, meanwhile, is not at all happy with his *falegname di fiducia*. Incredibly, this trusted man has tried to install one of the big new shelves the wrong way around, couldn't understand why it didn't fit inside a piece of wall that juts out, and smashed off a very large piece of plaster. What's more, he refuses to accept that the damage was his fault, claiming that he should have been told the alcove was not perpendicular to the main wall. They argue by the Visentinis' door for ten minutes until the carpenter hurries off, lamely pleading another engagement. My mop in hand again (for I still have the last flight of stairs down to the garage to do), I am persuaded by an insistent Giampaolo to come in and inspect the damage. His long slender fingers probe the smashed plaster. What do I think? It doesn't look that bad, I tell him. But he shakes his head. Obviously, he will have to call in his mason *di fiducia*. Yes, there's a man who's done a variety of jobs for them in the past. Because one could never plaster a corner perfectly right oneself. People would always notice. Worse still, he's going to have to decide whether to fire his *falegname di fiducia* halfway through the job or have him back. Again he shakes his head. The attachment to a person *di fiducia* is such a deep one; Giampaolo clearly sees the man's behavior as a kind of betrayal. Not to mention the added cost of the mason. Which on a *dipendente*'s salary is a tough proposition. Orietta brings in the vacuum cleaner to take up all the dust and plaster. *"Grazie al cielo,"* she sighs, "that we're getting near Christmas and there's the *tredicesima.*"

The *tredicesima*! Here's another little peephole into the heart of modern Italy. For what other country in the world has a *tredicesima*? None, I'm sure, unless at the end of some very slippery pole the Land of Cockaigne truly does exist.

Or perhaps Italy is the Land of Cockaigne. It's something the Italians like to say sometimes. Or they say: "Go to America? But Italy is America!"

The word *tredicesimo* means nothing more nor less than "thirteenth." But *la tredicesima*, the adjective turned feminine noun, means your thirteenth salary of the year. Thirteen, it's worth noting, is considered a lucky number in Italy.

What happens is that in the first weeks of December, the *statale* and *dipendenti* in general receive an extra month's salary. This is a legally required part of any employer/employee relationship. In the negotiations which originally brought the development about, I am told, back in the 1960s, the *tredicesima* was perceived as a productivity bonus to be paid only if the employee had behaved well, not been absent more than a certain amount, etc. But given that almost nobody takes it upon himself to judge the performance of anybody else, at least in the state system, payment soon became automatic. And some companies, notably banks, even introduced *la quattordicesima* and I believe in some cases a *quindicesima*.

Such extravagant arrangements give the hardworking *autonomo* perhaps his only real chance to gripe about the cushy lives of the *dipendenti*, though since he is aware that all the extra money will be spent on his goods and services in the general Christmas binge, he doesn't complain too much. Indeed, the imminent arrival of the *tredicesima* perhaps explains why Giampaolo and the ladies have all decided to get their carpentering done and bras made now. For, as pensioners, the ladies have their *tredicesima* too. They are briefly rich. Lucilla sets off into town for high heels and diamond-patterned black tights. Two men struggle up the stairs with Vittorina's new refrigerator. One can only wonder what they might do if they ever get the money they want for our flat. Give Giosuè a new headstone? Muffs and minks? A new parlor suite? Extra masses said?

Going back down to replace the doormats after the stairs have dried, I hear the postman's Vespa arriving, as it usually does, toward lunchtime. I wait for him. Apart from some junk mail for Patuzzi, there is a magazine for Vittorina, _I fioretti di San Gaspare_. My dictionary translates _fioretto_ as "an act of mortification." The magazine is published by _L'ordine dei frati del preziosissimo sangue_, the Order of the Brothers of the Most Precious Blood, which the saint founded. Most of it involves stories of miracles following hard upon praying to the saint. One reader writes to say that after years of painful prostatitis his problem was resolved by a single supplication to San Gaspare. Perhaps old Giuliano should have been informed. And it occurs to me that Italians have a long and uninterrupted tradition of miracles. Of which maybe _la tredicesima_ is just a recent and very civilized manifestation.

VIVA, VIVA, NATALE ARRIVA!

IT WILL SEEM ODD, perhaps, that having spent all my teens in London I had to come to Italy to discover real fog. It is a peculiarity of the Bassa Padana, the Po Valley. Protected by the Apennines from the prevailing west wind, the sun shines brightly on the vast triangular area of flat damp soil between Milan, Venice, and Bologna. The snow-covered mountains to the north keep a constant stream of icy air rolling down to meet the warmth steaming up from fields and ditches. And the result is the thickest fog imaginable stretching for mile after mile after mile. Sometimes lasting for weeks. The winter version of summer's *afa*.

When we step out onto our balcony this December morning, the world is milky white and quite silent. The terraced hill has gone, the castle has gone, likewise the abandoned mill. Along Via Colombare, the Madonnina has vanished and with her the woman with the twig broom, whose patient sweeping can nevertheless still be heard, pushing dirt she can barely see away into the fog. The dry sticks of Marini's vegetable patch opposite are somber pointed shadows, spear tips of an army of wraiths. A few poplar poles lean against a spectral fig tree, eaves and balconies drip, and all the street's railings are hung with dew-soaked spiderwebs.

Leaning on the marble parapet we never polish, we take such pleasure in breathing in this soft spongy air. It's as if the whole Veneto had been very gently, very efficiently anesthetized. Even the smells have gone, smothered where they rise. Everything is whitely quiet, waiting.

Then into this beautiful, hushed world comes a sudden fierce jangling, turning the corner from the Madonnina end. A grating jingle blares through a megaphone, followed by a voice speaking in dialect: "*Mamme, bambini, ragazzi, ragazze,* come and see, come and see, three *panettoni* for the price of one, three *panettoni* for the price of one!" The voice stops with unnatural abruptness. The jingle plays again, harsh, idiotic, strident. When it stops there is the unmistakable rumble of a diesel ticking over. The still, damp air begins to smell. And now I can just catch the ghostly shadow of a white Fiat Fiorino delivery van. Out blares the voice again, incredibly loud, the kind of volume one expects at the Last Judgment, booming through fog: "*Mamme, bambini, ragazzi, ragazze!!!*" Odd, I think, how he excludes fathers, unmarried adults, and the like. The van stops three times along the two hundred yards of Via Colombare, sells a dozen or so *panettoni,* and is gone.

As many as four or five of these *ambulanti* may pass down our semisuburban, semirural street in a single day, summer or winter, rain or shine. There's the man who sells brooms, dustpans, brushes, kitchen mats, pan scourers. He's a regular. He passes around ten o'clock, his wares piled on the top of his tiny Fiat 650 van. A broomstick lunges forward through the fog like a lance.

Another fellow sells mattresses. He has a dozen or so piled on the back of a small truck. Like the *panettoni* man he has a recording crackling through an overloaded speaker system: "*Un occasione d'oro per sogni d'oro.*" A golden opportunity for golden dreams. Every Tuesday without fail. He is burly, brisk, darkly mustached. But how many mattresses can he sell to thirty or so houses?

One suspects the knife sharpener of being willfully picturesque. He has a grindstone geared up to the drive of his moped and a little shelter affair arranged over the handlebars. He squints, hunched. In normal conditions you can see the sparks fly. Through the fog there's just the sinister shriek of metal on stone. You're reminded of the Green Knight, sharpening his ax; another sound heard in dead of winter.

Or there are the one-time-only *ambulanti* offering the most amazing deals. A huge truck noses along the street, squeezing between parked cars, watching out for shutters left carelessly swinging. Four best-quality wooden kitchen chairs for sixty thousand lire. Just fifty dollars. Is that possible? Or on another lucky day you may get the chance to buy a whole terrace set of tables and fold-up chairs for 100,000 lire. Sometimes one wonders if rather than being behind the truck when the stuff fell off, they didn't just take the whole truck and start driving around the streets.

Of the regulars, the cheese duo are the most impressive. These two fat jolly men have a super-long, purpose-built van which folds open at the side to reveal a cheese counter that wouldn't look out of place in Fortnum & Mason. Turning the corner by the Madonnina they have to reverse and maneuver. The relaxed megaphone announcement of *"Formaggi, formaggi, eccoci quà"* suggests far more confidence in their clientele. The vehicle ticks over in the fog. Orietta slips out in coat and scarf to buy some seasoned Asiago and Parmesan. It's cheaper, she says, than in the shops. One wonders why.

"Thieves" is Bepi's only comment when I mention the *ambulanti* to him.

Coming back, Orietta makes her usual detour to the *cassonetto*, heaving it so far the other way it's almost lost in the gray damp.

The *marocchino* is even more discreet than the *formaggi* fellows. Officially *marocchino* just means Moroccan. In reality the word refers to a stock figure in Italian life, the Moroccan carpet peddler. Male, anywhere between fifteen and fifty, he patrols the streets with a heap of carpets over his shoulder and colorful tablecloths on his arm. In summer one almost melts at the sight; if you bought anything it would surely be drenched in sweat. On winter days you suspect the carpets are worth their weight in gold. You're surprised he wants to sell them at all. In any event, the *marocchino* is admirably stoical. His face is a cipher. Apparently he expects nothing, fears nothing.

The bell rings. Rather than buzzing somebody in immediately, or even quizzing them through the intercom, I have learned to go out on the balcony for eye-to-eye contact. The Arabic man stands there in the damp cold, his rugs over his shoulders. Would I like to buy something? I say no thank you. He doesn't insist. And this is another admirable side to the *marocchini*; they will never bother you, never shout anything or use a megaphone, never try hard to persuade. Perhaps this one might have done better if he had tried. For the truth is we could use a few rugs on our freezing tiles. It's just that I'm not used to buying this way.

He presses Lucilla's bell. We can hear. Inevitably she lets him in. How many times have we been obliged to listen (for conversations on the stairs are audible everywhere) to Lucilla talking to Mormons, Jehovah's Witnesses, water purifier salesmen, survey interviewers, and the like. But this morning she actually lets the *marocchino* into her flat. He leaves about half an hour later, without having sold anything, I fear. For a *marocchino* could never be *di fiducia*, the way the cheese man is for Orietta. I hope at least Lucilla offered him a *gingerino* and told him he was *troppo gentile*.

From my balcony I watch the man walk stoically off into the fog. Even from this distance I can see that his carpets are not Moroccan at all. Most probably they are produced by some small sweatshop in Reggio Calabria operating from an illegally built prefab. He keeps a steady pace, stopping only at the house of the man with the Alfa 75, where the postman is mounting new railings on a low cement wall. Then the fog swallows him up. A short distance away there will be an old Fiat 128 serving as a base for him and three others. They keep the carpets in the trunk, move from village to village. Perhaps they sleep in the car too. The *marocchini* are rumored to be homosexuals without exception. Certainly they bring no women with them. And curiously they rarely aspire to a place in regular Italian life the way other immigrants do. I have never seen a *marocchino* here who did anything but sell carpets.

Since it's Christmas Eve, we drive into town for some last-minute shopping. When we leave the village, the fog is desperately thick along the narrow road, though no one is going particularly slowly. Each car hangs on to the taillights of the one in front and hammers through, even though this means being far too close to avoid an accident if one had to brake. And since we are one of the only vehicles on the road without fog lights, the car behind has to hang on even closer to us than we to the car in front. What this means in terms of the dynamics of an eventual pileup I've no idea.

Suddenly a carabiniere looms right in front of our hood, waving a red stop sign. And we realize we haven't even seen the big traffic lights. Comes the sound of sharp braking all along the line. Four officers in fluorescent plastic jackets are risking their necks to keep the junction operating. I wonder if we will see a parking spot even if we pass one.

In town, the medieval and Renaissance buildings are splendidly mysterious. The illuminated clock face comes and goes in the fog at the top of the fourteenth-century Tower of the Lamberti. The Roman arena is somber despite housing an exhibition of East European nativity scenes. Christmas carols, all English, are being efficiently cranked across the fog-draped trees of the main piazza, interrupted by the crackle of fireworks, illegal but abundant. In the shopping streets the stuccoed facades have been bled of all color by stabbing neon beneath. And anyway, nobody is looking up at them. Everyone has things to buy.

But despite the *tredicesima*, Christmas is not quite the spree it is in England. This is partly because, at least in the Veneto, the children have already had their presents. Santa Lucia, December 13, was the day. So the sidewalks are no longer choked with grandmothers determined to gratify excited infants. Decorations are everywhere evident, but fairly modest in the end: lights strung across the streets, red carpets on the cobbles outside shop windows, paper festoons in the three department stores. An unconvinced Father Christmas with the name of a shop on his armband is handing out candy. And of course there is the everyday streetlife, which takes on a special poignancy at Christmas: a gypsy woman sits begging in a doorway, the baby in her arms swaddled against the fierce cold; young blacks proffer trays of cigarette lighters and pirated cassettes; despite numbed fingers, a tramp is playing a popular tune on some kind of bagpipe: *Viva, viva, Natale arriva . . .*

In Standa, the cheapest of the department stores, people are picking up a few last-minute details to add to their homemade nativity scenes: an extra sheep or two, fake hay they forgot to get for the plastic manger, a star with a little bulb in it. There's an array of polyethylene packages. The magi are available separately or as a group.

But most interest is concentrated on food. Serious food. The delicatessens are packed, despite prices that would raise eyebrows anywhere. There is no one traditional Christmas lunch in Veneto, but it would be a mistake to imagine this indicates lack of interest in the occasion. On the contrary, it avoids any danger of getting into a rut. Parma hams and salamis are coming off their hooks at an extraordinary rate. All kinds of goodies—Russian salads, black olives, green olives, a sticky crystallizing orange mixture which calls itself *mostarda vicentina*—are being spatulated into plastic tubs. A bristling old fellow picks up a whole form of Parmesan. For how much? A hundred pounds? The butchers (*di fiducia*, of course) are unloading ducks, turkeys, geese, and chickens from the surrounding farms and factory farms, plus all the best beef cuts. The diehard *contadini* are looking for *cotechini* and the wherewithal to make polenta. A curious shop window offers fresh pasta of every color: green spinach pasta, swampy artichoke pasta, red pepper pasta, brown chocolate pasta . . .

We pick up the turkey we have promised our American friends and a few bottles of this and that from a display offering a remarkable range of cheap Scotch whiskeys, many quite unheard of, I suspect, in Glasgow and Edinburgh. Glenlivet, however, is cheaper than it ever was back in London, though slightly watered down to meet local proof regulations. Driving back to Via Colombare just as twilight stiffens the fog, we find our astonishing postman still messing with stones, bricks, and railings beside the Alfa 75, and we take the opportunity to give him his Christmas bottle of grappa.

He doesn't understand. He looks at us nonplussed in the foggy dark, his breath steaming warmly, white droplets on a black mustache. I explain that it's a tradition in England to give your postman something. The tracery of blood vessels on pink cheeks suggests that he is not unused to a glass or two. A token of our appreciation, I say, somewhat foolishly, for perhaps such words have never been addressed to a *statale* before. He takes the bottle, sets it down by the railings, thanks us, but remains somewhat wary, as if we must be expecting a favor in return. Perhaps in the end he will put it down to a fog mirage.

Giampaolo is unloading a Christmas tree from his car. In Italy they are not sold cut as in England, but with their roots in a pot. However, to get a cheap price, as every *dipendente* must, Giampaolo has driven some twenty miles to a convenience store where they sell trees that, yes, have their roots, but tied in a plastic bag. Very *valido* as an idea, and the price was *discreto*. He will plant it in a pot for Christmas, put it out on the balcony through January, then move it out into the garden before the spring to join Lucilla's sad madrigal of ornamental evergreens. Orietta seems dubious about its chances of making it that far. Probably it will have her vacuuming up pine needles every ten minutes right through the holiday. There must, after all, be something *relativo* about the deal.

Preparing tomorrow's food in the evening, we turn on the radio. Rita has recently taken a liking to Radio Santa Teresa, our local religious channel. Or one of them. Two priests are discussing the Madonna's house, believed to have been brought by angels to a convent in Loreto near the Adriatic coast. With sober enlightenment, the priests explain that in fact this is a tenth-century Palestinian dwelling brought over from Bethlehem by the Crusaders. Having chatted for a while, they open the telephone lines for questions. Immediately a woman's voice crackles through. She is very excited: "Don Marcello, Don Marcello, do you remember me, Maria, from Nogarole Rocca?" Don Marcello doesn't remember her. "You baptized my children." From the cracked sound of her voice this must have been some considerable number of years before. "Praise the blessed Virgin," Don Marcello says warmly.

Another woman phones, from Caprino this time, up in the mountains. She is so depressed, oh but so depressed. "Actually," Don Guglielmo reminds her gently, "we were asking for questions about the blessed Madonna's house in Loreto and the value of devotional relics in general." She bursts into tears. She is so depressed she doesn't think she can go on living. She would never have imagined life could be so awful. "Unburden your sorrows on the Holy Virgin," Don Marcello tells her. She has tried, she has tried, but she can't. It makes no difference. She honestly can't. She sobs loudly on our old tube-filled radio. And it takes these two embarrassed men literally ten whole minutes to get her to agree to unburden her sorrows on the Virgin and get off the line. "The Madonna be praised," she finally sniffles. There's an audible sigh of relief from Don Guglielmo.

After which about a dozen more women call, at least half of whom seem to know one or the other of the priests personally. Not one of them has anything to say about the tenth-century Palestinian remains in Loreto, or indeed about Christmas. Their menfolk, one suspects, are elsewhere.

Shortly after eleven we hear the clunk clunk clunk of the Visentinis turning their security locks about two hundred times as they prepare to go out for midnight mass. A few minutes later, Giampaolo comes up to our flat to inform us that our cat has got trapped in the garage and has walked over his white Giulietta, which he had just cleaned. There are black paw marks all over it. The Italian distaste, on Orietta's face rather than Giampaolo's, for animals which are allowed to penetrate the four walls of the domestic bunker is only too plain. I solemnly promise it won't happen again and mollify them both with Christmas gifts, which they weren't expecting: a scarf for Giampaolo, a simple brooch for Orietta, perfume for Lara. We have, as Italians say, made a *bella figura*, a good impression.

Best of friends, they offer to give us a lift to midnight mass to save us getting our own car out. Although we hadn't been planning to go, we accept. Walking out into the street, we catch the familiar sound of a small engine revving wildly, shooting off as the clutch is released, then whining, dying, and finally puttering into life again. Giampaolo goes down to help Lucilla get her car out.

The fog is impossibly dense, the traffic very brisk. The church parking lot, needless to say, is packed to overflowing. Inside, despite the fact that we're ten minutes early, the church is already a solid mass of fur coats. People obviously came some while ago to stake out their places and now there are no seats left. I am surprised at this lack of forward planning on the meticulous Giampaolo's part. Though perhaps the fault is our cat's.

We stand at the back near the nativity scene Lovato's son-in-law has been working on for so long. Stars wink in three phases, water runs in a little stream, ox and ass nod their heads. It's an elaborate affair. Though as in all nativity scenes there is no sign that the animals perform their natural functions. On the hill, the shepherds have a little carafe at their feet, which is a nice touch. They may not, after all, be so unused to UFOs.

More people crowd in. There's a buzz of chatter, greetings, handshaking, kisses. Everybody knows everybody. People you usually see smoking on street corners or double-parking outside the bar are queuing up to light candles. Some of the youngsters are obviously dressed, under their coats, for the discotheques they will be heading off to as soon as the service is over.

Things get under way a few minutes late. Don Guido intones the liturgy in a style my father, an evangelical Anglican, would no doubt have scorned. But there are advantages. The quickly read, toneless words impose a sense of order and ritual without one having to pay attention to whatever they might mean. The congregation are prompt with their responses and know very well when to stand and sit. They move as one well-trained animal. And they enjoy this oneness. Since we are anyway obliged to stand, my ignorance passes unobserved.

Looking about, as the others mouth prayers they learned in childhood, I can see Maria Grazia from the *sanitaria*, who supplies contraceptives at below list price. To her left is Montecchio's most famous politician, presently Verona's councillor responsible for traffic. His wife has a nice full-length fur, though surprisingly the family are on the list for the cooperative housing to go up behind the Madonnina. Beyond them stands the builder who is putting up the luxury villas on the hill above Via Colombare. Giuliano and Girolamo are there too, and *Un panino due*, and the woman with the twig broom, again in a fur.

But these fur coats seem to be causing problems. For although it's cold outside, it is desperately warm inside. Big modern radiators are pumping out heat. Before the altars, down the side of the nave, a thousand candles are burning. Orietta wriggles uncomfortably, frowns. But she hasn't put on anything sufficiently attractive underneath to be able to take her coat off.

Up in the chancel, a small choir of young people sings a very upbeat Christmas carol to the accompaniment of guitars and drums. Nobody seems to know the song. There is very little tradition of Christmas carols here. And anyway nobody is invited to join in.

Don Guido preaches a sermon from the chancel steps with the aid of a microphone on a stand. He also has a microphone on the altar. This means he never has to raise his calm dull voice and assume a rousing evangelical tone. He is not a leader, but a medium, a go-between. Predictably, he preaches generosity. We must remember the poor at Christmas. Christ was born in a stable. There is absolutely no criticism, veiled or otherwise, of his overwhelmingly bourgeois congregation. He is rehearsing the values on which their respectability rests. As so often with things traditional in Italy, I am unable to decide whether this is attractive or sinister, an expression of civilization or decadence. My Protestant truculence, no doubt.

And after the sermon we move into the Eucharist proper with the modern guitar band playing and a girl singing, very pleasantly and professionally. Indeed, it's a treat. People walk to the front, the host is popped into their mouths or placed in their hands. Moreno, the half-wit, goes up three times but is not turned away. To deal with such a huge congregation, Don Guido has four helpers, a young priest, three nuns. Other young people, many of whom shoot by me every day on *motorini*, are walking up and down the aisles with baskets, collecting money.

Then Orietta faints. The heat was too much. She should have taken her coat off. Fortunately there is such a crowd of people around her she couldn't possibly fall. Giampaolo rushes her out to the car and off home. No doubt this will mean a fair number of tests at the hospital. We stay behind for the hot chocolate Don Guido advertised at the end of his sermon and discover that below the church there is a very large *taverna* complete with bar, and drinks. Now this is civilized! In the crush, we come across Vittorina and Lucilla, determined to show off their furs to the last, though Lucilla's thick makeup is running a little in the oppressive atmosphere. *"Auguri, auguri, Signor Tino!"* she calls. *"Buon Natale, buon Natale."* Then she returns to her cemetery chat with other older widows. "The stingy niece," I can hear her telling them, "still hasn't ordered a stone for the *poveretta*. So I ordered one myself. To shame her. I told my lawyer to tell her lawyer I'd ordered it, and I didn't want to be paid, and do you know . . . "

Walking home in a freezing fog filled with car exhaust now as the worshipers disperse, I wonder where this morning's *marocchino* might be. Has he found a stable to sleep in, perhaps? With ox and ass. Not unfeasible in these parts. And I remember an article I read in the *Arena* only a few days ago: in the recent cold weather many *marocchini* have been sleeping in the empty *loculi* in the walls of the city's main cemetery, wrapped in their carpets. Well, at least they won't have to hear Vega barking.

BUONA FINE,
BUON PRINCIPIO

THE FOG PERSISTS, thick and extraordinarily white—not the gritty, yellowish variety I occasionally encountered in London. Penetrating even the narrowest streets, it deadens the anyway dead days between Christmas and New Year, muffling the sound of fireworks children are letting off between eating slices of pizza outside *Un panino due*'s. And when there is a deep frost the night of Santo Stefano, we wake the following morning to find every tree crystallized from roots to topmost twig: the clinging fog on their branches has turned to white ice. So that walking out in the country, breath tasting of blood in the throat, it's to find icing-sugar cypresses standing on a great cake of frostbitten landscape. The leafless vines have become disturbingly spectral, fields of crucifixlike contortions, bled white by frost and fog. The tall stone walls beside the road ring with the cold sound of our voices. Figures approaching through the murk intone the end-of-year greeting: *"Buona fine, buon principio."*

189

Happy end, happy beginning. It's been a week and more perhaps since we saw the sky.

And yet if one walks and walks, one can have that pleasure. For Montecchio is at the very northernmost extreme of the Bassa Padana and its fogs. The hills begin here, and you need only climb. Following more or less the same route we took with our neighbors in the mellow autumn, we head for Cancello, at the top of the ridge far above Via Colombare. And after a mile or two, there's a sudden thinning of the atmosphere. The fog becomes merely mist and haze. A pale disk of sun comes and goes. The landscape takes on pastel shades, a faded tapestry of beiges and dull greens woven up and down the steep slopes where farmland is retreating before heath and thicket. Another few hundred yards and, almost before you realize it, here comes the explosion of color and light: a sky more electrically blue than it ever is in summer, a low but whitely dazzling sun that immediately narrows the eyes, and, to the north, the vast, sharp panorama of the mountains sparkling with snow.

There are cars parked by the side of the road. Well-dressed people are stretching their legs. *"Buona fine, buon principio."* It's nice how these greetings are extended to every stranger one passes. Other cars race by with skis on their roofs. Immediately the light encourages a mood of fun and sensual pleasure. And with the light comes heat. The air is full of the smells of damp earth and vegetation warming in the sun.

Turning back to look at the plain, you appreciate how the fog stretches, like cloud cover seen from an airplane, as far as the eye can see: white, flat, monotonous, with just occasionally a church spire or radio tower poking spookily through. And having made it up here and rediscovered such things as brilliant light and scented air, you're furious to think you'll soon have to walk back down to that underworld and live heaven knows how many more days in the half-light and cold. Indeed, if you were in the habit of dividing people up into groups (and writers inevitably are), you could do worse than to distinguish between those Montecchiesi who are happy with their foggy lot, who sit it out stoically, like the Visentinis, seeking comfort in hearth, home improvement, and fifteen TV channels; and those on the other hand who are obsessed by that bright paradise only a few miles away and who pass the entire winter with their ski racks or bike racks on the tops of their cars, counting the days between one long weekend and the next. In between the two extremes are the hunters, country folk, like old Marini, quite at home in the fog, except that if they're going to see anything to shoot at they have to make the effort to get up here. Every few minutes the hills echo with gunfire. Little children gather the orange, yellow, and blue cartridges along the path.

This silent winter fog, that suffocating summer *afa*—they must play their part in forming the local character. The seasons here don't offer the exhilarating heroism of battling through strong winds, horizontal sleet, deep floods, and snowdrifts, the glorious centuries of stormy weather the British can boast. Instead, the inhabitant of the North Italian Plain faces these long periods of relentless attrition, a loss of sunshine, of visual clarity, coupled with oppressive heat in summer and damp penetrating cold in winter. Never the kaleidoscopic movement and brusque surprises of an English cloud formation. For day after day, heaven and earth remain inert, motionless, in an anemic torpor. The taciturn Veneto, a research student at the hospital tells me, consumes twice as many pharmaceuticals per head as other more fortunate areas of the peninsula.

Orietta is popping pills for her tachycardia as we prepare for the New Year's Eve celebration in the *taverna*. Lucilla knocks on our door and asks Rita to come and read the instructions in tiny print inside the box of some medicine or other. For her blood pressure. Could it combine nastily with the other drugs she is taking for her constipation? Vittorina won't take the pills that have been prescribed for her low pressure, counting rather on San Gaspare. Giampaolo, meanwhile, is congratulating himself on having decided to go for the flu vaccination this year. Everybody at the office has been down but him. Taking sick leave, most likely, Orietta thinks wryly, the *dipendente*'s only revenge. Sitting together in their flat, Giampaolo constantly fiddling with the remote control of the aerial on the roof, we watch the President's New Year message, in which, referring to the recent devastating bomb on a train in a tunnel between Florence and Bologna, he makes the famous remark: "They tell me that the secret services are honest, they tell me they are working nonstop to find the culprits. . . ." Later there is to be something live from the Moulin Rouge, which Giampaolo shows a lingering interest in. There's so much enticing soft porn on Italian TV. But now it's time to go down to the *taverna* for a big barbecue and plenty of wine and *prosecco*.

Toward midnight the fireworks begin to crackle in earnest. It sounds like a battle. Nearer to home, the Negrettis' adolescent boys have bought a full-scale discotheque outfit and installed it in their two-car garage, where they are making other young Montecchiesi pay a couple of thousand lire for the pleasure of sixteen-year-old Mario's disk-jockeying. Every time we stop talking in the *taverna* we are assailed by the line "Up, down, like a yo-yo, life is just a giddy up and go go." Lara asks me what it means, but I refuse to translate. It's too stupid. The reinforced concrete columns throb. Heaven knows how Vittorina and Lucilla are managing to watch their variety shows upstairs. Giampaolo tells me that legally he could phone the carabinieri and get them over, since doubtless the noise is above legally established decibel thresholds and the Negrettis certainly don't have a license for holding public gatherings. However, he feels this would be unkind at New Year. I ask him how he decides whether to call the carabinieri rather than the *polizia*. Do they have different duties? He tells me that their duties are exactly the same; indeed they frequently compete, refuse to share information in the hope of arriving at their criminal first. He calls the carabinieri merely from personal choice and because their station is a mile or so nearer. Isn't our Margaret Thatcher always talking about personal choice?

Toward one we go upstairs. The fog has lifted, as it sometimes will at night. The air is quite clear at a few degrees below freezing. From our balcony we can see rockets rising into the sky from surrounding villages. The restaurants offering their New Year's banquet at 200,000 lire a head will still be packed. Tomorrow's news will tell us exactly how many people the fireworks and celebratory gunfire killed in Naples, how many people who paid for their banquet in advance turned up to find the restaurant closed, the proprietor gone forever, how many people driving back at dawn in thickening fog went into walls and ditches. Obliged to put up with Mario Negretti's disk-jockeying into the early hours, we while away the time with the thousand-piece jigsaw puzzle the Visentinis have given us, showing the snowy peaks north of this fog.

The following morning, the Visentinis are off early to see their relatives in Venice, but Giampaolo has left precise instructions that I must go and see Lucilla before ten o'clock. I will be the only man in the house, and it is bad luck for a woman to see another woman first on New Year's Day. Thus before Lucilla can go downstairs to chat with Vittorina, I will have to go and greet her. Interestingly, the more religious, mysterious Vittorina doesn't insist on observing this superstition, while for Lucilla it's a matter of life or death. When I mentioned this paradox to Vittorina a couple of weeks later, I actually got a squeaky giggle out of her. Cilla just wants to see a man, she said.

And indeed when I knocked and announced myself, Lucilla was in a state of suggestive dishabille which twenty years ago might still have turned an *ambulante*'s head. *Buona fine, buon principio, troppo gentile, Signor Tino.* I bend down to kiss her on both made-up cheeks, and she tells me she hasn't even been answering the phone in case it is a woman. Actually she's not sure if the phone counts, but she thought she'd be safe. As always she insists I come in. Do I know how best to look after the plants she has been given? Four *stelle di natale* (poinsettias), a traditional Christmas gift, are lined up on the tiled floor, still in their transparent plastic wraps. They are so beautiful, but somehow she can never keep them for more than a month or so. *Sì, sì grazie*, she did get her seven bras, *troppo gentile* of me to ask, though she wasn't entirely satisfied. Il Professore, on the other hand, knew everything about plants. He used to advise her as to how . . .

Two weeks after these New Year celebrations, we receive a letter from Lucilla's lawyer advising us in the most grandiloquent terms that from now on we are to pay our rent to her. We show our ignorance of such matters by not appreciating that we could perfectly well ignore this. I immediately telephone Signora Marta, who says she will get her lawyer to send us another letter ordering us to continue to pay her and quoting the various articles of the law which justify this approach. "And how is the old lady?" she inquires as always. "She must be seventy-something, after all—why doesn't she just enjoy her old age?" I tell her that while Vittorina has been quite ill of late, Lucilla is doing just fine. Marta says that she herself is so upset by having these criminal proceedings brought against her that she is now being forced to take an assortment of tranquilizers. When she wins the case she will sue Lucilla for damages.

After which, the legal war goes on, with letter following letter. The first court hearing is finally held, then promptly adjourned— because Marta's lawyer doesn't turn up. A date some three months away is fixed. It is impossible for us not to reflect how all this is playing into our hands. Not only will nobody be able to sell the place until the case is settled, but it would take a very courageous Marta indeed to raise our rent in these circumstances. The affair seems to be without either *fine* or *principio*, which can only be *buono* for us.

STRADA DELLE ZITELLE

I DATE OUR FINAL ACCEPTANCE as first-class citizens of Via Colombare to the moment when it became generally known that Rita was to have a baby. It would have been carnival time, February, the shops full of monster masks and d'Artagnan outfits for five-year-olds. It was also around then that we discovered the Centro Primo Maggio, a place which has always made me that little bit happier about living in Montecchio.

Rita wanted tests done at the hospital and asked Orietta how to go about it. No one could have been better informed. Nor more delighted about the news. A baby in number 10, *meraviglioso!* Giampaolo too was genuinely delighted. His serious man's face broke up into excited boyishness. The vibrations in this spic-and-span, austerely stylish apartment were suddenly very cozy indeed. Lara almost jumped for joy. The little brother or sister she hadn't had! she cried.

Of course, the Visentinis were discretion itself. They respected your privacy, spoke to no one. It was a point of honor. With them any remark, however banal, was considered highly confidential. But about ten minutes after Rita had mentioned the development to Lucilla (since every secretive society must have its source of gossip), the whole of Via Colombare was informed. And our social status rose vertiginously. We were no longer two fly-by-nights who did strange jobs and brought queer visitors in scruffy cars with foreign plates. We were responsible people putting down roots. We were creating a family and thus probably Christian even if we didn't go to mass. Along the street now, there was no question of people not responding to my *buon giorno* and *buona sera*. On the contrary, everybody smiled with complicity. Rita was buttonholed by women who had barely spoken to her before. When was it due? Was she suffering from morning sickness? Did we want a boy or a girl? Which hospital were we thinking of going to? Heads nodded sagely in the cold air. For there was no fog now, just a long dull wait for spring. After which, the baby.

Anyway, it would probably be a girl. Yes, it would certainly be a girl. Why? Because every child born in Via Colombare in the last few years had been a girl. And oddly enough all their names started with M: Marta, Monica, Milena . . . Perhaps we could call ours Mariangela, or Miranda. Although not that many children had been born in the last ten years, of course, because not only was this the street of the little girls (at this very moment playing volleyball over railings in winter sunshine), but it was also *la strada delle zitelle*, the street of the old maids.

It hadn't occurred to us before, but now that we came to think of it there was a marked preponderance of unmarried middle-aged women in the street: the woman with the twig broom, for example, and her slimmer sister; then the dark-haired sprightly sister of the insurance peddler; and the woman at the corner by the Madonnina who sat at her window behind a loom and had a dog on a chain outside which barked ferociously behind tall iron gates and appeared to answer to the name Book.

"Perhaps it's because of the Virgin," the woman with the twig broom laughed, all of a sudden on very easy terms. She had wirily permed blond air and a fierce mole at the base of the nose. We didn't understand. "The Madonnina," she said, pointing to the statue with its patient sad face. And she added with a note of disappointment, "I don't suppose you'll be leaving number 10 now—my nephew will have to buy in the cooperative."

Walking back home, I objected to Rita that the Virgin had surely only been a virgin prior to the birth of Christ. After that she had had other children, whom Jesus referred to as his brothers. It was thus unlikely that she would want to influence the women of Via Colombare to become old maids. Rita told me I was wrong. The Virgin had never had other children. But I have a whole youth of church attendance and Bible studies behind me. I was sure. "And Joseph?" I asked. "What became of him then?" We were walking by the low pink wall of old Marini's garden. He was pruning his fruit trees.

"Celibate."

"But if . . . "

"Well, he could hardly go to bed with the mother of Christ, could he?"

I'd never thought about it in quite this crude way. I suggested we go and talk to Don Guido about it. Even if he chucked away his encyclicals he could surely clear up this one for us.

But in the end it was enough to inquire of an authority like Vittorina. Yes, of course the Virgin had remained a virgin for the rest of her life. Anything else was unthinkable. Otherwise how could she be the model of virtue? She would come down to our level. The old woman, herself childless, seemed genuinely puzzled that anyone should have imagined otherwise.

I quote this banal misunderstanding only to show how even a supposedly well-educated Protestant like me can for so long be unaware of some key piece of dogma underpinning the Catholic culture he is living in. Joseph had thus been forgotten. Jesus hadn't had any brothers, as I had been taught. Mary was the model of celibacy, which was a blessed virtue. She had somehow managed to combine this self-denial with pious motherhood, thus making herself the perfect woman. Indeed, a statue of her was still reputed to be crying in Colognola Veneta after more than three months, though the priests were refusing to allow the tears to be analyzed. Radio Santa Teresa had discussed the matter, but without ever taking on the question as to why the Virgin might be crying. Because she was still unhappy about her son's crucifixion despite His resurrection? Because the local congregation was sinful? Or to demonstrate that devotional images were more than mere blocks of wood or stone? Sometimes Radio Santa Teresa would broadcast a whole rosary, repeating *Santa Maria, madre di dio*, time after time. It was quite relaxing. And now the Virgin was also being held responsible for the preponderance of female births in Via Colombare. And likewise for the fact that so many of the women in Via Colombare remained unmarried. . . .

Naturally, I began to hope that our baby would be a boy (as the Virgin's had been, come to think of it).

But such a hope was precisely what was expected of me anyway. "I imagine you'll be wanting a *maschio*, Signor Tino?" Lucilla said. "It's only natural for a man to want a *maschio*." And she laughed, as if to say, "Too bad for you the creature was conceived in Via Colombare of all places."

I thus decided to say to other inhabitants of the street that I would rather like to have a girl, while secretly hoping we would have a boy, and at the same time feeling irritated with myself for getting drawn into this superstitious mare's nest, which in the end nobody on Via Colombare particularly cared about, just as none of them particularly cared whether the Pope insisted that contraception was murder, or whether a visiting priest had once dared to tell them not to come forward for the host if they hadn't paid their taxes. There is this magical duplicity about Italians. I'll never get used to it. You think they're superstitious bigots, but then they're more open-minded than you are. None of them would ever have criticized Christ for plucking ears of corn on the Sabbath. It's as if they were a nation of Protestants, or even freethinkers, who just happened to be deeply attached, for reasons of style and aesthetics, to the Catholic way of worship. Because they appreciate its richness. It fills their lives.

But a more pressing question than the sex of the child was whether we should use public or private health care for this pregnancy. Giampaolo Visentini, being the new man, favored use of the public health system, which was, he claimed, extremely *valido*, though he appreciated that some people might doubt that. Indeed, he himself had paid privately when Lara had had to see a dermatologist over a rash she'd had, because the waiting list at the state hospital was so long. And he'd been furious, he added, when the consultant's secretary had not given him a receipt after he'd paid his seventy thousand lire.

The problem, Orietta explained, was that if you went to the hospital for your visits, you couldn't be sure of seeing the same gynecologist every time, nor could you know whether he'd be there when the child was born. The doctors had plainly decided on this system in order to further their private practices outside the hospital.

We were thus persuaded to go private. A gynecologist *di fiducia* was recommended by a friend, and we went. Disconcertingly, despite having an appointment, we had to wait just as long as one usually waits in the doctor's office. Then at the end of his examination, the little man, who went by the apt name of Dolcetta, prescribed a list of tests so long one wondered if there would be time in the remaining six months to perform them all. And since a scan was urgent, he said, we should do that privately too, not waste time at the hospital; and he gave us the name of a clinic, where we very quickly discovered he himself worked, and presumably took a cut of the 100,000 lire or more they wanted for a scan. At which Rita decided to drop the man and go for the lowest of the low, a health service gynecologist who came to the small public clinic in Montecchio once a week. Not being a hospital consultant or even a hospital doctor, he was generally spurned, and so making an appointment was refreshingly easy. The man turned out to be a southerner with a light, jolly patter, and a determination, he surprisingly boasted, to make the public system work. We couldn't have been better served.

CENTRO PRIMO MAGGIO

IT WAS ACCORDION MUSIC which first drew us to Centro Primo Maggio. We were walking behind a little footpath that leads off the main road behind the new church, where Don Guido keeps his rabbits and hens. Running between two deep ditches, the path is ill-kept. To the left is a patchwork of vegetable plots behind crumbling houses, plastic bags over warm-weather plants, plane trees pruned to knobbly trunks, dogs on chains, sulking cats, and a complex crisscrossing of lively streams. I am conscious, as I describe this, that it does not sound especially attractive, whereas in fact the rich haphazardness of it all and the general rejection of any recognizable geometry is constantly picturesque. Someone has built a little raft to push from one side of a ditch to the other: a chair strapped to a wooden door over gas-can floats. There's an old man in his plot asleep in a decaying armchair, with a hat and a bottle of wine. A woman is dropping sprigs of rosemary into her apron. On precarious scaffolding, an older workman and young apprentice chip at the ruined stucco of a house. And there is bric-a-brac from the past: a complicated pattern of stone walls guides one of the streams into an old sheep dip; here and there steps lead from a house down to the water and a large flat scouring stone. A sturdy middle-aged woman will appear and descend the steps with a red plastic basket full of dirty laundry. Where the houses back right onto the water, you see pipes gushing out suspicious effluents into the stream. All these people have color TVs and decent cars.

We had just begun to hear the strains of jolly accordion music when we came across the ascetic Lorenzo, standing thigh-deep in the larger of the two ditches, almost a river at this point, patiently hacking away underwater with a sickle tied to a long metal pole.

He is cutting the choking underwater weeds, he explains, which are a result of excess oxygen in the water because of extravagant use of fertilizers up on the hills, plus the dumping of waste by pig breeders.

On his own?

He laughs. He and some friends have formed a cooperative, a non-profit-making company, which is paid by the town to keep the village's streams and ditches in good order. It's a victory won after a decade of protest about public lack of concern for the local ecology.

But isn't it cold in the ditch? A great clump of weeds detaches itself from the bottom and floats clear with the current. Lorenzo has a big bag tied to his belt into which he drops a muddy Coca-Cola bottle.

Not at all. The water is warmer than the air, and he has his waders on. He likes the job. But has decided to leave Montecchio.

Lorenzo has ginger hair, tightly curled, and a thin nose. Despite his having left the Jesuits, his sharp features betray the stubbornness of the man with a cause.

Because the people here are so traditional, he says, so timid, so cynical, so set in their ways. They're never willing to get out there and fight the environmental battle. Lorenzo turns out to be another of those Italians who aspire to escape provincial claustrophobia.

"I'm thinking of going abroad," he says, just as Bepi does, though the two men couldn't be more different.

First he tried the church, he said, where they wouldn't allow you to have a single thought of your own. And it is not much different in the end trying to improve the situation here in Montecchio. Every new idea is greeted with suspicion.

He begins to press us to come to the next meeting about the overpass the town is planning to build right by the hill with the castle. Feeling guilty, we agree to come—the cause is certainly a good one—but to change the subject we ask him what the accordion music is. Lorenzo gives us directions to the Centro Primo Maggio.

The path ends in a flight of steps climbing to a road where cars chase down a desperately narrow, crooked strip of asphalt with no space for a sidewalk below the tall walls of three- and four-story houses. Opposite the path, however, the houses end and the road opens up into the village's second lake, which is much like the Laghetto Squarà, though without the Roman blocks. A battered crash barrier keeps the hurrying cars from falling in. To the left of the lake are the gates to a large old factory covering acres of land. This was once a tannery. Now Mondadori, Italy's largest printing company, is using it as a paper storage warehouse. One thus steps out from a path to find a huge German truck with two trailers rumbling back and forth to get out of the gate, around the crash barrier by the lake, and then on into the forbiddingly narrow canyon of the street beyond.

On the other side of the lake there's a grassy pasture, and to the right, a group of *case popolari*, public housing. We walk down toward them and toward the sound of music. Other people are converging there too, in carnival outfit. Or rather, the adults are for the most part in ordinary clothes while their little children are fairy queens and assault robots. Carnival is fairly tame in Montecchio. So tame we didn't even know the procession was today. In any event, no inhibitions are being dropped behind demonic masks. For a more extravagant celebration people will go to Verona, where bizarre floats wind through the streets for hours and youths cover shop windows in shaving foam.

The *case popolari* look really okay. True, the stucco is cracking here and there and the balconies are smaller than they might be, but by London standards they look fine. And the people living in them seem to be doing all right too. There are plenty of expensive cars about. Like the *statale* (and very often he is a *statale*), your *casa popolare* occupant is on to a good deal. He pays a rent way below the market rate, and after twenty-five years the flat will automatically become his. Meanwhile, he polishes his Alfetta. The only drawback being that ten years after the place was built, the town still hasn't found the money to put in sidewalks or to pave the parking spaces. The ground is grit and stones. One thus has to wash one's Alfetta rather more often than even an Italian might want to.

And the little princesses are getting their silver slippers dirty. The accordion speeds up. We follow a small d'Artagnan through the development to find, on the other side, just where the country begins, a rusty green gate in a sagging fence and the legend "Centro Primo Maggio." Inside, under a bare pergola, a small group of middle-aged men in Sunday best are playing accordion, guitar, and drums. Despite their changing the tune every couple of minutes the sound and rhythm are always the same:

Der-der-der-der, di dum, diddy dum, diddy dum, der der der der, di dum, diddy dum, diddy dum. A table is stacked with paper cups; there are big plastic bottles of lemonade at one end and even bigger bottles of wine at the other. In the middle are plates of *galani*, fried dough cakes dunked in icing sugar. The children hurl handfuls of confetti, some of which gets in my wine. And a little boy bursts into tears because he has got his Zorro outfit dirty.

Then the Re Magnaron, the carnival leader, arrives. The *magnaron* is a tiny fish that swims about in the dikes and ditches here and once formed the traditional carnival dish. With his scaly head and sequined cloak, the man playing the role looks like something from a Ben Jonson masque. Guffawing loudly, tossing clouds of confetti, he leads off the fifty or so cowboys, penguins, Batmen, and fairy queens on their infant procession through the village. But we have already fallen in love with the Centro Primo Maggio and decide to stay behind. There will be time for the parades when we have our own children.

It began as a Communist Party social club. Immediately to the left of the gate is a large low prefab with bar, cluttered tables, a pair of Space Invader machines, a copy of *Unità*, the Communist paper, a poster of Berlinguer, a hammer and sickle, and an assortment of those ubiquitous old Montecchio men with their hats and wine bottles. Playing cards. Opposite the hut is the pergola, perhaps twenty yards long, vine tendrils stretching over a curving iron frame to offer a shady space on summer days and a small dance floor for festive evenings. There is a strip of concrete for bocce, which is fenced in to prevent the heavy balls from flying out at passersby. A notice exhorts customers not to argue. Beyond, a very large scrubby lawn is scattered with rickety chairs and tables as far as the flood embankment and emergency ditch fifty yards away. To one side of this lawn a big barbecue stand prepares hot sausage meat, *bruschetta*, and eggplant slices on toast for lunch. Then there are a couple of tennis courts, a children's playground, a concrete table for Ping-Pong, and at the very end of the complex an ambitious dirt track for BMX bikes. For the Communists must appeal to the younger generation too.

But it is not the facilities which make Centro Primo Maggio what it is. I haven't spent a hundred lazy Saturday afternoons here for that. It's the extremely attractive atmosphere of laissez-faire, the civilized and gentle nature of the people who use the place. There's nothing aggressive in the culture of Montecchio's working and peasant classes. At least not that I have observed. And if they drink too much, they do it slowly, sitting on the veranda of the prefab, watching the crimson wink of Bardolino in the sunshine. They are at ease, relaxed, there is never the slightest threat of hurry or unpleasantness. Nor does one experience that sense of claustrophobia you get in downtown middle-class Verona, and even in Pasticceria Maggia sometimes, that obsession with fashion and elegance, fur and leather, the scrubbed faces of the men, the heavy makeup of the women, the crinkly dyed blond hair of respectable girls fanning out onto sheepskin shoulders, the hubbub of posh Veneto la-di-da.

None of this at Centro Primo Maggio. It's the sort of place, I have sometimes thought, that Orwell must have dreamed of. You salute your faith-healing barber, who clearly appreciates you more now you have admitted to sensing a tingling feeling when his fingers touch your head. You salute the shoemaker, who runs a little Elvis Presley fan club and has pictures of the King all over his tiny shop. You wave to the supermarket boys as they play tennis, the girls who serve in Bepi's shop. And Ercole, tall, lantern-jawed, who fills up your car at the local pump and ran as an *Indipendente di Sinistra* in the last elections, nods to you as he helps the younger boys with their bikes. Prices are comparatively low, though it would be a mistake to buy a cappuccino here. Wine or espresso or both are the thing. Just inside the door of the prefab, a small space is made available for a couple of *marocchini* to show their wares without going about and bothering people. And there's a black man selling cheap leather goods and Russian watches. You pick up your wine, take it out into the garden, and wonder how long you can resist the smell of sizzling pork and eggplant.

Not that there aren't encroachments from the modern yuppie Italy and its well-heeled pieties: the anxious mothers, for example, who are watching their children do as tennis teacher tells them on the new, carefully groomed clay courts; and then the bright young men who have just finished playing and are ordering, instead of beer or wine, the fashionable, healthy, super-vitaminized mineral drinks heavily advertised on television. They are so conscious of their virtue, these young men, as they discuss the technicalities of their game with TV-expert solemnity, that somehow one feels almost sorry for them. Outside, hordes of eight-year-olds in the uniform of the Montecchio biking clubs are strapping on their helmets before tackling the BMX course. Every single child has his or her special biking shoes, biking pants, biking gloves. . . .

But it all coexists so happily at Centro Primo Maggio: as if the contemporary fads were nothing more than pink froth on the same old blood-red wine. And it's fun watching the bocce, or on summer evenings the people dancing to the squelchy tunes of the accordion beneath the now fragrant pergola: der der der der, di dum, diddy dum, diddy dum . . .

Whenever I go, I always feel this is Montecchio at its best.

IL FRATE INDOVINO

Aɴᴏᴛʜᴇʀ ᴛʜɪɴɢ ᴛʜᴀᴛ ʀᴀɪsᴇᴅ my status in Via Colombare, and at number 10 in particular, was that I was the only man around one morning when disaster struck. We were sitting in the kitchen. The news was reminding us it was time to make our VAT declaration. It is touching the way the public service seeks to prod the citizens' memory in this way. People in such-and-such a category, the newscaster tells you—artisans, shopkeepers, solicitors—have just three days to make such-and-such a declaration. Or people with cars registered in January have just a week to pay their car tax, though there may be a reprieve, since not enough forms are available.

The apologetic Roman voice was suddenly interrupted by a pounding on the front door. Lucilla, in her pink brushed-nylon dressing gown, face harrowed by melodrama, was hopping from one foot to the other on the landing by the remains of her Christmas poinsettias. She had been unable to get Vittorina to come to her door.

This then was what all the shouting had been about earlier on.

Had she tried the phone? Vittorina has a phone by her bed. Lucilla rushed back into her flat and was so upset she couldn't dial the number. *"Che agitassión, che agitassión, Signor Tino!"* she cried. We helped her. A tubby hand grabbed the receiver. There was no answer.

Could Vittorina be out?

No. Lucilla claimed she had heard her moaning behind the door. At which Rita phoned for an ambulance while I rushed downstairs. Orietta came out, and whereas I would have imagined this was just the kind of thing that would bring on her palpitations, she was in fact very cool and sensible. We must try to get into the flat. Lucilla's spare keys, perhaps? But Vittorina had left her own in the door inside. So, a window, Orietta suggested.

I went outside and pulled myself up onto Vittorina's terrace balcony, beneath which I had watered grass all the long summer before. Forcing apart the slats of her shutter just a crack, I was able to see that the French window behind was open to let some air in. I asked Orietta if she had such a thing as a bread knife and she hurried off to find one. It was late February. Rain was falling in the street behind me, and, unusual for these parts, there was wind with it. I remember the cheese van turned the corner with a coolly megaphoned *"Formaggi!"* Then Orietta brought out a selection of useful-looking knives and only a very few moments later I had sawed two small squares out of the plastic slats so as to be able to reach in and release the catches inside. I heaved the shutter up a little, crawled underneath, and found Vittorina stretched limply on her cold dining-room tiles in nineteenth-century underwear.

On being let in, Lucilla had a fit of hysteria. It was plain she could already see herself beating her fists on the coffin. She howled out loud and tugged at her short hennaed gray hair to feel the pain. Neighbors rushed in from the street. Together we got Vittorina into a sitting position on an armchair. The women rubbed her hands and feet. Others comforted Lucilla and helped her loosen her girdle.

Somewhat embarrassed, I decided I had better retire to the kitchen until the ambulance came. It was thus that I found myself reading a rather odd calendar pinned to the door of one of Vittorina's freshly carpentered cupboards. *Il calendario del frate indovino*, it said. And this immediately struck me as curious, for a *frate* is a priest, a friar (the calendar was published by a religious order), while an *indovino* is a decidedly secular fortune-teller. Another peculiar thing was the way the colors and graphics of the poster-size pages seemed to come straight out of the early sixties (old cornflakes-box illustrations spring to mind), whereas the dates referred unequivocally to today. In the middle of the page were the days of the month with saints' names in bold type followed by runner-up saints in small print; for example, March 1, SAN SILVIO, Sant'Albino, Sant'Ercolano. Then around the calendar proper, a series of different-colored boxes offered oodles of advice, predictions, maxims and mottos, information for farmers, satirical jokes, cartoons, and ominous sayings. Plenty for me to while away five minutes with:

"*Seeding*: Given a waning moon, now is the time to plant peas, beets, and spinach in a sheltered area."

"*Women*: Diehard reactionaries refuse to recognize that in a Christian society women have responsibilities as great as those of men, and sometimes greater. Like motherhood."

One wondered quite who the reactionary here might be. And if the piece on seeding had been written by the *indovino* persona, was the comment on women the work of the *frate*? Vittorina, of course, had had no children, no motherhood to justify her femininity. Nor even virginity. Though she subscribed to this same potent mix of the religious and secular: the quote from the Bible and the day's horoscope beside. And then my eye caught this disquieting reflection:

"*Thought for the Day*. Every morning in Africa the gazelle wakes up and knows he will have to run faster than the lion if he is not to be killed. Every morning in Africa the lion wakes up and knows he will have to run faster than the gazelle if he is not to die of hunger. When the sun rises, it doesn't matter if you're a gazelle or a lion, you'd better start running."

Clearly this boded ill indeed for poor Vittorina.

The Croce Verde ambulance arrived, an orderly offered a possible diagnosis of stroke, Vittorina was swathed in blankets and carried off. The stretcher bearers refused to let the sobbing Lucilla into the vehicle, so a neighbor, the insurance salesman's sister, one of Via Colombare's *zitelle*, traveled with her. At the last moment Orietta hurried out with a plastic bag containing nightdress, cutlery, soap, towel, and toilet paper, all of which Vittorina would need if she had to stay in a hospital for any length of time. Lucilla retired to her bed with its pink canopies and called the doctor to come and measure her blood pressure, slipping the man twenty thousand lire for doing what the state already paid him to do. Imaginatively, he prescribed tranquilizers. *"Troppo gentile,"* Lucilla told him, and called us in to ask if we would go and get her prescription.

The druggist is still a figure of some authority in provincial Italian society. A long queue of people with no time to go to the doctor were thus waiting for his advice. And unfortunately there is only one druggist in Montecchio, since the town has not given permission for another to open. This gives our druggist a powerful monopoly, especially since such simple products as aspirin, milk of magnesia, and the like can only be sold by druggists. The prescription charge is around two pounds, then you pay a percentage of the cost of the product, this depending on the nature of the medicine required and your own particular status.

The process is complicated. The druggist has what looks like a plasticized logarithm table on the counter and taps on a calculator, doing percentages, adding and subtracting. I wait, but then the woman in front of me doesn't have a prescription for the Valium she wants. Which must only be sold under prescription, of course. *Sotto voce*, a long argument begins. *Per favore, dottore*, she pleads. After furtive glances to check who is in the shop, he finally gives her what he shouldn't. At the full price. Then he asks me to sign two petitions, one to have the flood ditch outside paved over for more convenient parking, another to complain that the government is being very late in making its payments to druggists for medicines sold under prescription. Politely, I refuse. Down south, in Calabria,

I think, there is an area where pretty well every druggist has been kidnapped at some time over the last few years. Ransom payments have not presented an insuperable problem. Walking home, I observe that I am already feeling that peculiarly Italian envy of the more fortunate employment categories.

We go and visit Vittorina in the hospital. The building compares well with the National Health ones I knew, though there are a few beds in the corridors. The nurses are mainly small slim southern men and wear green pajama affairs and slip-on clogs. At night Marisa has been sitting on a straight-backed chair by Vittorina's side. Almost everybody who is seriously ill has a relative spending the night.

But Vittorina is recovering fast. She's sitting up and smiling. It's just that she can't move her left arm or leg. In a slurred voice she is embarrassingly profuse in her thanks. She does hope Lucilla will let us keep the flat. And driving home, it occurs to us that, yes, we do have a strong card to play here. I will point out to Lucilla that since I mostly work at home I am generally on hand to deal with the kind of emergencies that might befall old and ailing women. Whereas a new tenant, even one as capable and *gentile* as Signor Giampaolo, would probably not be.

Always assuming Lucilla wins, or that the case is ever settled at all.

Arriving back in Montecchio, we noticed a small knot of people outside the church, elderly women and children, one or two of the latter furiously rubbing their foreheads. How odd. Until we recalled it was Ash Wednesday. "From dust you came and to dust you shall return." Don Guido had been signing the cross in ash on their foreheads. This was one religious festival that it was as well perhaps Vittorina had missed.

Though death, as they like to say, is not always unwelcome. And if the saga of Marta vs. Lucilla was to be interminable, it was not long after Vittorina's return home that the final curtain did at last fall on another long-running drama. The weather had turned rough: spring storms, March winds. And at night, when the wind blew, you couldn't keep the shutters down, because the plastic slats would rattle irksomely. This meant that if Vega chose to bark, five or six yards from our window, the noise was even louder. It seemed to ring in your skull.

One night we were kept awake for ages as the dog yelped, howled, and bayed, railing at the stormy wind, we imagined, participating in her doggy way in the change of the seasons, the approaching equinox. Right through the small hours it went on, urgent and tortured, as if the creature were barking inside our brains, tugging us back from the threshold of sleep with her teeth. How we moaned and swore and wondered at our own impotence. Until the following morning, wearily brushing my own teeth before some lesson, I pushed open the frosted glass of the bathroom window, for no other reason really than to feel the air on my face and see the world I knew was there. Except that today it wasn't, quite. For under the budding *cachi* tree was stretched, as if in sacrificial offering, the horribly distorted corpse of our canine tormentor. Poisoned.

Rita! Rita! A moment's delighted celebration, an enthusiastic embrace. At last, at last! Someone had done in the mutt! How splendid life was going to be!

And then came the first doubts. Everybody must imagine it was us. Oh no! The Negrettis were only too well aware how much Vega disturbed us. We had talked quite openly about poisoning the creature. And there had been those phone calls we'd made. In the early hours. Those calls alone must make us the prime suspects. Not that we feared Rocco Negretti would go to the police. It wasn't his style. But what if some stupid vendetta were to begin? After all, we had the cat now. Would it be safe for her to go out?

That evening we talked to Giampaolo and Orietta. Vega, they had heard through the grapevine, had definitely been poisoned, but nobody knew by whom. They looked at us intently. We denied any knowledge. There was a rumor, they said, that the animal had eaten some rat poison Negretti had used in his cellar. But this seemed extremely unlikely, given that the dog was never allowed into the house. Vittorina, grim-faced, mouth twisted as she spoke, was mysterious: "That animal got on one too many people's nerves," she said darkly. Across from my study window, the old skull face between lace curtains was sibylline as death itself.

Other inhabitants of Via Colombare seemed not so much reticent as genuinely uninterested. Who cared who had killed old Negretti's dog, as long as the next one he got didn't bark so much?

We mulled over this strange case of wish fulfillment for some time. And watched our cat carefully. Nothing happened. In the end our conclusion was that Negretti must have poisoned the animal himself to be rid of her. For only forty-eight hours after Vega's death, he came home with a huge black Doberman and launched into a breeding experiment that is still going on to this day. The sight of the great black creature terrified us at first; how loud would this monster bark? Until we realized that a Montecchiese breeding a dog is quite a different proposition from a Montecchiese merely keeping a dog. For a breeding dog is worth money and hence deserves respect. With the result that first Ursa and later Sirio, Musca, and Canope (this obsession with the night sky was one of the more attractive sides to Negretti's character) were well fed and regularly brushed, and barked very little at night.

PRIMAVERA

I DON'T KNOW WHY, but I picked up a copy of the *frate indovino* calendar myself. I had noticed it hanging in three or four houses now. It seemed popular in a sort of *Reader's Digest*, ready-source-of-wisdom way. And who would be without a ready source of wisdom? Thus, come springtime, an entry entitled *Per Tutti* tells me: "Remember that love exists regardless of age, and that the love that lasts longest is also the strongest. However, we should also remember that young people are a constant prey to sexual impulses, especially at certain times of the year. Fortunately, these can be quietened and actually disappear in individuals who manage to establish loyal relationships with their parents, their true friends, and their spiritual guides."

A world where adolescents are not troubled by sexual impulses! One's first reaction is to burst out laughing, to assume that our *frate* is way out on a celibate limb here. Who could ever want such a thing? Yet when I begin to pay attention, it does seem that a very large proportion of my students at the university not only seem to want but actually to have achieved the God-fearing serenity he describes. And a fair number of youths in Montecchio too. There is a decorousness and calm about them at once admirable and disturbing. "No, I don't want to leave home," they tell you. "I like living with *mamma e papà*. There's nothing I'd like to do that I can't do at home." Or: "Francesca and I will get married and live together in about five years' time when I pass the state exam to become an accountant in my home village of Buttapietra." They seem quite untroubled by matters sexual.

I ask how many of my students go to mass (one can pretend this is a linguistic exercise when teaching English). More than half regularly and most of the rest occasionally. Yes, they go with their parents. Even their grandparents. (Of course, in a way, this is wonderful, even enviable.) I ask what they did last weekend, and hear from three or four students that they went on a spiritual retreat. To be together and pray for peace. The girls dress with Latin elegance and seem very self-composed. But Friday night they went to a discotheque. Oh yes, Federica, and what did you wear? Black skirt, black tights. And you, Cristina? Black skirt, black tights. And you, Monica? Black skirt, black tights. Do the boy wear ties when they go to discotheques? Some do, some don't. And what did you have to drink? Fanta, Coca-Cola. No wine? No wine.

One constantly suspects that some cover-up is going on. Something you can't understand is happening. Surely they can't all be like this, so very sure of themselves, untroubled by life's passing. And I ask questions at random. How did you get to the discotheque? In *papà*'s car. What kind of car does he have? A Mercedes station wagon. Oh, and how long did you stay? Till two in the morning. And does anything actually happen at these discotheques? What do you mean, happen?

Is this truly serenity, the wise calm of the youth who has a good relationship with loyal friends, sensible parents, and spiritual guide? Or reticence and obtuseness? And how does it square up with those unmarried mothers of Montecchio, disconsolately pushing their prams around the broken fountain of Piazza Buccari?

"By far the most widely practiced method of contraception in Italy," explains Maria Grazia in her *sanitaria* (she loves these conversations), "is coitus interruptus. You know? Not something young men are notoriously good at." A rueful expression crosses her face. "And then spring comes so suddenly here."

It certainly does. Late March, early April's the time: San Francesco, San Sisto, Sant'Isidoro . . . The lingering mists, the cold colorless days, the heavy rains, are suddenly gone. The sun powers through, so hot you find you're desperately overdressed. And the women would have loved to wear their furs just one last time. But it's too late. You wake up one morning—San Celestino, my calendar tells me—and the sky is awhirl with swifts and swallows. How they liven up the hills and farms and river bridges with their voracious, darting search for food, and sex presumably. Cherry and peach blossoms simply explode. All the trees at once. Line after line of them up the hills between the still-gaunt vines. Already the bees are crawling in and out of sugary petals. The polyethylene comes off the lemon trees. The earth releases all its pent-up smells. And in the evening dusk, white cherry flowers glow like beacons, to the croaking of a thousand frogs converging on Montecchio's ditches— to lay their spawn.

How loud those frogs will croak! It's obscene! And no wonder that one or two of the spiritually less well-guided tend to fall by the wayside: in the soft grass, the primroses and periwinkles. After all, the *frate indovino* did warn that there were vulnerable times of the year.

At number 10 a condominium garden committee agrees to have a man come in and prune all our flowering shrubs just before they can bloom. He cuts and clips, returning a year's growth to austere geometric shapes. And the buds had looked so promising. Rita is furious and sticks the cuttings in jars about the flat. If she had had more time, Lucilla says, she would have moved the hibiscus to the other side of the little cypress. But what with Vittorina being ill . . .

On Palm Sunday all the parishioners come out of mass with olive branches in their hands. Specially blessed by Don Guido. The children make a pretty picture. Their well-dressed parents look rather sheepish. *Il frate indovino* says:

> *La domenica dell'olivo, ogni ucello fa il suo nido,*
> *e se gioccola la frasca, sarà bello il dì di Pasqua.*
> (On Olive Sunday, all the birds their nests do lay
> And if the branch drips rain, Easter will be fine again.)

In the event, *la domenica dell'olivo* is fine this year, and likewise *Pasqua*. So much for our *indovino*.

On Easter Monday, *Pasquetta*, as it's called, the tradition is to set off into the hills for a mammoth picnic with barbecue equipment and bottles of wine. As always, the formula of religious festival plus heavy eating appears to be invincible. Everybody is on the move with baskets and ice chests. Marisa and Leone take the two old ladies up to Cancello. Bepi is throwing a party on his grounds at Rivoli. More modestly, we walk along the valley to Mizzole with Giampaolo, Orietta, and a well-prepared picnic basket. As we cross the main road a stream of cars drives by with sacks of charcoal strapped to luggage racks.

Outside the village, the valley is luridly green today, and the spring light, one notices as one saunters along, is different from in England somehow. At first you think it's clearer, perhaps because after weeks of mist and rain, you can see the mountains again now, far far away. And it gives you a tremendous sense of space to see them there, still in their majestic winter white. But it's not really a question of clarity. Nothing could be clearer than the light in England when a gusting wind is blowing every scrap of haze and exhaust away so that you feel you could see the whole length of the Edgware Road, if only you wanted to. Anyway, by ten o'clock, as seen from Montecchio, the Alps have already disappeared in a gathering heat haze. Visibility soon loses that sharp edge it will keep all day in windier climes.

No, it's the suffusion of the light that gives the spring its power here, its distinctly erotic feel. Quite simply, the light seems to have got in everywhere, to be on all sides of everything. Perhaps because it bounces off the pastel stuccoes so, and the white limestone of the window surrounds, simmers dazzlingly on terra-cotta roofs, shoots off dusty gray asphalt—a light that is glare, haze, and heat all together. So that the clothes simply fall off the women. In the space of a couple of weeks we've gone from furs to thin blouses and fashion T-shirts. People move in a bath of fragrant brilliance, which somehow gives you a feeling that things are happening in slow motion. For the light has that effect too. Especially if you are in the habit of taking three bottles of wine on a picnic, stretching out under the first cherry blossoms, and simply watching as the more adventurous hikers push on.

And lying there, you hear your first cuckoo raise its cheeky call, and the larks twittering high in the sky, and the urgent hum of a thousand bees (for many orchards have their own hives), and the frogs and toads croaking shamelessly as they flop through the long grass to the water.

What chance for spiritual guides at moments like this? Surely even the best of biblical armor can offer no real immunity to such a strident call to be living and doing. What hope for Montecchio's Catholic youth? The *frate indovino* must be tearing his tonsure.

Then across the heavily scented grass comes an insistent modulated drone. Nearer and nearer, louder and louder. Until all at once a leather-clad figure bursts out of a nearby ditch, roars through the vineyard where we are picnicking, and attacks the first slope of the hill in a spray of dirt and stones. Followed by another, and another, and another . . .

For ironically, it's science that comes to the old church's aid. There is the internal combustion engine. With the same ritual inevitability that lifts the sun higher every day and draws the sap up in the trees, the local adolescents answer migrant birds and reawakened bees with a great shriek of unsilenced mopeds and motorbikes. Throttles are opened and closed, opened and closed, revving rhythmically in the spring air. Cannily, Don Guido, a man who knows the lesser of two evils when he sees it, permits the lads to go around and around the church parking lot in frenzied circles. Then they race to *Un panino due*'s for a slice of pizza, then to Giulia's at the other side of the village for Coca-Cola fresh from the refrigerator.

While back in Via Colombare, the Negretti boys gun their mother's Cinquecento back and forth, back and forth across the big terrace among the broken flowerpots and clothespins: three yards in reverse, a great screeching of brakes, three yards in first, three yards in reverse, three yards in first. The blue smell blots out all the stirring scents in the air. The noise drowns the seductive cries of the *ambulanti* with their seasonal offers of deck chairs and skimpy beachwear.

Walking the winding sidewalk-less village streets to the bar of an evening becomes hazardous. Hordes of *motorini* scream by, rearing up on their back wheels, skidding and swerving. Could this be, one wonders, some pact between Fiat and the Holy See, a conspiracy to displace the libido of Latin adolescence and restrict casualties in the spring offensive to a minimum? Orietta confides that she and Giampaolo are now worried about Lara, who has taken to hanging around with the moped brigade outside the church and is reported to have been seen holding the hand of a tall blond boy. I suggest she should consider herself reassured.

Mid-April. We cycle through a cherry-blossom countryside. In the hills the hedgerows are so full of primroses, narcissi, violets, hyacinths, it's almost unbearable. The strips of winter corn are shooting up. Everybody's busy with his vegetable patch. The farmers are spraying their trees with the usual assortment of noxious chemicals.

And then it turns cold and rains again. Not only rains, but sleets, for an hour or two actually snows. The snow lies ice-white on the white cherry blossoms. Old Marini shakes his head. Not a year for fruit, he says.

Giampaolo is shaking his head too. It is almost time for us to bottle the *prosecco* he has been keeping in three huge wicker-covered demijohns down in his cellar. The problem being that *prosecco* should always be bottled when the atmospheric pressure is high or rising. This sudden return to winter is a disaster.

But the weather is going to be good next week, I tell him. I have heard the long-range forecast. All we have to do is hang on and we'll have sun and blue skies again. The pressure will rise.

He frowns, twists his mouth.

What's the problem?

Prosecco should really be bottled with a waxing moon too, he says. And the full moon is Sunday. He knows the weather is supposed to be fine next week, but by then the moon will be waning.

I protest that I thought he was a man of science. Surely his encyclopedia doesn't believe in any of this lunar stuff. This is the realm of the *frate indovino*.

Giampaolo is such a nice man because he knows when he is being ribbed and rather enjoys it, yet at the same time he persists perfectly seriously with his line of argument. His encyclopedia, he says, doesn't actually say anything about bottling *prosecco*. But the fact is that he has a certain amount of respect for popular wisdom. He believes that someday the scientists will find some reason behind the farmer's attention to the moon. More pertinently, we have spent quite a lot of money on our sixty liters of *prosecco* and he doesn't want to risk its coming out wrong.

But what could happen?

It might turn out flat, he tells me glumly. It's the waxing moon that makes it bubbly.

Well, I'm as anxious to avoid that as he is. For the next few days, every time I meet him, on the stairs, in the garage, or out on the lawn trying to remember where he puts his bulbs so we won't mow over them (for we'll have to start mowing the lawn again now)—every time I meet him, our conversation is about rising and falling pressures, waxing and waning moons.

Couldn't we just wait for the next waning moon?

We could. But that will take us to mid-May. It will be absolutely our last chance. Otherwise the fermentation process will have gone on for too long.

Giampaolo hangs a barometer on his balcony and wears a worried look. We discuss the expediency of bottling willy-nilly on the last day of this waxing moon, regardless of pressure. My own instinct is to bank on the atmospherics, rather than the moon. He looks at me, wondering if I know something. I hasten to assure him I don't. He must decide. Or perhaps he should ask old Marini. No, these Montecchiesi, Giampaolo tells me, only deal with local wines. They would have no idea what to do with a *prosecco*. Thus, while worrying about the moon, he nevertheless manages to express his Venetian, modern man's superiority to the provincial locals.

The days pass. The moon is now a perfect round silver coin in the sky. How can it possibly affect our *prosecco*? I stand on the balcony, watching it rise full as full between rain clouds over the derelict factory. To wax no more. Mid–May it will have to be.

IL 25 APRILE

On April 25, flags hang from windows and balconies along the main street through Montecchio. It's Liberation Day. People whose homes face onto major thoroughfares are obliged to fly the flag. Most of them do. Somebody has forgetfully left a pink towel over the railings of a balcony. In a beam of sunshine it clashes gorgeously with the red, white, and green.

Walking toward Centro Primo Maggio, for it's a public holiday, we hear the strains of a brass band. In dark uniform an endearing mix of adolescents and middle-aged stalwarts are playing a military march. They arrive at the monument to the fallen more or less as we do. Not the monument in the main square dedicated to the soldiers who died—they have already been there—but a more modest, modern affair located at the corner below the former tanning factory where another small development of *case popolari* begins. Here a copper plate records the names of eleven civilian

Montecchiesi killed in the bombing. A recycled wreath lies at its foot.

The band lower their instruments. A couple of youths in jeans are busy setting up an amplifier. A small crowd gathers, families in their Sunday best, shifting weight from one foot to the other, children tugging at coats. Every few minutes they have to part to let a car or a team of racing cyclists through. On the opposite corner is one of the noisier bars for village youths, its window daubed with a cartoon view of the New York skyline, symbol of unimagined decadence.

An old, portly man in uniform, complete with medals, starts to speak into a microphone, though there are only thirty or so people. He begins with the normal introductory formalities employing the pompous Italian of public discourse, so that for a moment I imagine this will be one of those politician's speeches one grows accustomed to here where any possible message is mystified by an interminable clutter of qualifications and relative clauses ("It depends"—I quote more or less at random from a newspaper by my side—"if this development is to be seen in the light of a possible rapprochement between forces by their nature intrinsically unsympathetic to what I think one would have to call the future interests and indeed hopes of the nation, conceived as that group of people who, for reasons of history, race, and culture, consider themselves to form an identity distinct from, though not opposed to, other national identities, or whether . . . ").

But no. Having got over his carefully prepared introduction, his list of names to be thanked and organizations mentioned, the old man has given up on his notes and is talking in a very simple way about the war and the dead now. He remembers how Italy fought on the wrong side, how soldiers went to freezing Russia in light summer uniforms, how these civilians were killed by the bombs of their ex-allies. He pauses, clears a hoarse throat. "If their death is to have any meaning at all," he says, gesturing to the monument, "it must lie in the kind of Italy that we have managed to build after the war, that we are able to build now. And at the moment, this Italy of

Mafia, tax evasion, and public corruption does not do honor to their names—we cannot feel we have built on their sacrifice."

He continues in this remarkably strong vein, though speaking calmly and intelligently. His old man's sincerity is impressive, the more so because of his scrubbed red nose and the deep wrinkles, weather-, age-, and drink-induced. He has none of the professional speaker's polish; he ers and ahs, feeling for what to say next. Turning around to the monument, having problems with his microphone, he begins to read out the names, one by one, as if they were people he knew. And maybe he did. "Albertini Mario, Pizzini Giuseppe, Stefanelli Emanuele . . . " The little gathering listens gravely; and it's a moment of unusual candidness, this old man in the spring light, speaking hoarsely into a microphone, reading out the names of the dead, surname first, then Christian name, as if at some impossible roll call. Then the band strikes up the national anthem and everybody disperses for their cappuccinos. On our way to the bar, we find a bunch of fresh daffodils has appeared by the plaque to the three who fell under enemy fire as the Germans retreated. It would be interesting to know who put them there. The Dalmatian imprisoned behind jumps on and off the old bidet that serves as its water bowl.

In the bar the price of our cappuccino has gone up another hundred lire, but since this price is fixed by a government body, we can hardly complain at Pasticceria Maggia. The price of an espresso is fixed, the price of a cappuccino is fixed, the price of a newspaper is fixed, the prices of gasoline, diesel fuel, and heating oil are fixed, the price of bread is fixed. Is this in line, I ask Lorenzo, with the spirit of *liberazione*? And paying at the cash register, I ask the pretty Cinzia if the price of brioches is fixed too, since I notice they always cost the same everywhere. "Not officially," she says, smiling, and is careful to give me my receipt.

Returning to Via Colombare, we find Lucilla and Vittorina sitting on their backsides in the middle of the lawn, legs stretched wide apart in dark old wool skirts. Vittorina has her big straw hat against a sun that's getting perceptibly stronger every day. Each woman holds a knife, and they have an old shopping basket between them. They thrust their knives into the lawn, wiggle them vigorously about, and pull out the fresh young dandelion plants. The roots are cut off and tossed away and the leaves dropped into the shopping basket to be washed for salad or boiled like spinach. They chatter and sing as they work. I have never seen them so happy. Lucilla has put on a green kerchief, peasant-fashion. When they've exhausted the garden, they say, they'll go off to the orchard and vineyard fields to try there. And indeed, in the countryside in spring, the meadows are full of crouched figures with plastic bags or shopping baskets, gathering dandelion and other leaves.

Giampaolo comes out to discuss lawn-mowing rotas, and they give him some of their harvest. *Vado matto*, he says, I'm crazy for them. We accept too, though I can't say I'm wildly enthusiastic. The locals have a taste for such rough, bitter salads: leaves with the texture of a cat's tongue and the taste of herb medicine. Terribly good for her constipation, Lucilla confides. To me it seems the kind of taste one could only have developed in darkest wartime.

Old Lovato watches us from over the fence, wondering what we'll do with the garden this year, how much our hedge will grow and steal his light. Behind him, and stinking with fertilizer, his peas are already rising thick as Persian spears at Thermopylae. With Vittorina not being able to do much after her stroke, Giampaolo's encyclopedic, ecological approach has got us no further than a few weedy rows of snail-ridden spinach and salad greens. The sun may well follow its dazzling trajectory above Via Colombare, the railings and cement, vines and cypresses may drip and drip with light, but somehow that dank little patch below the old cinema wall and Negretti's terrace is always in the dark.

Then incredibly, in May—but as a *dipendente* Giampaolo seems born to bad luck—the weather breaks again right on the new moon. Once again it seems the combination of rising pressure and waxing moon is to elude us. The brilliant Mediterranean sky is suddenly replaced by the kind of cloud you expect to find over Halifax or Slough. The rain is desperately heavy. Via Colombare is

not crowned, and surface water gurgles about looking for a gutter.
Lovato stands at the window, staring at his peas, willing them to
stand firm. Our lady of the twig broom cycles by under an umbrella,
climbs off at her house, and despite the torrent, kicks a cigarette stub
away from her gate. Old Signora Marini is another one pedaling
under an umbrella. Lack of wind makes this possible as it would not
be somewhere else I know. On the third day of uninterrupted rain, I
even spy one-armed Negretti, his good hand on the right handlebar, his new dog, Ursa, tied to the left, and a red umbrella tucked
under his stump.

Montecchio being in the drainage path of countless miles of
limestone hills above, the ditches are soon full to overflowing.
Even the emergency ditches begin to fill, something that happens only once or twice a year. The water is a muddy brown
flecked with white as it bears away the heaps of litter people have
thrown there. Before the week is out, water floods the section of
road by the Cassa di Risparmio di Verona, Vicenza e Belluno, the
village's one bank. The Communist Party is quick to get out posters
complaining that while the town has plenty of money to spend for
all sorts of other projects, it has never solved this simple drainage
problem. The head of the local Christian Democratic Party ducks
(as it were) the question at a meeting held in the local library, which
is temporarily closed for book borrowing because the librarian is
away for his military service. Finally the rain becomes so violent that
it fills the emergency ditch to the brim, bursting the stout wall that
protects the main road and covering it with water and broken
masonry.

How can we possibly bottle *prosecco* in this? complains Giampaolo.
He taps his barometer. I've never seen it so low. We watch an
evening's TV together over the last of the previous year's bottles.
On one of the local channels there are frequent ads for talismans (by
post) and the services of local astrologers, but nothing on how to get
the right combination of atmospherics and lunar cycle for our sixty
liters of bubbly. The news quotes the huge sums the government has
already promised in compensation to keep the farmers happy.
Should we perhaps prepare a claim for our possibly ruined *prosecco*?

Until the miracle happens. The weather clears two days before the weathermen said it would. The pressure is suddenly rising. Giving us a twelve-hour window to do our stuff before the full moon.

L'IMBOTTIGLIAMENTO

Amid ancient accountancy reviews and stacks of *Nuova Alta Tensione* in Patuzzi's cellar stand about a hundred cobweb-ridden wine bottles. Giampaolo inspects them, turning them over in his hands, looking inside, putting his nose to the neck. There's a grave expression on his face. It's Friday night. Saturday is our last day for the waxing moon. His own bottles stand in sparkling ranks by his cellar door, each with a square of plastic wrap on top to keep out the dust. Clearly we should have thought of this problem before.

Our neighbor goes away and returns with a bottle full of metal shot and a big cast-iron tub. His instructions are precise. We boil the bottles ten at a time in the tub and for at least five minutes; we then half-fill each bottle with the metal shot and, thumb over the top, shake vigorously, up and down and around and around. The shot must be rinsed between each bottle. After which the bottles can be washed in normal fashion, rinsed three or four times to remove the soap, and placed in a position where they can drain off thoroughly before tomorrow morning. Already I'm beginning to wonder if we mightn't perhaps have stuck with supermarket bubbly.

Rubber gloves are required. And infinite patience. But the radio has just the thing for us. As we work late into the evening there's a quiz show which involves people answering questions about the intricacies of bureaucratic red tape: "In what situation might you be asked for a document of *esistenza in vita*?" "Should an application for a no-parking sign for your garage or gate be made on plain paper or stamped paper, and if the latter, how much does the stamp cost?" "How many years less does a woman teacher have to work for her pension if she has three children?" "When a couple is selling a secondhand car, is it sufficient for just one spouse to take an oath before the lawyer, or do both spouses have to go?" "When one is given a prescription for an X-ray, for how long is it valid?" The respondents are quick on their buzzers. We try not to slosh too loudly, because the answers are frequently surprising. Actually, it's a pretty useful program.

Then Saturday morning early, with a blond thumbprint of moon only a sliver away from being full, it's straight down to Giampaolo's cellar to do the deed. Like his mind, this tiny space of four or five square yards is admirably tidy and well-ordered. There are only two shelves of wine bottles, all carefully hand-labeled to record the type of grape, the area they come from, the harvest year, the date of bottling: *Cabernet—Friuli—vendemmia 1981, imbottigliato il 2 Maggio, 1982; Traminer—Alto Adige—vendemmia 1982, imbottigliato il 15 Aprile 1983* . . . In the shelves below are boxes and cabinets full of tools, hardware supplies, and the like. Again there are painstakingly prepared labels: 2cm anchor nails, 1cm self-tapping screws, 5mm expansion plugs . . . The air rarely moves down here. Along the top shelf are hundreds of editions of the topical magazine *Panorama* (which may be worth something one day), plus twenty or so volumes of a now outdated but still formidable encyclopedia. Almost at once I feel I'll have to be on my best behavior.

Out comes the equipment, handled with the special care due to the fetishistic object. A clear plastic siphon with a tap, lengthily boiled and rinsed the evening before. A bottling tripod with handpump-like lever. As you bring this down the fat cork is squeezed pencil-thin and forced into the top of the bottle. *Molto valido*, this piece of equipment, and a bargain at fifty thousand lire from a friend. The action is *discreto*. Though of course the quality of any bottler is *relativo*, since what counts above all is the quality of your cork.

And we swing into a long lecture on the various corks the market offers. Giampaolo has purchased different kinds for the different wines he is planning to bottle, though there is also an element of experiment, he explains. He is eager to see how much effect different corks will have on the same wine bottled the same day from the same demijohn. He has corks made from a single piece of quality cork; these are the most expensive, since they retain their springiness and breathe well. Careful to wash your hands before touching them. Then there are some cheaper corks made from putting together pieces of cork in layers. These are okay as long as you're not planning to keep your bottle too long; they'll do for the *prosecco*, which will last a maximum of a year, but not for the Cabernet he's got, which should improve with age. And finally he has a bagful of plastic stoppers, which have the advantage of being very cheap: you can insert them by hand and remove them by hand, but of course they don't breathe. It will be interesting to see if this makes any difference to the *prosecco*.

He's also going to do five bottles of each wine he's got in clear rather than green glass, to check how much the light factor affects the quality. I point out that to do this he will have to open two bottles at once, otherwise he won't be able to make a direct comparison. But he's aware of that. When the in-laws come to lunch, it won't matter if one bottle is not quite up to scratch. Apparently the tight space of the cellar is breeding a sense of complicity.

We lift the first demijohn onto a chair to get the height required for siphoning. This has to be done with immense delicacy so as not to disturb the sediment at the bottom. Bent over, muscles tense, it is as if we were shifting a tactical nuclear warhead. Then with the Murphy's-law cussedness which upsets even the best-laid plans, the chair turns out to be rickety, or the floor uneven, and the big jar tips perilously from side to side, doubtless displacing clouds of sediment inside, like mud in a pond. There's a hunt for pieces of paper and cardboard to slip under the chair legs, but the damage is done now and we will have to wait at least half an hour for the sediment to settle. In the meantime, we siphon off half a jugful, examine it for cloudiness, then pour a little in and out of our first ten bottles (dark green) to rinse and prime them. Immediately the dankish air down in the cellar takes on a very heady smell.

We line up the bottles, ready for action stations. There's a pleasantly conspiratorial feel to mucking about in a cellar that stinks of drink. We are beginning to enjoy ourselves, and at last the siphon is gently lowered into the demijohn. Giampaolo kneels on the clean-swept concrete, head down low, to suck the precious liquor through.

At which precise moment, with a great banging of brooms, mops, and buckets (the doors are iron down here and resound tremendously), fat Lucilla appears. And announces that she had planned to do the garage spring cleaning today. There are a lot of tire marks on the floor and one or two drops of oil. A rather shell-shocked but determined Vittorina appears behind her, thinning hair tucked into a kerchief. They stand there in the doorway looking at us. Orietta has also been informed and press-ganged. Rita has pleaded the excuse of pregnancy. That is, having observed Lucilla's cleaning methods, she is concerned about exposure to noxious fumes.

So at this extremely delicate and exciting moment, Giampaolo and I are obliged to go and move our cars out of the garage, where, hairy upper lip working nervously, Vittorina (despite all doctor's orders not to exert herself) is already splashing detergent on orange bricks. Lucilla is strewing handfuls of sawdust. Orietta has a grim look. For the first time I notice a Sacred Heart above the four electricity meters. Cars removed, we excuse ourselves hurriedly.

Bottling turns out to be both boring and demanding. The siphon nozzle goes down into the first of a hundred and more bottles. The wine flows slowly, but you have to keep an eye on it so as to stop it an inch or two from the top. Meantime, you're checking that the next bottle has been primed, or, once the process is underway, trying to cork the bottles you've already filled. With a dipstick, Giampaolo examines the wine in the other demijohns and tells bottling stories. How the year before last, for example, all but two of the *prosecco* bottles came out flat and were more or less undrinkable. Though he'd had excellent atmospheric and lunar cooperation. This is just one of those imponderables that make it so exciting.

I ask him why the *prosecco* I buy from the supermarket, admittedly at three times the price, is never flat, despite the fact that the bottling factory can hardly be observing the moon and the barometer. Additives, he says contemptuously. Sugar, fizzing agents. Give you a hangover. That's why store-bought *prosecco* can never equal the perfect home-bottled variety, just as Bepi's vegetables are never at the same level as those grown in the garden without any pesticides.

Although this particular choice of comparison hardly seems to warrant the gleam of faith and enthusiasm now shining in Giampaolo's eyes, the delicious fumes are sufficient to quell any further objections and keep me more or less merrily at work for the rest of the morning. At least, I reflect, we have escaped the assault on the garage, which we might otherwise have been expected to get involved in. Leaving the cellar in a daze toward lunchtime, we find Lucilla shoveling up bleach-sodden sawdust in an atmosphere suggesting chemical warfare. The ferocious vapors cut right through our tipsiness, would quite probably clear the nose of a man long after he had ceased to be eligible for a certificate of *esistenza in vita*. "Signor Giampaolo, Signor Tino!" the old woman calls to us. "See, all the tire marks and oil stains are gone!" Likewise gone is Vittorina, who apparently felt faint. Orietta has her kerchief around her mouth, her eyes streaming.

FIACCOLATA

Is it a complete coincidence that the *fiaccolata* occurs toward the end of May, only a few days before tax declarations are due? "The financial administration," says the form in front of me on the kitchen table, "has tried to streamline and simplify the contributor's obligations. . . ." There follow sixty-four pages of instructions on how I am to fill in my income tax return, not many of them easily comprehensible, some referring me to paragraphs and articles of laws which I should apparently somehow procure and study. So that I am just reflecting that I will, after all, have to go to an accountant, when a faint murmur of *"Ave, Ave Maria"* takes me out onto my balcony.

It's a balmy, almost summery evening. The cherry blossoms have long gone. The foliage is thick on everything but vines and fig trees. Winter's dry sticks are no longer in evidence; new ivies twine the fences, smothering sharpness and starkness under soft leaves. And all the street's roses have flowered at once, small bright blossoms climbing up stuccoed walls. But not up the railings. Good iron railings must be kept clear. Our cat, who goes by the name of Toro, is scratching at Marini's cypress tree. The swallows whirl about the rooftops, in a hurry to catch their supper before retiring. And Simone's car has just drawn up in the street below when, from around the corner into curdling twilight, turn the first of a candlelit procession, the *fiaccolata*.

They are coming from the village end of the street, the derelict factory end, led by Don Guido and chanting the *Ave Maria*. They are enjoying holding their candles. Among them, as they approach our house, are most of the people I regularly see in the street: Mario, the insurance salesman, and his *zitella* sister; old Marini; the Lovatos, man and wife, daughter and son-in-law; the salmon-faced mechanic; the wife and children of the man with the Alfa 75, though not the busy *imprenditore* himself; the elderly, bent, straw-hatted fellow whom the mongol-looking woman plants on a chair outside her front door every morning; Lara with various youths usually to be seen straddling their mopeds, bags of potato chips in hand; the woman with the twig broom, of course.

With others from the village, there are perhaps a hundred people altogether, walking rather self-consciously along Via Colombare through the gathering dark toward the Madonnina at the far end. The patient little statue has been freshly painted, and a small electric light adds to the halo effect. A bunch of spring flowers has been placed on the ledge below.

Vittorina goes down to join the chanters. Lucilla does not. She comes out onto her balcony for a moment to nod to everybody, then goes back inside, where the business of entertaining ex-carabiniere Simone is doubtless a demanding one. The dirge grows louder, and, as always at this hour, bats begin to flit back and forth, taking over the warm skies from the swallows in a peculiarly appropriate changing of the guard. They swoop below the eaves, filling the darkness above the procession's slow candles with quick demonic life.

Disappointingly, just as the picture is at its most evocative, the streetlights go on, reducing the candles to pinpoints. And immediately afterward, any mystery that might have persisted is promptly dispelled when, the procession having reached the Madonnina, an amplifier and microphone appear from somewhere for Don Guido to speak into. His uninspiring voice thus has a loud electronic ring to it, with now and then a whine of feedback. And he speaks for almost twenty minutes. What he actually says I don't know, for the words are as distorted as they are loud and uninflected, and after a few moments I cease to pay attention. In any event it seems unlikely he will have any useful advice on how I'm to fill in my tax forms. Nor do I imagine my joining in the ceremony will afford me any particular protection against eventual errors I might make. And I go back inside to wade through the sixty-four pages of instructions.

The alignment of social forces bearing on the payment of taxes is not quite perhaps what one would have imagined. Of course, the radio news has been reminding us with some insistency these last few days of our forthcoming civic duty as *contribuenti*. But not so the calendar of the *frate indovino*, who, despite his conservative attitudes on such questions as women and the family, despite his frequent appeals on behalf of all kinds of missions, does not hesitate to tell me at this crucial moment in the financial year that "Italy is not, as the Constitution claims, 'a republic founded on labor' (of which there is less every day), but a republic founded on taxes (of which there are more every day)." Not satisfied with this inflammatory talk, he inserts, only shortly before the declaration deadline, the reflection, "The criminal is not obliged to testify against himself. The taxpayer is."

What is the church's position here? Far from generating a sense of guilt in the would-be evader, the *frate indovino* seems to assume an attitude of solidarity with an oppressed population, as if we were still in the days when spendthrift Bourbon princes sent heavily escorted bailiffs about to wring the last centesimo out of a starving peasantry. The complicity will stop when we get back to sex, of course, but on questions of rendering unto Caesar what is Caesar's, our Rovigo-based friar has a demagogue's infallible eye for the popular line. "To make sure that VAT is collected," he winds up the section entitled "Predictions," "the Italian government intends to subject the

Italian people to a machine that most nearly approximates a meat mincer." It's as if, tipping us a wink, he were saying, "Don't worry, folks, do as you feel with your declaration and the church will be on hand to shrive your peccadilloes afterward."

Sometimes, when I pick up my bread of a morning at Bepi's, my friend invites me out for a quick espresso, and in these tense days toward the end of May we inevitably find ourselves discussing what is on everybody's mind. "The government is a thief," he announces almost at once. It's a stock phrase, *governo ladro*. You frequently see it sprayed on walls and railway bridges. He shakes his shaggy head as though over an irretrievable and pitiful situation. I make the mistake of remarking a little piously that I do believe in a state where everybody pays what he ought to, so that everybody can pay less, and I say I think the church, with the hold it has over a lot of people, should tell people to cough up rather than conniving with them. Bepi's response is somewhere between the incredulous and the irate. Am I mad? His head-shaking speeds up. His scorn is all too apparent. But then it occurs to him that this is merely my Englishness talking—of course, I'm from a different world, I don't understand it—and now he becomes concerned, his big forehead creases up, he fears that I may be about to make a big mistake and declare more than I need to. He leans over the table, his voice urgent and conspiratorial: "What you have to remember"—there's a bright light of conviction in his green eyes—"what you have to remember is that they are attacking and you are defending. It's naked aggression. And self-defense is always legitimate."

"The balance of indirect to direct taxation is fairly *valido*," pronounces Giampaolo more reasonably that evening. He is weighing his words carefully in this sad period when last year's *prosecco* is already finished and the stuff we bottled last week isn't ready yet. "Then the level of fiscal pressure has been established *discretamente bene*; but all this is rendered *relativo* by the fact that the government makes no serious attempt to collect. Except from *dipendenti*."

And indeed the *dipendenti* have announced a protest to coincide with the tax filing deadline. They will be marching on Montecitorio, the parliament, to demand draconian measures against the demonic *autonomi* who aren't paying their fair share. To hot things up the newspapers amuse themselves by publishing figures indicating the average level of earnings declared by various categories of *autonomi* the previous year. Your average jeweler claimed he earned just five thousand pounds, the average doctor even less, the average lawyer not much more, etc. It's ludicrous. But everybody has his justification for behaving as he does, and the *dipendenti*'s protest is quickly followed by a series of articles showing how the government only wastes what it receives anyway, is generally corrupt and inefficient, and always will be until Italy is more or less taken over by the European Community.

In the event, the administration of this year's income tax collection does little to improve the government's image for fairness or efficiency. As May progresses and people go from one tobacconist's to another in search of the appropriate forms, it becomes clear that not enough have been printed. Or perhaps they have been printed, but they are certainly not being distributed. Then to make matters worse, somebody discovers that an important mistake has been made on one of the pages. We will have to return to the tobacconist's to buy a revised form. So that as well as reminding us of our civic duty, the radio is also talking about the possibility of a two-week postponement of the deadline for filing our returns. Indeed this now seems more or less certain, the newscaster tells us, with a noticeably congratulatory tone to his voice. Until, just three days before we are supposed to pay, the Minister of Finance is interviewed and says that there will be no postponement, he has never mentioned such a thing, nor does he see why he should be obliged to deny any old rumor as soon as it starts circulating, even if it has been given credence by the public broadcasting network. People should never imagine anything has changed until he personally announces it has. And it hasn't. There will be absolutely no concessions to anybody, and people who don't file their returns before the deadline will be fined in the regular fashion.

My accountant is thus in a state of desperation when I finally see him at nine in the evening the very day of the deadline. Out come all the invoices, the registers. His fingers incessantly tap the three-zeros button that distinguishes Italian calculators. As usual, I understand little of what he is saying about the various deductions available to me. I notice in my instruction book that if my wife was dependent on me I could reduce my taxable income by a splendid 120,000 lire, or sixty pounds, and when I have a child I will be able to reduce it by a whole 48,000 lire, twenty-four pounds.

Yet despite this evident meanness (there is no child benefit here), I am always surprised at how little I have to pay. "First," the accountant says briskly, "we reduce your income by fourteen percent. Now, let's see." Fourteen percent! Why? "Because in the category you fall into, or rather that we have chosen to put you into, taxable income is reduced by fourteen percent, which is considered to be your expenses. If the category were different, the reduction would be different. As would the percentage of national insurance you have to pay, and so on."

When finally we get to the end of the whole business, it turns out the government actually owes me money. Which I can expect to be refunded in about four to five years, the accountant remarks. "But it definitely will be refunded. With a modest interest. And it's always welcome when it comes, isn't it?" We finish toward eleven. The accountant has a whole stack of completed forms to be delivered to an office at the station which remains open until midnight the day of the deadline.

Then the following week the Minister of Finance calmly announces that although he didn't postpone the deadline for filing returns, there will now be an amnesty for those who didn't get them in on time. They have until June 14. Another two weeks. Perhaps the *fiaccolata* and the power of prayer are not entirely to be overlooked.

MAMMA!!!

GIVEN THEIR ENTHUSIASM for children, it will at first seem curious that Italians produce so few of them. Lara is an only child. Marta, the daughter of the mongol-looking cleaning woman, is an only child. The woman with the twig broom has a little nephew who visits and at age six rushes up and down Via Colombare on a tiny motorbike with two-stroke engine making an awful racket. He is an only child. Many of my adult students have just one child. If they have any at all. The population is expected to fall by two or three million before the end of the millennium. Only in the house next to the cadaverous old lady does a very jolly signora have three children, all daughters. "How many girls," asks an article in the newspaper, "owe their existence to the elusive quest for a male child?"

It's interesting that those who prefer vegetable gardens to dwarf cypresses and do not clean too obsessionally, or have their blood pressure checked with fanatical regularity, tend to be those who produce more than one child. Again much seems to depend on the family's relationship to the rural past, the extent to which they are influenced by the general clamoring for security. For children are so expensive. They must be provided for from start to finish. First a gynecologist *di fiducia* must be found, and then a pediatrician *di fiducia*. The little ones must spend their summers in *pensioni* or second homes by the sea to breathe the iodine; in winter they must go to the mountains to escape the fog. Very probably they will have to attend a church rather than a state nursery, paying more. Then perhaps a private school, of which there are many. Everything they have must be new. Who would buy a secondhand stroller or cot for their dear little child? Who would buy anything but the most expensive leather shoes for their toddler? And it will be a costly business sending heir or heiress to university, for this takes an absolute minimum of four years, usually much much longer, and there are no grants. Anyway, the child will be engaged by then, and most likely the family will have to buy the couple a flat, since they can't marry before they have been bought a flat, can they? And all the furniture. And all the appliances. Nor would it be wise for them to marry until family contacts, or personal successes, have secured them a steady job. In the local area. It's a major undertaking.

"We didn't have another child," Orietta tells a rather bitter Lara, "because it wouldn't have been fair to you. How could we have given you everything you need?"

A certain Antonio and Sabrina come to talk to Lucilla about the possibility of buying our flat. Their voices boom in the hallway. They now have jobs in the Banca Popolare di Verona in town. But they can't get married until they have bought a flat. And when they buy a flat it must be within walking distance of his parents. They have been looking for more than a year. Via Colombare would be ideal. Antonio's father is with them. A gruff dialect voice. Money isn't a problem, he says, and promises, "all in cash."

The Veronese don't usually look for cheap "first homes" as the English do. Indeed, the very notion of first and second is in naked contradiction to the word "home," isn't it? Because a home is for always, for keeps. Looking for a "first home" would thus be as absurd as looking for a "first wife." And while one might eventually fall out with one's wife and desire to change her, it's extremely unlikely that one would ever want to change one's home. Only a bomb could shift the people in Via Colombare from theirs. No, you protect your home with iron railings, remote-control gates, shock-resistant glass, armored doors, and locking shutters. It's your palace, your bunker, your life sentence. Even the modern Giampaolo will never leave Via Colombare, though his company has offered him positions in Rome and New York. For where would Orietta be without the marble and ceramics she has polished so often? The carefully chosen bathroom porcelain? *"Aggràppati al mattone,"* says a character in Natalia Ginzburg's *La casa e la città* when her brother announces he intends to sell his flat: Cling on to the bricks.

The upshot is that most of the people buying in Montecchio are youngsters being eased (regretfully) out of the old nest (to a place not too far down the road). Antonio's gruff father will pay a fortune to sort out his child. While he himself lives in a decrepit cave of a place off the main square. Because this is what parents must do for their children.

Understandably, then, the people at the prenatal course we go to in town are all on their first child. And their last, is the general consensus. For the most part they are reserved and serious. Veronese. A poster shows a pregnant beauty in flimsy, fashionable nightdress looking out of a window into some spiritual distance of mother-hood and self-realization, the faintest smile on her face. On the wall opposite, a smaller photograph shows the blood and gore of birth itself. There is a crucifix, of course, though I haven't spied a Madonna yet, which is odd.

An attractive woman social worker arrives and, sitting on a stool, discusses at length all the clothes we must prepare for the *esserino*, little one, when he arrives. She smiles constantly as she talks, and a relentless use of diminutives generates a warm, cozy feeling in her audience. It's something I'm going to have to get used to over the next few years: *la gambina, la testina, il braccino, il piedino, le manine, i ditini, la boccucia, le spallucce, i ginocchietti, il nasino, il sederino*; and then the clothes: *la tutina, le scarpine, il vestitino, i guantini, il maglioncino, il giubbottino, i pantaloncini* . . . Together they create an overwhelming impression of lovable tininess to be cuddled and coddled and kissed and tweaked and generally thoroughly and triumphantly spoiled.

The previous evening we had seen a news program showing Italian sailors setting off for their UN mission to Beirut. The camera zoomed in on a young southern boy weeping his heart out at the rail as his ship pulled away. And it didn't take a lip reader to hear what he was screaming to that crowd on the dock. *"Mammaaaaa! Mammaaaaa!"* His face was broken up with fierce emotion. *"Mammina!"* In a way it's wonderful, this lack of shame.

And when we come out of the prenatal course at nine o'clock, full of warm feelings about our child-to-be, there are young conscript soldiers everywhere, monopolizing the phones in the main square in an attempt to get a call through to Mamma before they have to return to their barracks. Verona is a big army town with two major barracks. One of these is out on the road to Montecchio, so that our bus going home is packed despite the hour. And the same boys who five minutes ago were desperately trying to get through to their mums are now rowdy and rough, jostling the one or two Montecchio girls on the bus, hoping perhaps to find the future *mamma* of their own only child. But the girls won't answer back. There seems to be a kind of rule that the locals will have nothing to do with the soldiers.

"Signor Tino, Signora Rita!" As our key clunks, Lucilla emerges from her door in a state of some excitement. She's in the pink brushed-nylon dressing gown, her television grinding out its variety show behind her. Do we know, she shouts, can we for one moment imagine what Signora Marta has just done? Obviously we cannot. Do we know what she had the brazen cheek to do this very afternoon? No, it's beyond us. She telephoned, she telephoned to suggest that they both give up the court case, sell the flat, and go halves on the money.

"O Dio!" Rita says coolly. I close my eyes. This is it. Eviction.

"It means she's guilty!" Lucilla is winding herself up into her usual semihysteria. "Guilty, guilty, guilty! It means she knows she can never win in court. Because the flat is mine. It's mine. It was built with my money, and Il Professore left it to me, if only they hadn't destroyed his will. *È mio, mio, mio!*"

If she switched to dental care some of the time and resources presently allocated to housecleaning, it would be much easier to talk to Lucilla at moments like this.

"So what did you do?" Rita asks.

I hold my breath.

"Le ho detto mai—never. *Mai mai mai mai.* Because she is evil. *Maligna! Una carogna!*"

And we are safe again. You can rely on Lucilla.

Upstairs my *frate indovino* tells me that I must be "parsimonious with hatred," as hatred nourishes itself with my blood, my hopes, my life. I also notice that every single page of the calendar carries an ad for a book called *Cara Mamma* . . . written by none other than the *frate indovino* himself. On the page for May it says:

"Looking for a present for your sweetheart and mother-to-be . . . why not give her the fantastic *Cara Mamma* . . . It's worth more than any gold ring . . . and it costs much less."

GIUGNO

THE MONTH OF JUNE is breathtaking, mainly because of the poppies. The wheat stands thick in the broad fields of the plain, or bristles in undulating strips between rows of cherry trees and vines up on the hills. It is light green at first, turning a duller, denser color through May as it grows. Until, with the first truly hot days around the beginning of June, the green is suddenly transformed into a sizzling carpet of red, laid by some magical hand (while you were having your siesta, it seems) to usher in the summer. It's quite overwhelming. One walks for hours up the valley to absorb field after field of it. Or we cycle southward into the plain. The dazzling, dazzling red stretches majestically away, waving above the wheat, miragelike, desperately intense, seductive, screaming life as colors will.

Giuliano and Girolamo are not impressed. It's a great pity these scientists haven't found a good spray to get the poppies without damaging the wheat, they say. Or I think they say. I can never be entirely sure I have understood these two old farmers. We find them up on the hill with their tractor, dousing the cherry trees one last time before harvest. The marginally younger Girolamo is at the wheel, steering between the terraces; bent forward at 45 degrees, Giuliano stumbles along beside him. From a tank trailed behind the tractor, clouds of filthy-smelling chemicals steam up into thick foliage where here and there ripe cherries peep. I ask Girolamo how he measures the dosages he's giving. He shrugs his shoulders. He just sprays a lot, he says. They need a lot of spray to keep the maggots out. He comes down with us to mix the next tankload in the farmyard, and it's clear he does so *ad occhio*, by guesswork. I remind myself I must tell the ecological Giampaolo, just to see him shake his head. Giampaolo has now collected a huge number of snails from our sad lettuce patch and imprisoned them in a bucket with a pane of glass on top, but can't decide if it's worth the effort to wash and eat them.

Ciliegge avelenate—poisoned cherries—proclaim crudely daubed notices in all the orchards from Montecchio to Mizzole, trying to scare off scavengers by warning of noxious spraying. From the sound of giggling children in the leaves, the ruse would appear to be no more effective than the empty tin cans and strips of plastic strung up against the birds. *Ciliegge avelenate*—when Rita points it out, I am delighted to notice that the dialect-speaking locals have no better grasp of double letters than I do. It should be *ciliege avvelenate*.

Bepi doesn't stock cherries in his shop, because everybody, he says, either has a tree in his garden or steals from the orchards. As usual his reflection comes complete with a tone and expression which suggest his disillusionment at the local situation (beneath contempt) and his confidence that he is smart enough to keep a step ahead all the same. Indeed, very few of the shops sell cherries. The farmers, it seems, mostly export their fruit to Austria and Germany. They have quotas to meet and the harvest was bad this year, thanks to that late flurry of snow. With the result that despite all these hills upon hills of orchards, I personally end up eating very few cherries indeed. There are none at Via Colombare 10, of course, because fruit trees are very much a peasant thing, not part of a city person's garden.

"How long is it now?" the woman with the twig broom rushes out to ask, as we return from a shopping expedition. Everyone wants to talk to Rita. There is a ground swell of solidarity which rises with the curve of her belly. We are just a few yards from where the Madonnina is clutching her own son. Beside the statue, a notice has gone up to tell us the name of the builder who will be converting the orchard behind into terraced housing. Like all notices in Italy it gives the reference number, section and paragraph of whatever law it is that sanctions whatever is being announced.

"Another two weeks," Rita says. "Election day more or less."

This stout *zitella*'s brow knits as she thinks and calculates. "The full moon won't be until a week after that. The third I think."

I smile politely.

Lucilla and Vittorina are disappointed because they are going to be away. Their annual holiday. They have us over to say goodbye and show us photographs of a multistoried modern hotel on the Adriatic coast east of Venice where they go every year. No more those magnificent adventures—Vienna, Prague—with Il Professore. Lucilla's wistful face is clownish this evening behind approximate make-up. The photo shows miles of beach and the usual evenly spaced rows of brilliant sunshades, ten deep, all the same green and purple pattern, like soldiers on parade. "The sea air is so good for one's pressure," Lucilla is confiding to Rita. "That's why we go." Vittorina, with her rather dazed post-ictus expression and ever thinning hair, manages a faint, squeaky laugh, twisting her mouth. "Lucilla only goes for the men," she croaks. "Sitting in the bar chatting up men in the evening. And wearing her bikini on the beach naturally." The image is so bizarre one would like to ask for confirmation. But how? Far from chiding her sister-in-law, Lucilla grins a grin of unqualified self-satisfaction. She has invested a lot in this image of herself as *femme fatale*. She and Vittorina are a good act.

But on popping downstairs to inquire of Giampaolo whether I

can start opening my *prosecco* bottles yet, it is to find the Visentinis seriously concerned. And precisely about the question of Lucilla and Vittorina's holiday. Because, yes, sea air is good for high blood pressure, since the atmospherics tend to lower it, so the sea suits Lucilla and always has, but it is most definitely *controindicato*, a bad idea, for low blood pressure, which is Vittorina's more serious problem. Vittorina should really go to the mountains, since atmospherics there tend to raise pressure. Orietta can't understand why the doctor, who came today, hasn't explained this to them. There is general agreement that the man just takes his money and runs.

For a while voices are urgent and low. Giampaolo and Orietta see the situation as posing a real moral dilemma. Ought they to go and enlighten the two women, encourage them to change destination, at the risk of merely making Vittorina anxious without actually convincing Lucilla, who always has the last word and is very eager to go to the sea and talk volubly to bronzed widowers on deck chairs? Or should they leave be and let the women have their fun, despite concern that the climate could bring on the notoriously fatal second stroke? Really, it was up to the doctor to talk to them about this. . . .

Forgetting my *prosecco*, I get drawn into a discussion about the Visentinis' own holiday, still to be settled. And like every Montecchio conversation on the subject it soon develops into a rehearsal of the pros and cons of the invigorating mountains, the enervating sea. For any other destination is just too hot in holiday time when factories and offices close. Only a foreigner, for example, would visit Florence or Rome in August, or embark on some walking tour of Tuscany.

Giampaolo declares himself for the mountains, the cool air, the great unspoiled panoramas, the brisk walks, the modern man's righteous ecological pride when he doesn't throw away a sandwich wrapper but tucks it back in his knapsack. Orietta is for the sea and lazy days under a sunshade which will never bring on her heart murmur, copies of her favorite women's magazines, evening barbecues with other members of the holiday village, in Puglia, Calabria, beneath palm trees. Lara just begs and begs to be sent somewhere else, anywhere, to some camp or something, it doesn't matter, so long as she can go on holiday without the family. But Orietta would worry too much.

In the end, as it turns out, Orietta will get her way on all fronts. Giampaolo will go to the travel agency at the last minute in a calculated piece of brinkmanship, hoping to pick up a cut-price place in an undersubscribed holiday village, a cancellation with any luck. Then, doing everything at the same time as they always do, he and twenty million other Italians will load the car in early August to face a four-hundred-mile drive in blazing sunshine with miles of waiting cars at every toll booth. But at least the expedition will justify the twin carburetors. . . .

Bepi scorns them all, these provincials. For his first holiday since he set up shop, he goes off to the Seychelles. Where he meets more Italian greengrocers than he does at the market of a morning. Paradoxically, he seems quite pleased about this. He has made some useful contacts. New suppliers. Sheep's cheese from a distributor in Lessinia. And on returning he asks me to translate a letter for a friend he made there who wants to get in touch with a native girl he fell in love with. The letter is touchingly ingenuous, swearing the writer's determination to go back next year. Bepi seems very eager for me to finish it. His big burly presence and bright green eyes are extraordinary somehow against the funereal backdrop of Patuzzi's bookcase. I tap it out for him: the girl's beauty, their unending love. He watches the letters appear in sickly yellow on my processor screen. Is English the language he will have to learn to speak to the girls? Somehow I already know he will not go back.

And no you can't open those bottles yet, Giampaolo says, when I go down to ask him again. Not for another three weeks. There is an element of masochism about it, a casting about for virtue and self-esteem. His *dipendente*'s long-suffering life. If he just bought the stuff from the shop, he wouldn't have to survive this two-month period without. But having decided to bottle his own—because then it's the real thing, alive, not pasteurized, dead, and immortal on a supermarket shelf—he will never go out and buy a case or so to tide him over. It's a point of honor. And he's rather disappointed when I do. Only to savor the difference when ours is ready, I tell him.

ELEZIONI

I T IS AS SUMMER GETS into full swing that you are reminded you are living in a foreign country. A strange breed of wasps, more than an inch long, have made their nest in the eaves above our balcony and will occasionally whir into the flat, causing intense alarm. Opposite the church we see a snake, head held high, sliding rapidly along the wall of the flood emergency dike. Typing away at Il Professore's desk, I become aware that a baby lizard has come in through the French window and is soaking up the sunshine on the tiles by my feet. Outside, freed from their winter covers, lemon and orange trees flourish again in tubs by lowly back doors shrouded with bead curtains against the flies.

Meanwhile Montecchio is being made ugly by preparations for the forthcoming general and local elections. It even seems possible our child could be born right on election day, though what kind of omen this might be I don't know. The local authorities erect long lines of ramshackle scaffolding outside the church and in the main square. These are then hung with laminate billboards decaying with age, thus giving the political parties free advertising space. At least fifty yards of scaffolding and sheet metal are required just to make sure that every party will get space. For of course there are many.

It was my first Italian general election, and despite the imminent domestic upheaval I was eager to get a handle on the political life of my adopted country. I read all the editorials in national and local newspapers, I spoke about it to everybody I knew, I went to meetings in the local library. I thus passed from confusion, to disbelief, to further confusion, and, ultimately, to a quiescent state of total disillusionment. Which I have maintained ever since.

Of course, every nation is disillusioned with its politicians. Everybody is half aware that a politician can never represent the people who voted for him, for the simple reason that anybody who runs for election is fundamentally different from the mass of people who don't. And if he isn't when he decides to run, he most certainly will be once elected. The idea of a representative parliament is a pipe dream. However, in the other countries I have lived in, one is at least left with the consolation of choosing between, if not different ideologies, then at least different emphases. This party will spend more, this less, this party believes in social security, this doesn't, etc. So that elections can be expected to focus (reductively, perhaps, but usefully) on some issue such as should we give more money to the health service, should we possess nuclear weapons, and so on. There is also the government's record. The governing party has done this, this, and this. Do you like it, or don't you? Italian elections have none of this refreshing naiveté.

In the early days—heady May and the first half of June—most comment in the newspapers and on TV seemed to be concentrated on which member of the five-party coalition had been responsible for bringing the government down and provoking these early elections. Given that the public generally perceives elections as a great evil (if only because the squares are cluttered with scaffolding, and the TV monopolized by dull talk shows), this is a matter of some importance. Apportioning blame could prove a potentially effective weapon.

So, were the Socialists right to vote against such-and-such a clause of such-and-such a bill (usually something quite obscure)? Were the Christian Democrats right to insist on this clause and make it an issue of confidence when they knew the Socialists would vote against it and the Liberals abstain? Why did the Republican Party minister attack a government policy he had just subscribed to in a cabinet meeting? Why wouldn't the Social Democrats agree with the others as to who should be chairman of some bank or TV network? And so it goes on. Blame is never effectively apportioned. In the eyes of your average Montecchiese, they are all responsible. They become responsible the moment they are elected. And anyway, it wouldn't have mattered if such-and-such a clause of such-and-such a bill had been passed, since everybody would have ignored it just the same.

"The Socialists, a Modern Party for a Modern Italy"—Bettino Craxi, the party's leader, is pictured with somebody behind him working on a computer. Despite the fact that their emblem is a carnation, the Socialists are using green posters this year to steal a march on the Greens. Who have unfortunately split into the Rainbow Greens and the Smiling Sun Greens and are arguing heatedly about who was responsible. "A New Role for Women in a Fair Society," says the Communists' poster. But will it cut much ice in *la strada delle zitelle*?

All in all, there is a curious lack of imagination about this advertising. Especially given the Italians' usual verve and flair for such things. A weariness. As if none of it really mattered. "Working toward a United Europe," boasts the Christian Democratic Party. But then so, if we're to take them at their word, are the Social Democrats. The Republicans trumpet their "Honesty and Integrity," clearly hinting what everybody already knows, that the others have neither. But then do the Republicans? And is it what people want? The Movimento Sociale, inheritors of the fascist tradition, think it is. "Firm Government and an End to Corruption," they proclaim. Well, it's a step forward from the "Believe, Obey, Fight!"

of their predecessors, a motto still provocatively visible under a thin coat of whitewash on the town hall of a nearby village. "The Right Choice," say the Liberals about themselves, feeling that no further explanation is necessary. Or perhaps possible. "Toward a Real Alternative," plead the Communists, their hammer and sickle reduced to a sixpence. "Stability, Prosperity," thunder back the Christian Democrats, making much of their own emblem of the Crusader's red cross on a white shield. Well, who would ever argue with stability and prosperity?

In the end you have to turn to the extremist fringes to get any hint of policies. "Rome = Mafia = Taxes," says the slogan of the separatist Liga Veneta. And another poster warns: "Bringing Blacks to the Veneto = Slavery." Obviously somebody has a penchant for perverse equations. At the other extreme, the Democratic Proletarian Party wants "Nuclear Weapons Out Now." The Pensioners' Party demands social justice for the elderly. Predictable stuff. The Radical Party, splendidly idealistic as ever, proclaims: "No to World Famine."

Responsible modern man Giampaolo Visentini is thus profoundly depressed. "They don't even bother trying to hoodwink us anymore," he observes. Bepi just snorts. He won't talk about it. It's too ridiculous. In the *sanitaria*, herbalist Maria Grazia's husband thunders for the Liga, the separatists. There are too many *meridionali* moving into the area. Have I heard that they're setting up yet another cooperative to build houses for themselves in Mizzole? Have I? With that and the new high-security prison going up next to the barracks, we'll have the Mafia here in no time. Amusingly, work on the prison is stopped the following week because it's discovered that the contractors involved paid bribes to politicians to get the job. A student of mine tells me she was a Democratic Proletarian activist once, but then she realized they were just the same as all the others.

Meanwhile the debate on TV has switched to the technical question of whether parties should declare their allegiances with other parties before the election, so that people know what kind of coalition they are voting for. This is an age-old Christian Democrat ploy to have people suspect that the Socialists might desert the present government to form an alliance with the Communists after the election. Which would be the end of everything, of course. The Socialists insist that each party must simply present its policies and that is that. Whereas so far nobody has presented any. The Communists accuse the church of using the pulpit to encourage people to vote Christian Democrat. The smaller parties try to have us all imagine that behind the scenes Christian Democrats and Communists are planning to get together and change the electoral system in such a way as to exclude all the others. There is an enormous amount of talking, much of it deployed about the furthest outposts of comprehensibility, and absolutely no debate. Nobody mentions interest rates, or inflation, or unemployment, or defense spending, or levels of home construction, or anything that might remotely have any bearing on day-to-day life. Nobody presents a program or manifesto. As for the government's record, it is never considered, since each party in the coalition always claims that the other members were responsible for everything bad. Oddly, there are no opinion polls, no suggestion that things are running one way or another. If I could vote, I reflect, I would have absolutely no idea who to vote for.

Election day finally comes around. The baby is due now, but taking its time. We wake to a perfect Sunday morning and hear the radio reminding the population that it's not just a right but a duty to vote. They must get along to their polling station before dashing off to swim at the lake or picnic in the mountains. They mustn't let the election be won by apathy and indifference. "And if you really can't vote today, remember that you have the right to take time off work to vote tomorrow morning. Up to two o'clock." The amount of concern suggests fears of an abysmal turnout. Which I would find only too understandable. We shall see.

Being a dutiful citizen, Rita sets off to vote. Who for, I have no idea. We follow the dusty road over the first and second bridges, where people take the corners so courageously. The parking lot is full for early mass. Six girls pass us on three bicycles. In each case the passenger stands on the saddle with her hands on the shoulders of the rider. One has an ice-cream stick in her mouth, another a cigarette. The vines are stretching their tendrils across the pergola of the Bar Centrale in Piazza Buccari, where Moreno the half-wit, in deer-stalker hat despite the heat, is cadging cigarettes and being gently mocked by men reading *La gazzetta dello sport*. And it's only half-past eight. One learns to rise early here to get the best of the day.

We arrive at the other end of the village, where the local school has been closed for the last three days to prepare it as a polling station. Though it's difficult to imagine why so much time was needed. In the main entrance, a computer printout has each person's name and, for some reason, profession. There is an obsession about categorizing people by profession. One then goes to vote in one of a variety of classrooms, and in each classroom there are two *scrutatori*, observers. Not surprisingly, these are mainly the children of local bigwigs, glad to pick up the eighty thousand lire they get for their services. In the booth, one puts a cross over the emblem of the party one wants, and then, if one likes, the name of one of the many people who are running for that party. Each constituency returns a number of deputies, and each party can offer a whole range of possible choices to fill those positions. Which means you can vote for someone in some particular faction of your chosen party, or for the man who has already done you a favor. Or is going to if he gets in. It makes counting terribly complicated.

Curiously absent from the whole process is any real suspense about the result. The evening news offers no "swingometers," no eager experts discussing marginal states or constituencies, no surveys taken of people leaving polling stations. This is partly because the quite extreme system of proportional representation removes any seesaw effect. A swing of 5 percent means nothing more than a swing of 5 percent. Not the difference between one government and another. And anyway, no such swings are likely to occur. Perhaps 2 or 3 percent will leave this party, but only to disperse among five or six others. Perhaps at the end of the day one party will have crept forward the few points required to shout victory. But in the main the status quo will be left untouched. For the truth is that disillusioned as they are, most Italians will always get out there and vote for the same party they always have. The football supporter mentality, Giampaolo calls it: "You stay with them even when they're losing every game and charging you more to watch every time."

Thus, despite the carefully deployed anxiety of the public broadcasting service before the event, and despite the fact that so many people hold residency and thus voting rights in cities far away from where they live, the turnout is a huge 90 percent. This truly amazes me, and I bully everybody I know to try to extort some satisfactory explanation. To no avail. A love of secrecy, writing down the name of a friend of a friend in the polling booth perhaps? A residual concern that not voting might prejudice one's position in some *concorso* to become a teacher, or caretaker?—Vittorina and Lucilla were both unaccountably worried about missing the election. Genuine fear of a Communist government? Or perhaps—and it's the explanation I would plump for—perhaps, despite all disillusionment, a very profound, heartfelt satisfaction with the way things are and a determination that they should remain so. I plump for it because it has the hallmark of that profound schizophrenia, which is also the charm, of all matters Italian: the Pope adored and ignored, the law admired and flouted, politicians despised and reelected. The gulf between officialdom's facade and private thought could not be greater than it is here. But in the secret of the ballot box that facade is always supported. Nothing changes. Italy, one sometimes thinks, is as if frozen in the high noon of its postwar prosperity.

I played a little game with my students on our last lesson of the year. I suggested they write down who they think their barber or hairdresser votes for and why. Normally responsive and fun to teach, my request left them nonplussed, diffident, reticent. It was as if one had asked some ancient Athenian to explain the Eleusinian mysteries. A completely taboo subject. Montecchio, in the event, returned the Christian Democrats with 75 percent of the vote, but I have yet to meet anyone here who will speak well of the party. "The only good thing about elections"—Bepi deigned to mention the subject over an espresso with grappa at eight in the morning—"is that the results are so complicated that for a month and more afterward there's no government at all. And so for a while, *non possono rompere le palle!*" Which loosely translated means "they can't get on our fannies."

"If the country," comments *il frate indovino*, ear perfectly tuned to the popular mood, "could buy politicians for what they're really worth and then sell them for what they claim they're worth, it could pay off its deficit in no time at all."

Doubtless our witty priest votes Christian Democrat.

LA LUNA

THE BABY WAS LATE. Rita was finding the heat and summer *afa* oppressive. We bought a fan and she sat at her typewriter in a stream of dusty air. When the Visentinis learned about the fan, Orietta felt it her duty to come upstairs and warn us that fans were *controindicati.* You sweated, then sat in the air from the fan, and inevitably caught a cold. She was also worried that we hadn't got rid of our cat. Cats could cause all kinds of diseases when one had a little baby in the house. I often wonder if perhaps Italian houses of the future won't be designed with some sort of disinfectant footbath in the entrance-way. We liked our cat.

Meanwhile, whenever I bumped into anyone in Via Colombare an eyebrow would be raised. Any news yet? If there's anything I can do . . . Even the mechanic at the end of the street, smelling strongly of grappa after lunch as always, was in the know. Did I want my car looked over before the all-important trip? The last thing I needed was a breakdown on the way to the hospital. I thanked him and got filters, plugs, and points changed at a very reasonable price. *"Buon giorno, Signor Teem,"* said old Marini's wife. "And how is your signora this morning?"

What a far cry from the kind of reception I had been getting a year before! Clearly, I thought, a child is the ultimate passport to society here, a blank check to draw against vast reserves of Latin sentiment. Far from having my greetings rejected, I now had the opposite problem of having to discuss the relative merits of the various local hospitals with the vaguely mongol-looking woman, while the woman with the twig broom came to clap me on the back and tell ghastly stories about the gynecologists at Borgo Roma, where her sister-in-law had given birth. *"Macellai,"* she insisted. "Butchers. They jump on your belly to push the child out." And she asked who would be coming in to look after me while my wife was away at the hospital. I wondered for a moment if I had understood this correctly.

"Who'll cook for you?"

"Nobody. I can manage myself."

She shook her head, whether in admiration or despair at a changing world, I don't know. *"Troppo bravo, troppo bravo,"* she said. "You English are so tough." And she added by way of valediction: "The full moon will be the night of the third."

Inspired by the consultant gynecologist who gave our prenatal course, we have decided to go to his hospital in the small town of Zevio. He is the only consultant in the Italian state system practicing the Leboyer method. Or so he says. Obviously we've driven over there once or twice to check out the route: fifteen miles of twisting country roads, with the last stretch, unfortunately, being repaved and hence bumpy as hell. A useful stimulant, perhaps, but also another complicating factor in that delicate equation: when to set off. We time the trip at thirty minutes. Getting out of the car to stretch our legs, we find a sleepy, overgrown village with a truly vast main square, in the middle of which is a villa-cum-castle surrounded by a moat. The rest of this inexplicably huge open area is just a desert of asphalt crisscrossed by fading white lines indicating where five or six roads might intersect. On Sundays, we discovered on our second trip, the space is packed to suffocation point with a bustling provincial market selling cheap clothes, fruit, vegetables, and adventurous underwear of mammoth proportions, presumably for ladies like Lucilla. The traffic was backed up for a mile. Another factor, then, is that one must not go into labor on a Sunday morning.

The hot days drag on. We sit under the pergola at Centro Primo Maggio listening to the accordion. People with houses by the streams hang watermelons in the water to keep them cool. They're too big for the refrigerator. Despite the predictable election results, the politicians, as Bepi had foretold, have so far been unable to come up with a government. Nobody's concerned. The shops begin to close as everybody goes off on holiday. There are the usual scandals about poor old people having to walk miles in suffocating heat to find a grocery open. By law, shops are obliged to run a rotation system, but the fines are so small they tend to ignore the problem. You go to the post office and find it closes for the afternoon in July and August. There is alarmist talk about the unavailability of doctors in hospitals. We begin to get nervous.

And then the big day arrives at last. Or rather night. Toward two in the morning the terms of the equation are finally and ruthlessly satisfied: fierce contractions. We bundle into our despised orange car and head south across the *bassa* to Zevio. We're about halfway—San Martino, Campalto, Mambrotta—driving along roads that twist and turn unaccountably through perfectly flat countryside, when, over a distant dike, what should sail up into the sky but the moon, a perfectly, round, splendid, shining white moon, full as full can be, and apparently drawing us to Zevio as the natal star to Bethlehem. How infuriating! I can just see the satisfied smirk on the face of our lady of the twig broom. Even Giampaolo will consider it as confirmation of his *prosecco*-bottling technique. Yet one feels strangely satisfied to see it too. *La luna*. So bright! So large! We speed on through field after field of silvery peach orchards under that presageful ghostliness lunar light tends to have, especially at important moments in your life. And it does cross my mind for a moment that perhaps the moon has more influence in Italy than it does back home. This would explain so much.

The Chiarenzi hospital in Zevio has long corridors paved with cheap black stone. The porter gives a direction with his thumb, barely looking away from a TV screen. In a spare room a nurse with nun's headgear takes down the details. Then more corridors. At the entrance to the maternity ward a little waiting area is heaped with flowers, and there is a small white statue of the Madonna. One gets to rely on her after a while: that simple passivity, absorbing all, at crossroads, hospital wards, cemeteries. Though somehow, through her very ubiquitousness, the quiescent figure becomes not so much a protecting presence as a reminder that whatever happens, all will go on as before. Without her and her crucified son, usually much smaller and hidden away by some dusty central heating pipe near the ceiling, you might imagine that what was happening to you here and now was unique, and desperately important.

Rather surprisingly, I find myself wondering if the Madonna doesn't have some quality in common with the moon.

In the ward, a bright young nurse speaks to us in dialect and listens to the baby's heartbeat through a wooden trumpet pressed against Rita's belly. Interestingly, she is called Stefania, which is the name we have chosen if the baby is a girl. Which no doubt it will be. I'm pretty well resigned to that now. Not that I in any way mind having a girl. On the contrary. What could be more delightful than a little girl? Just that I had hoped the Via Colombare influence would not be confirmed. I'd far rather have a random world than a determinist one, however benevolent.

We spend the night in a tiny room with Rita in labor and me fighting sleep. Enticingly, there's a pasticceria right across the street, which will surely open at seven o'clock. Shortly after dawn, while a crow sits on a branch not a yard away, a priest leads four men carrying a rough wooden coffin out of the hospital into the street. I decide not to remark on this to Rita. And when a light goes on in the pasticceria around eight o'clock, I selfishly hurry out for a cappuccino, only to hear that the bar is closed for the holidays. The man has merely come to do some decorating work. And the pasticceria on the other side of the village is always closed Monday mornings. A test of the extent of your Italianization is whether you still grind your teeth when you hear that something is closed.

In the event, the low lights and soft music of the Leboyer method have to be forgotten, because that room is already occupied. "Full moon," explains the nurse. "Haven't had a birth for a week, and then six in a single night." Okay, okay, I give in. But the baby, when it finally shows up, is a big bouncy boy.

The first duty of an Italian father is to buy a rosette, blue for a boy, pink for a girl, and stick it on some highly visible part of his house. Driving home that day, I found a *tabaccheria* in San Martino that sold me one for what seemed a rather expensive ten thousand lire. The lady at the cash register was desperately eager to engage me in conversation about the joys of parenthood: "*Sì, sì, sì*, a great change in your life, you can't even imagine yet," she says excitedly as I walk out in a daze without my receipt. Back in Via Colombare I taped the thing high on the front door of number 10 and hoped that all the *zitelle* in the street would see it immediately and eat their hearts out.

My second duty was to find two witnesses and take them along to register the birth. Since public offices are open only in the morning, this would have to wait till the following day. Giampaolo and Orietta were more than happy to help me out, and we set off early next morning so he wouldn't be too late for work.

Registration had to be in the village of birth, so it was back along the winding road to Zevio again. The *comune* was a baroque *palazzo* in the huge main square where traffic crisscrossed with impressive confidence across the open asphalt. At the top of flights of eighteenth-century stairs, a huge room with ornate ceiling and a long wooden counter was occupied by just two women toying with computers.

The man who registered births was out for a minute, they said. Could we wait?

I generally accept this kind of thing now. But Giampaolo looked at his watch. "We'll give him five minutes," he said ominously.

As with his behavior over Negretti and his dogs, phoning the police at the drop of the hat, I was surprised at his immediately tough, legalistic, though always reasonable approach.

"We have come to a public office," he told the women calmly. "There is no queue, and hence no reason why we shouldn't be dealt with immediately."

Orietta tugged at his elbow. "Giampaolo!" she muttered.

But after five minutes Giampaolo again politely demanded to be served. The younger of the women, lavishly if not seductively made up, fashionably if not attractively dressed, said the man couldn't possibly be much longer. Giampaolo asked where he was. The girl flustered. Nobody had registered a birth for a week or so, she said. And then they were so pushed still with the aftermath of the elections. Surely we could understand that. But if we were really in a hurry, then she would try to handle the matter herself. Her voice echoed petulantly in the big room, designed, presumably, for nobler purposes. A great chandelier gathered dust above a video terminal. The lighting was fluorescent.

We were in a hurry, Giampaolo said. We had come early because he had to get to work. People noticed, he remarked pointedly, when he was absent.

The girl, clearly resentful of the fact that her colleague hadn't budged, came over to the counter, pulled a huge book out from a drawer beneath, and asked us for our documents: Giampaolo's, Orietta's, my own. But when she saw the British passport, she shook her head. Was I the father? She couldn't possibly take it upon herself to register a foreigner's birth. And she turned to the older woman: "Do we have any special conventions with England?" The other didn't know. I suggested that the conventions would be the same as for all European Community countries. "Is England a member of the European Community?" the girl asked her colleague. _"Credo di sì,"_ came a monotone response. But the girl shook her head all the same. We would just have to wait for _il responsabile_.

"But where is he?" Giampaolo returned to the offensive. "We have no intention of waiting here all morning."

The girl looked to the woman behind for support. This dusty

creature said sourly: "Running an errand at the hospital." And she wouldn't look up from her keyboard.

"Call him up."

My neighbor, I was discovering, had the disturbingly professional belligerence of somebody who not only knows when to pick a fight but is also perfectly confident of how he is going to go about winning it.

The two hesitated.

Giampaolo announced: "This is a public service. The office is obliged to have somebody present who can register births. It is now officially open. You have admitted the man is not ill. At this point I am left with no alternative but to *sporgere una denuncia*"—report the matter to the police.

We had been waiting only ten minutes. It seemed perfectly normal to me.

"Giampaolo!" Orietta protested, *sotto voce*.

Turning to us, the usually wooden Giampaolo grinned broadly and whispered: "The man's in the bar. You'll see. He's having his breakfast."

At the word *denuncia* the two women, rather than protesting or growing more hostile, had begun to confer quite urgently under the cover of their computer printer. After a moment they pulled out the phone book and began to leaf quickly through it.

"They'd have the number to the hospital written down," Giampaolo whispered. I was all admiration.

The girl picked up the phone, dialed, asked if Lucio was there, hung on. And then the obvious occurred to me. "It's because the pasticceria at this side of the village is closed. He's had to go to the one opposite the hospital and it's taking him longer than it usually does."

And indeed, just five minutes later Lucio could be heard hurrying up the stairs. There was icing on the bristles of his fine mustache. *"Bene, signori, vediamo."* He smiled broadly, rubbed his hands together, and scribbled down my passport number as if he saw a dozen a day. To my relief, the delay was not mentioned. Everybody was extremely polite and friendly, and we all wished each other *buon giorno*. But Giampaolo, walking down to the car, was gloating. If there's one thing an impotent *dipendente* can do, it's demand his rights from a *statale*. Such was the world into which my child had now been officially introduced.

MANIFESTI
FUNEBRI

So MUCH GETS SAID about the inefficiency of Italian public services that I feel it my duty toward the end of this book to remark on how extraordinarily fast, even in the holiday season, the gas, water, and cemeteries board (AGSM) will authorize a death notice. On every wall or space where ads and announcements are pasted up in the villages of the Veneto—behind the bus stop, or higgledy-piggledy on a wall at a crossroads—you always find a couple of these simple *manifesti funebri*, giving their sad news. And from time to time, while picking up your newspaper or going for a haircut, you will turn a corner and see a familiar name. One knows in Montecchio when one's neighbors go. The cemetery encroaches on the shopping streets. Rightly so, perhaps. And while birth may be a frilly silk-blue or pink, death has no sex and, of course, only one color. So you quickly learn to recognize the black borders and Christ's upturned face with the crown of thorns at the top in the center. Across the middle of the poster there will be a name in large letters, and perhaps a nickname too, since nicknames are common in Italy ("Dino Chiericatti," and beneath, *"detto, il capitano"*). The age is placed in brackets, likewise the married woman's maiden name. There is the time and date of the funeral, gratitude in advance for those who attend. And a brief comment such as "mourned by all her loved ones," or "lost to the affection of family and friends"—some appropriate, conventional formula, nothing fanciful. "Authorized by AGSM," they have stamped askew in the bottom left-hand corner. The very day after Vittorina died, the posters were already up all over the village.

Rita returned from the hospital just two days after Michele's birth. In the meantime the old women had come back triumphantly sunburned from their holiday and were fussing and clucking to see the child. We had barely laid the portable cradle on the table before they were knocking on the door, bringing gifts in extravagant packages. They peeked under the covers, went into ecstasies: the first male child born on Via Colombare for heaven knows how long! A jinx had been broken! And again Lucilla made herself cry by recounting the story of her own little boy: the fever in the night, the hot poultices applied to *quel povero corpicino*, that poor little body. Again we said we were sure she had done everything that reasonably could be done. And I glanced up to check that I had written our pediatrician's number on the board by the phone.

Giampaolo came upstairs. He didn't want to disturb us. They would see the baby when we all had the time to settle down. He just wanted to let me know that I was released from my duties of watering and mowing the lawn for a little while. Then whenever we felt ready, we could pop the first of those bottles of *prosecco* together. He now had three in the back of the refrigerator.

The following afternoon, a day of stifling *afa*, Vittorina did not wake up from her siesta. Lucilla's yells brought me running. Leone and Marisa were visiting, and the three of them had discovered the corpse together. When I got downstairs, Lucilla had already recovered sufficiently to start pulling open drawers and thumbing through papers. It was intriguing that for all the closeness of their friendship, Vittorina never told her where she kept the will.

Leone lowered the shutters. Marisa lit a candle on each side of the bed. I withdrew. On the threshold of her spic-and-span flat with its millimetrically positioned lithographs and carefully dusted knickknacks, Orietta had tears in her eyes. That low pressure at the seaside had been a terrible, terrible mistake. Criminal, on the doctor's part. At which the culprit himself drew up on the road outside, a practiced smile on his face as he stepped out of his Porsche. *Troppo, ma troppo gentile*, sobbed Lucilla. It occurred to me I had better remove the blue rosette from the door.

Today was Friday, and the funeral couldn't be arranged until Monday. With Giampaolo still at work, Orietta came upstairs around five to say she was worried about the possible smell. No, the undertakers didn't take away the body here. The relatives had to pray over it until the funeral. They would put her in her coffin tomorrow, but the body would still be lying there until Monday, and with this weather . . . Mightn't it cause some kind of disease? After all, *la poveretta* was only just the other side of the wall from their own bed.

As the *cassonetto* with its rubbish was only the other side of the street.

Rita was trying to breast-feed the little baby. I couldn't imagine there was any serious health risk, I said. But it wasn't my field. Orietta, it appeared, had already consulted Giampaolo's encyclopedia. And now she stayed in our flat to phone various offices of the health service. There was a corpse just the other side of her bedroom wall. Could it cause disease? Their reassuring answers didn't convince her. She would keep her windows tightly closed, however hot it got.

All Saturday and Sunday the people of Via Colombare trickled by to pay their respects to the deceased and offer *condoglianze*. Lucilla managed to be overdressed in mourning, bursting with energy and self-commiseration, playing the protagonist's part. *"Gradirebbe un gingerino, Signora Rosa, una tazza di tè?"* And yes, Vittorina had left the flat to her, though she didn't want to talk about that kind of thing now. Word spread like wildfire. Bank workers Antonio and

Sabrina stopped by with Antonio's father, all in black, though they had never known Vittorina.

It occurred to me that with the flat downstairs to dispose of, the heat was probably off as far as we were concerned. And a baby is such an attraction.

Then on the Monday, perhaps a year and a month after we had arrived, I got to see another of Lucilla's balcony performances. About twenty or thirty of us had gathered in the street, trying to keep out of the mud a bulldozer had left, for they had just begun to plough down the cherry trees behind the Madonnina. More work for our lady of the twig broom. Perhaps because of the heat, people were not overly formal. Only Lovato, who had presided so long over Vittorina's gardening, had a suit and tie. Giampaolo had taken time off work and was smartly though casually dressed. Faces were waxy with sweat. Don Guido arrived in his battered Renault, dents front, back, and sides. There was subdued chatter, the bright whistle of a blind blackbird in the dusty morning air. Old Signora Marini whispered to me that we could come and get some figs when they were ripe. Black or green. She knew my wife liked figs. How was little Michele? Weight? Sleeping habits? *Che caro!*

The hearse turned the corner from the derelict factory end, its polished gray flanks bearing the sublimely comforting announcement *Azienda Municipale Servizi Funebri*—another branch of AGSM. Men dressed in blue overalls went in beneath the Californian eaves of number 10 and lifted the coffin in the shuttered, candlelit room. They were careful with their feet on the polished marble. The ailing tropical plants were moved aside. Then out they came between the two dwarf cypresses that guarded the bourgeois spirit of the glass front door. In the street one or two people stepped forward to place flowers on top, but Vittorina had not been a Montecchiese by birth, it was not a big funeral. The hearse had long side windows cut specially low to make an elegant display of the polished wood. Don Guido had to slam his damaged car door twice.

And then just as the hearse got into gear, just as the crowd was preparing to follow, Lucilla, with a perfect sense of timing, burst forth on her terrace balcony and began to shriek and tear her hair.

She had been betrayed, betrayed, betrayed! By life, by death. Her only treasure had been taken from her. The only companion of her old age. "Vittorina, Vittorina, *tesoro, cara,* how could you? How could you die on me? *Maria santissima, oh Gesù, perchè, perchè?*" Curiously, there was at least as much anger as sorrow in the performance, as if her sister-in-law's death wasn't so very different from having been cheated out of Il Professore's flat. Another loss, another encroachment. She bared her crooked teeth and howled, she pulled at her hair. Truly grief-stricken, and truly theatrical. She railed against God and spat. But this time one didn't feel inclined to find anything cartoonlike or caricaturish about it, as one had a year ago. One was part of the crowd now, and one watched and listened respectfully, offering the tubby woman the audience she needed. One reflected that there would always be occasions, many occasions, even in the modern, high-tech, all problems-solved world Giampaolo yearned for, when appearance on one's balcony and a wild raw wail in stifling heat before a gathered crowd would be both understandable and appropriate.

Late that evening, we opened the first bottles of *prosecco* with the Visentinis and wondered who our new neighbors would be. One bottle was flat. The second frothed splendidly. There was just no telling why. The moon, the pressure? "*Salute!* Health!" Orietta was quick to say, clinking glasses. "*Molto valido,*" I said, taking my first sip. "*Discreto,*" Giampaolo nodded, not wanting to go overboard. "But *relativo,*" Rita added, "if only one bottle out of two is good." Sharp young Lara giggled.

AFTERWORD

SOME FOUR OR FIVE YEARS AFTER I arrived in Italy, in a moment of nostalgia for milk floats and the busy racial mix of Acton High Street, I reread Browning's "Oh to Be in England." It wasn't April and there are no melon flowers in Montecchio; nor, if there were, would I find them gaudy, for nothing pleases me more than bright colors. Then the things Browning remembered about England are not the things I remember. I go for the back seat up top of a Victoria-bound bus, or gusting wind on the upper Edgware Road. The orchard bough, the swallows, the thrush, are not part of my memories of home. And anyway, all these things can be found in abundance in both Tuscany and the Veneto. There is no need to feel nostalgic for what is all around you. So that perhaps rather than making any real comparison between the two countries, all Browning was saying, in his very beautiful way, was that he was homesick. And also, by curious implication, that he was not coming home. Anyone whose homesickness can be so exquisitely relished, so effectively deployed, has long passed the point of no return. Browning remembers England the way a happily married man, surprised by a scent some warm spring evening, might remember an earlier girlfriend: with thanks, with pleasure, even a ghost of regret, but no real urgency. If this book is anything, I hope it suggests how I passed that point of no return. Which is a process of immersion in details, whether they be pleasant or unpleasant. For details are sticky as spider's silk; you are very soon caught. And rather than a travel book, perhaps if there were such a category in the libraries I should call this an arrival book. For by the end, this small square handkerchief of Italy I live in has become home for me. I hope that for just a moment the reader will have been able to feel at home here too.

About the Author

TIM PARKS is the critically acclaimed author of six novels, including *Goodness*, *Family Planning*, and the recent *Juggling the Stars*, a thriller set in northern Italy.